TEACHER'S BOOK

ESSENTIAL ANTHOLOGY

COMMUNICATION AND INFORMATION

Christine Brookes
Caroline Davis
Ken Haworth
Beth Kemp
Judith Rippeth
Nicola Williams

OXFORD
UNIVERSITY PRESS

Great Clarendon Street, Oxford, OX2 6DP, United Kingdom

Oxford University Press is a department of the University of Oxford. It furthers the University's objective of excellence in research, scholarship, and education by publishing worldwide. Oxford is a registered trade mark of Oxford University Press in the UK and in certain other countries.

First published in 2014

British Library Cataloguing in Publication Data
Data available

978-1-40-852341-4

10 9 8 7 6 5 4 3 2 1

Paper used in the production of this book is a natural, recyclable product made from wood grown in sustainable forests. The manufacturing process conforms to the environmental regulations of the country of origin.

Page make-up by OKS Prepress, India

Printed in Great Britain by Ashford Print and Publishing Services, Gosport

Text acknowledgements

We are grateful for permission to reprint extracts from the following copyright material.

Telegraph: *Speed Mating*, Telegraph View, (The Telegraph Online 3 April 2012)

Guardian: *Bob Marley obituary, 'Bob Marley, the eloquent ambassador of reggae'*, (The Guardian, 12 May 1981) (http://www.theguardian.com/theguardian/1981/may/12/fromthearchive).

Daily Mirror: *Kung Fuel Fighting*, the Daily Mirror, (30 March 2012). Caption to photo.

The Times: *A Fuel Crisis made in Downing Street* (The Times, 30 March 2012). Caption to photo.

Telegraph: *Teenagers: they don't drink, they don't smoke. What do they do?* (Julia Llwellyn Smith, The Telegraph Online, 28 February 2012)

Stainton: Emma Hearts LA, (Keris Stainton, Orchard Books 2012).

Shaw: *Pygmalion*, George Bernard Shaw.

Clairol: Slogan from Clairol Nice 'n Easy advert.

Amnesty International: Amnesty International's Open Letter to members of Pussy Riot - http://www.amnesty.org/en/news/scores-musicians-urge-russia-release-pussy-riot-2013-07-22.

Blair: Extract from Tony Blair's speech on education, (23 May 2001).

Dahl: *Boy: Tales of Childhood*, Roald Dahl, (Puffin, 2008) first published in 1984.

Chang: *Wild Swans: Three Daughters of China*, (Jung Chang, HarperPress, 2012).

Bryson: *Down Under*, Bill Bryson, (Black Swan 2001).

Theroux: *Dark Star Safari: Overland from Cairo to Cape Town*, (Paul Theroux, Penguin, 2003).

Scott: Diary of Captain R. Scott, 1912.

Huffington Post: *Coming Full Circle: My meeting with the Dalai Lama*, Sophia Slater, (The Huffington Post, 1 August 2013).

The Sunday Times: Restaurant review of Oblix, The Shard, AA Gill, 'Table Talk' in The Sunday Times, 21 July 2013.

McCourt: *Angela's Ashes*, Frank McCourt, (Harper Perennial, 2005) first published 1996.

Pepys: Diary of Samuel Pepys, 1666.

Guardian: Review of the Tavern Restaurant, Jay Rayner, Guardian, 20 October 2013, www.theguardian.com/lifeandstyle/2013/oct/20/the-tavernrestaurant-review. Copyright Guardian News & Media Ltd 2013

Telegraph: Review of *Despicable Me 2*, Tim Robey, The Telegraph, 27 June 2013, www.telegraph.co.uk/culture/film/filmreviews/10145597/Despicable-Me-2-review.html.

Cycling Weekly: Product review www.cyclingweekly.co.uk/tech/bikes/12964/1/merida-sculturacomp-904. **©Cycling Weekly/IPC+ Syndication**

Bella: Clothing feature, http://shop.bellamagazine.co.uk/browse/womens-clothes.

Daily Mail: Review of *One Direction: This is Us*, Paul Tookey, 30 August 2013 www.dailymail.co.uk/tvshowbiz/reviews/article-2406227/One-Direction-film-This-Is-Us-review-Chris-Tookey.html.

Herr: *Dispatches*, Michael Herr, Picador, 1978. Copyright Random House

Although we have made every effort to trace and contact all copyright-holders before publication, this has not been possible in all cases. If notified, the publisher will rectify any errors or omissions at the earliest opportunity.

Contents

Introduction

This book accompanies *Essential Anthology: Communication and Information Student Book*, an anthology of texts collated for Key Stage 3 students. The texts are divided into five distinct units grouped by genre or theme. These texts were chosen for both their intrinsic qualities and their capacity to facilitate the development of specific skills in English. In amongst them, you will find a wide range of stimulating and exciting texts, which have not formerly been anthologised, alongside a few tried and tested favourites.

How the anthology is organised

The anthology is organised into five sections:

- Unit 1: In the news
- Unit 2: Language out loud
- Unit 3: The power of persuasion
- Unit 4: Real-world stories
- Unit 5: Horror

There is an introduction to each of these sections which you will find helpful to read with your students and consider the points raised in them. Each section is based around key areas of KS3 Schemes of Work and provides a route leading directly to KS4 areas of study.

Progression is built into each unit with notionally 'easier' materials and tasks at the start, increasing in complexity and challenge as the unit develops, with some of the later texts being designed to stretch the most able students. Texts have been selected to allow, where appropriate, for comparison studies to be undertaken within and between units.

How to use the anthology with the teacher's book

Students do not all develop at the same rate – either in the materials that they want to read or in the tasks which they are capable of doing. Across Key Stage 3, students vary greatly in maturity and ability. The texts within each unit of the anthology vary in subject matter and complexity, giving you the freedom to choose those most appropriate to the age, interests and ability of the students in your class. Whilst an indication of the target audience of each text is given in the teacher notes, this is in no way intended to be prescriptive.

The range of activities and the detailed guidance provided in this book are designed to enable the teacher to choose the tasks most appropriate to the students. Whilst you may wish to work through all the activities linked with a given text, there is the option to be selective and to create your own individualised scheme of work.

The format of the units

Each unit starts with an overview and questions designed to help you establish students' prior learning. There is a group of key questions which define more specifically the main areas to be covered, as well as a list of key words and the outline of a medium-term teaching plan, which presents a six-week overview of how the texts and activities could be put together to form a teaching sequence. Guidance is given with regard to the relative complexity of each text, likely learning outcomes and suggestions for exploring links between texts.

The teaching notes for each text provide a clear indication of the Assessment Focuses and helpful contextual detail about the text. There are two starter activities of different levels of challenge, from which you can choose the one most appropriate for your students, before embarking on the reading and close study of the text. Whilst it is not essential for the texts to be read aloud, whether by you or your students, this is often a helpful way of engaging interest from the start. This is particularly the case with the more demanding texts. Weaker students can often be helped to tackle and understand material beyond their reading age by an initial perceptive reading of the text. These teacher notes contain a wide range of approaches to the first reading of a text. These are often interchangeable and can be used with texts beyond the anthology.

The activities in each unit are designed to raise the students' skills in all areas of their English. There are, for example, activities designed to move students on from literal reading to comment, and from comment to inference and exploration; activities designed to focus on the structure of sentences, paragraphs and whole texts; activities designed to build confidence and competence in speaking and listening and to increase understanding of the appropriate use of Standard English. In addition, each text carries an activity specifically designed to focus on and improve technical accuracy in spelling, punctuation and grammar, presenting you with an excellent opportunity to teach these essential skills in a relevant context. Learning outcomes are clearly indicated and opportunities for differentiation are regularly highlighted.

Additionally, each unit contains ideas for further resources, and suggests ways in which these could be used for development beyond the remit of the unit. These include recommendations for individual student reading or for class study, helpful links to websites, or DVDs that may be of interest.

At the end of each unit, there is a unit assessment task designed to test the skills developed in the activities. It is suggested that you use this once you are confident that students have completed a range of texts in the unit.

A bank of worksheets, produced to enhance specific activities, aid differentiation, and further develop technical skills, is provided after the units.

Online resources

A range of helpful, user-friendly online resources accompanies this book and the anthology. Working alongside the print resources, it provides:

- editable Word versions of all the worksheets from this book
- PowerPoint versions of a student-friendly format of each task that teachers can use in front of class and clear indications of the outcomes for each task
- exemplar annotated student work.

Flexibility

The key to using the *Essential Anthology* range of resources successfully is flexibility. In them, you have an excellent range of texts and detailed guidance on potential approaches to these texts. There are many ways in which these can be used: you might decide to work through a specific unit in the order in which the texts appear; you might select texts from across a number of units to provide a concentrated focus on a particular theme or the development of a specific area of your students' skills in English; you might choose to use individual texts to support other areas of study which you are pursuing. You, the teacher, know your students best. This book provides ideas and activities designed to stimulate interest and offer structured routes to learning but it is you, and the way you use these ideas and activities, who will ensure this learning happens.

UNIT 1 In the news

Overview of unit

This unit aims to give students an understanding of the various forms of broadcast and newspaper, as well as the linguistic and presentational features used to engage the reader.

Key words

Caption
Column
Editorial
Emotive
Purpose
Sensationalism
Strapline
Tagline

Assessing learning prior to this unit

1. What types of newspaper have students read?
2. How familiar are students with a range of linguistic and presentational devices?
3. What are students' current levels of reading, writing, speaking and listening?
4. What curricular targets do students have?

Key questions for this unit

1. Can I comment upon the differences between red top, broadsheet, local and international newspapers?
2. Can I develop my understanding of linguistic and presentational devices?
3. Can I write in various forms and conventions to suit purpose and audience?

Example scheme of work

A six-week overview of how the texts and activities could be put together to form a teaching sequence.

Week 1	Week 2	Week 3
• Introduce the unit using the light-hearted headlines from Texts 1 and 2. There is an introduction to linguistic devices in headlines and use of adjectives in Text 1. • Further work on headlines could be covered through Text 3, Activity 1. • Speaking work is offered on Texts 1 and 2 including a 90-second radio report, a debate on what is newsworthy, and reflection and target setting related to student performance.	• Complete language analysis and a summary using Text 3 about Edinburgh Zoo. • Writing activities offered include a factual report, a non-fiction leaflet and writing a counter argument using Texts 3 and 4. Text 3 links to Text 1, which is also about an animal. • Other activities analysing language are Text 5, Activities 1 and 3, and Text 6, Activity 4.	• Link pictures to newspaper stories using Text 5 on Asbos, which links to the activities on pictures using Text 6. • Emotive language is analysed using Texts 5 and 6 and factual reports on the texts are created. These link to factual reports earlier in the unit using Text 3.

Week 4	Week 5	Week 6
• Obituaries are studied using Text 7. Activities focus on connectives and structure before creating an obituary. • Fictional writing is covered in the form of a diary. • Social networking is considered as a form of news using Text 8. • Activities include speaking tasks and transformational writing (changing a piece from one style to another). This links to transformational writing in Texts 3, 5 and 6.	• Two newspapers from the same day, reporting the same story, are studied using Texts 9 and 10. • Activities compare the headlines and use of picture before considering the qualities of broadsheets and red top. • This can be linked with earlier activities on headlines and pictures using Texts 1–3 and 5–6.	• Text 11 offers a positive view of teenagers and focuses on speaking activities using a variety of approaches including Socratic Circles and role play. This links back to speaking activities on Texts 2, 6 and 8.

Assessing the learning outcomes of this unit

Reading tasks in this unit focus primarily on exploring issues of audience and purpose, and on analysing the effect of language choice and authorial viewpoint.

Writing tasks in this unit include writing news stories, magazine columns and obituaries.

Grammar and vocabulary tasks in this unit focus on alliteration, figurative language and spelling rules.

Spoken English tasks in this unit include debate, discussion and use of Socratic circles.

Links between the texts

Texts 1 and 2 look at analysing headlines which Texts 3, 9 and 10 build on.

Texts 3, 5 and 6 deal with language analysis. Emotive language is analysed using Texts 5 and 6.

Transformational writing (changing a piece from one style to another) is covered in Texts 3, 5 and 6.

Texts 9 and 10 are more challenging and look at different reporting of the same news story. This can also be linked with earlier activities on headlines and pictures using Texts 1–3 and 5–6.

Text 11 builds on work covered in speaking activities from Texts 2, 6 and 8.

Online resources

There are editable PowerPoint versions of all activities and Word versions of all worksheets available in Kerboodle.

In addition, there are exemplar student outcomes plus teacher notes and additional activities for the following activities from the Teacher's Book:

- Text 4: Activity 3
- Texts 9–10: Activity 1
- Text 11: Activity 3 (video)

1: Mugly by name, ugly by nature

Context

This is a story with international interest because it features a British dog winning a competition in California. The story is typical of the light-hearted style of stories that red tops print to amuse and entertain their readers. The photograph is large to attract readers and the language is simple. The headline, subheading and caption all use language in interesting ways to make the reader laugh. People usually enjoy animal stories.

This text would be suitable for Year 7s of all abilities.

Getting started

Introduce this text by asking students: 'Who likes animals?' Perhaps show them the picture without the story. They may like to guess what type of story has been written about the dog and guess its name. Discuss how this story will not interest everyone, but the cute picture and animal interest is widely appealing and provides a fun opportunity for writers to play with words and entertain the reader with something a little more amusing than the usual serious news. Students might like to consider other stories of this nature that they have read, or when it may be appropriate or inappropriate to include this genre.

Starter 1

Show students the picture only and tell them the dog's name is Mugly. They can discuss and feed back possible headlines that use the dog's name and hopefully a student will successfully rhyme this with 'ugly'.

Starter 2

Students can discuss the camera angle for this photograph. They should consider why the dog appears to be looking directly at the viewer and why the owner is not included in the picture. This will lead to a brief discussion about how newspapers create empathy from a reader through visual techniques as well as the written word.

Further resources

Further examples of people's views of ugly animals can be found at:

- www.bbc.co.uk/news/science-environment-24040130
- www.bbc.co.uk/news/magazine-20323753.

Activity 1

Response to the headline

Programme of Study link

Reading

- Knowing how language presents meaning
- Discussing reading with precise and confident use of linguistic and literary terminology

Description

Ask students to read the headline 'Mugly by name, ugly by nature: Chinese Crested from Peterborough wins World's Ugliest Dog'. Then ask students: 'What do you notice about the headline?'

In groups students should each be given one linguistic feature from the headline to find and comment upon, such as assonance (words that sound the same: Mugly, ugly, ugliest), play on words (words that sound like another word: Mugly) and alliteration (words that start with the same sound: Chinese Crested). Their comment should include a personal opinion about their own response to the headline and whether they think it captures the reader's interest. Students can use the point, evidence, explanation (PEE) technique for their comment. For example:

P: The headline uses assonance

E: Mugly, Ugly, Ugliest

E: The repetition of words that include 'ugly' stresses just how ugly the dog is, and that ugliness is the centre of the story

Groups of students can each present their linguistic feature to the class using the glossary if needed. Pairs then use this new information in their discussion of the overall effects of the headline and what they would expect the story to be about.

This can be followed by a one paragraph paired written response to the question, 'How does the headline engage the reader?'

Learning outcomes

- Students will be able to identify the basic features of language used in the headline and make a simple comment.
- Students should be able to apply appropriate terminology in identifying various features of the writer's language and make detailed comments.
- Students may show sophistication and begin to develop precise perceptive analysis of how language is used.

Differentiation

Lower ability students can be provided with a glossary of terminology.

Higher ability students should explain the meaning of terminology to lower ability students to demonstrate their understanding and should identify and comment upon more than one device.

Assessment opportunities

- Reading: critical analysis
- **RAF 5**

Activity 2

Creating a 90-second radio report

Programme of Study link

Spoken English

- Rehearsing and performing a play script

Description

Ask students to identify the key points in the article. These will be used to create a 90-second national radio news item reporting on and dramatising the event covered here. Students can use the Who? (who was involved), What? (what happened), Where? (where did it happen), Why? (why did it happen), When? (when did it happen) approach to locate appropriate information from the text or highlight a projected version of the story on a whiteboard. They can then write two sentences for each of these with separate opening and closing sentences for each. You may decide to complete this with the whole class before students work on their radio broadcast. Remind students that a radio broadcast needs to be short and sharp, portraying the key information quickly and simply. Current examples can be used, such as from BBC iPlayer (www.bbc.co.uk/radio).

Following the performance, the news items should be reflected on using Key Stage 3 Speaking and Listening criteria. Recording may help reflection. Students can mark one another for role play and drama (SLAF3) and then set targets for improvement (SLAF4). The next activity will take this reflection further.

Learning outcomes

- Students will be able to convey straightforward ideas about characters and situations making deliberate choices of speech.
- Students should be able to adopt a convincing role through flexible choices of language.
- Students may be able to reflect on and evaluate their own and others' discourse.

Differentiation

Lower ability students can be allowed three minutes for their radio news item. Listen to example radio news items before starting the task and list their features.

Higher ability students can mark one another using the Key Stage 3 criteria, applying key phrases from the criteria to demonstrate their understanding of it.

Assessment opportunities

- Spoken English: reading aloud and drama
- **SLAF 3, SLAF 4**

Activity 3

Reflection and target-setting

Programme of Study link

Writing

- Considering how their writing reflects the audience and purposes for which it is intended

Spoken English

- Giving short speeches keeping to the point

Grammar and vocabulary

- Discussing spoken language with precise and confident use of linguistic and literary terminology
- Drawing on new vocabulary and grammatical constructions and using these consciously in their writing and speech to achieve particular effects

Description

Following the reflective work in the previous activity, ask students to set themselves a clear target for improvement in Spoken English which they would hope to achieve during this activity. On completion of the activity, students should revisit their targets and assess whether they have achieved them.
It may be possible to look at Key Stage Spoken English criteria (SLAF3, SLAF4).

In pairs or individually, students should write a three-minute voice-over for the competition final leading to the announcement of Mugly winning the title of World's Ugliest Dog. The voice-over will feature a presenter or presenters introducing Mugly to the crowd, stating his name and age, the country he comes from and breed, before describing him as he walks out onto the stage in the final and is announced as the winner. The description should include a sentence about his physical appearance using the picture as a stimulus and an imaginative sentence about the types of activities he enjoys.

Learning outcomes

- Students will be able to reflect on their performance.
- Students should be able to demonstrate how they have achieved their target.
- Students may be able to demonstrate how they have exceeded their target.

Differentiation

Lower ability students can view some voice-over examples from television news reports where a reporter talks over a film sequence or a sports presenter comments on an event such as the build up to a horse race. A series of pictures can be selected or drawn by students to match key parts of the voice-over.

Higher ability students should include an interview with Mugly's owner to follow the voice-over. They can extend their evaluation to include a reflective written comment about how well achieved their target, using the assessment criteria as justification of their assessment. This can be extended to the evaluation of other performers.

Assessment opportunities

- Writing: style and vocabulary
- Spoken English: reading aloud and drama
- **WAF 7, SLAF 3, SLAF 4**

Activity 4

Adjectives

Programme of Study link

Writing

- Writing for a range of purposes and audiences
- Applying their growing knowledge of vocabulary and text structure to enhance the impact of their writing

Grammar and vocabulary

- Drawing on new vocabulary and grammatical constructions and using these consciously in their writing and speech to achieve particular effects

Description

Remind students of the definition of an adjective – a describing word, such as large or grey in the large elephant or the grey elephant. Ask them to list all the adjectives in Text 1, or they can highlight them on a whiteboard projection.

Now ask students to think about adjectives that are the opposite of 'ugly' and to change the report so it tells the story of a beautiful dog winning the World's Most Beautiful Dog competition. They should do this by swapping each identified adjective for a suitable word that changes the tone and subject of the report. A thesaurus can be used to expand vocabulary.

Learning outcomes

- Students will be able to demonstrate deliberate vocabulary choices.
- Students should be able to choose a range of vocabulary for effect.
- Students may be able to consistently and imaginatively match vocabulary to purpose and audience with precision.

Differentiation

Lower ability students can be supported through building a word bank in groups prior to writing, or through looking at an extract from Crufts for ideas about how to describe the dog.

Higher ability students should change the direction of the report completely by rewriting it as a critical account of the competition from the point of view that animals should not be entered into competitions to gratify their owners. This can be developed into a debate to pursue both sides of the argument and could include relevant speakers from the RSPCA, those running the competition, dog owners and perhaps representatives of the newspaper or the general public who were there.

Assessment opportunities

- Writing: style and vocabulary
- **SLAF 3, SLAF 4, WAF 7**

SPAG focus

Alliteration is when two or more words in a row start with the same sound – white whiskers, short snout, Chinese Crested. This is used to emphasise what is being described.

Using alliteration, write the missing word in each of these sentences:

- His .... face wouldn't win him any prizes in a beauty contest.
- The .... puppy followed its owner.
- She was wearing a .... dress.
- Are you looking at my dog's ....feet?

2: Whitstable mum in custard shortage

Context

This story appeared in a daily evening newspaper in Kent and is an example of one of the more light-hearted stories that newspapers report on from the local area. The headline is overly dramatic, suggesting a much more serious report than is presented, whilst the exaggeration adds a humorous tone to the story. The story is similar to the 'and finally ...' section of the evening news, which traditionally offers an amusing reflection of the day's stories to counteract the more dramatic and serious news.

This text is suitable for Year 7 students of low and middle ability.

Getting started

Introduce the text by referring to how, at the end of *The News at Ten*, there used to be an 'and finally' section with a light-hearted story. This story is much like that – not of interest to everyone, but fun and an opportunity for writers to play with words and make a drama out of nothing. Students might like to consider other stories of this nature that they have read, or when it may be appropriate or inappropriate to include this genre.

Starter 1

Ask students to name as many newspapers as they can.

This can be followed by a sorting exercise using the categories of broadsheet, red top, local, international. There may be scope to explore these categories depending on the previous learning of the group.

Discuss the change of name from 'tabloid' to red top due to some of the broadsheets changing size and why they changed size.

Starter 2

Start a class or group discussion about why people read newspapers (to find out about news/gossip/sport/TV, etc.). This could lead to a class survey asking students which newspapers they or their families read. Students could then create a bar chart or pie graph to collate the responses.

Activity 1

Headlines

Programme of Study link

Reading

- Making inferences and referring to evidence in the text

Spoken English

- Participating in structured discussions

Description

Using Worksheet 1.1, students discuss then decide which headlines are fictional and which they think could have actually appeared in print. The headlines are all for unusual stories, so students will need to consider how far-fetched they think real headlines can be and anticipate the stories that may accompany the headlines. They should look for over-dramatisation of simple events. Students can then write a few sentences justifying their decision regarding one or more of the headlines.

Learning outcomes

- Students will be able to read a range of newspaper headlines and make inferences based on evidence.
- Students should be able to justify their view by reference to particular words and phrases from that headline.
- Students may be able to argue and evaluate their view through reference to key words and phrases. They will consider counter arguments.

Differentiation

Lower ability students can be given one headline per pair or group to discuss then decide upon the nature of the story reported, if indeed they think it exists. Students can be asked to stand on either side of the room to indicate their preferences.

Higher ability students can write the opening paragraph to the story for one of the headlines with a focus on the five Ws – Who, What, Where, When, Why?

Assessment opportunities

- Reading: comprehension
- Spoken English: discussion and knowledge of language
- **SLAF 2, RAF 3**

Activity 2

Linguistic devices

Programme of Study link

Reading

- Knowing that language, including figurative language, provides meaning

Description

Ask students to reread the strapline (the secondary heading) 'A Mum of three … fruitless'. Using the table below, ask students to identify the linguistic devices used here and their effects before going on to the rest of the article to identify further examples of these devices and their effects (puns, humour, exaggeration, alliteration, etc.).

Devices	Examples	Effects
Pun	'fruitless'	Adds humour as it indicates the search for custard was a waste of time but also tells us the woman did not get her fruit pudding.

Learning outcomes

- Students will be able to identify a linguistic device from the text.
- Students should be able to explain the effects of the linguistic device on the reader.
- Students may be able to evaluate the effects of linguistic devices in Text 2 and create a glossary of linguistic devices for other students.

Differentiation

Lower ability students can be given a glossary of linguistic devices used in the article.

Higher ability students can locate different devices before teaching them to the other students. They can also write their own glossary of linguistic devices based on the article.

Assessment opportunities

- Reading: critical analysis
- **RAF 5**

Activity 3

Debate on what is newsworthy

Programme of Study link

Reading

- Making inferences and referring to evidence in the text

Spoken English

- Participating in formal debate summarising and/or building on what has been said

Description

In small groups, ask students to discuss what they consider news is, and then write a definition of 'news'. Groups should then discuss who the audience of this piece is and whether that makes a difference.

Ask students if they agree or disagree with the following statement: 'This type of article is not newsworthy and should not be given print space.'

They should complete a list of points that support their argument including evidence from the news article. They should also consider opposing points of view and what might be used in the argument against them. The teacher can chair the debate by inviting an opening argument from a confident student that is then countered by a group arguing for the opposite point of view. This pattern can continue. You may need to play devil's advocate if discussion dries up or you may need to address a student directly to encourage participation.

An overall vote can be taken on the worth of this type of story.

Students can use proximal learning groups or can work in groups of six and use de Bono thinking hats, which give individuals a defined role in a group as shown below.

- Blue hat – planning – How will we tackle this topic?
- White hat – facts – What do we know about the types of stories in newspapers?
- Red hat – emotions – How do we feel about serious stories and about amusing stories?
- Black hat – problems – Are there any weaknesses in these arguments regarding the inclusion of trivial news?
- Yellow hat – benefits – What are the advantages of light-hearted unimportant stories?
- Green hat – ideas – Are there any alternative or unusual solutions to including silly news?

Learning outcomes

- Students will be able to express an opinion based on their reading of Text 2.
- Students should be able to justify their opinion and consider the opposing point of view.
- Students may be able to argue their points logically and in detail whilst giving well thought out evidence against the counter arguments.

Differentiation

Lower ability students might need to be given points for both sides of the argument. They can sift through these and select those that they want to use in their presentation. Others may wish to use PowerPoint or other ICT to enhance their presentations if available.

Higher ability students can be encouraged to use role play to further challenge and support lower ability students who could take on the roles of an editor, journalist, Jules Serkin from the article or a local reader.

Assessment opportunities

- Reading: comprehension
- Spoken English: presentation and communication; discussion and knowledge of language
- **RAF 2, SLAF 1, SLAF 2, SLAF 3**

SPAG focus

the = definite article a/an = indefinite article

For example, 'Let's play the game,' means a specific game. 'Let's play a game' means any game rather than a specific one.

Explain to students the appropriate use of articles, using examples from the text – the Co-ops, a Co-op; a corner shop, the store.

Ask students to rewrite these newspaper headlines as normal sentences. Include the article *the* or *a/an* where necessary.

Bank cut up about losses

Racism law derailed

Government wrong on animal rights

United manager faces sack after string of defeats

'Video games corrupt youth' says Minister

Death of singer leaves band in chaos

Rising tide of divorce

3: Speed mating

Context

The *Telegraph* website is linked to the *Telegraph* broadsheet newspaper where different aspects of the newspaper can be accessed online. This contains a headline, photo and readers' comments about the story. This article appears under the heading of 'Telegraph View'. The story is concerned with Edinburgh Zoo's attempts to breed from two newly acquired pandas and will appeal to animal lovers as well as those interested in science.

This text is suitable for Year 8s of all abilities.

Getting started

Generate a shared context for reading this text through these starter activities.

Starter 1

Ask students what they think about the headline. 'Speed mating' is a clever pun on 'Speed dating' where potential lovers may meet. It thus implies the pandas are being encouraged to breed. Provide students with the picture from Text 3 and ask them to write a suitable caption for the photograph. Their caption can be relevant to the actual story or it can imply a completely different story.

Starter 2

Students can list the purposes of zoos, which will hopefully lead to the point that zoos breed endangered species. Broaden the discussion to consider what other species may be endangered and what is meant by 'endangered'. Students should be encouraged to express their opinions about how animals become endangered, and humans' role in this, as well as why protecting an endangered species is considered to be advantageous.

Activity 1

Headline switch

Programme of Study link

Reading

- Discussing how language features present meaning

Writing

- Applying their growing knowledge of vocabulary, grammar and text structure to their writing, and selecting the correct form

Description

A pun is a form of wordplay that suggests two or more meanings. It is effective because it has a humorous or rhetorical effect. Ask students to discuss, in pairs, the effect of the pun on 'Speed dating' in the headline and consider other stories that the headline could refer to. Ask paired students to compare their ideas with a different pair to see how others reacted to the pun. Ask students to write an alternative headline for this story using a different technique, such as one of those discussed in Text 1, Activity 1. Students should justify their choices and explain their effects by annotating the headline.

Learning outcomes

- Students will be able to discuss the headline and write an alternative.
- Students should be able to explain the effect of the pun and justify their alternative with reference to language features chosen.
- Students may be able to analyse the effects of the headline and their alternative and be able to justify their preferences.

Differentiation

Lower ability students may need support through the provision of a range of alternative headlines for Text 4 which they should rank in order of preference before justifying their choices.

Higher ability students can be challenged to provide further broadsheet and red top pictures with accompanying strap lines for analysis and creation of alternatives.

Assessment opportunities

- Reading: critical analysis
- Writing: style and vocabulary; grammatical range and accuracy
- **RAF 5, WAF 7, WAF 5**

Activity 2

Sum it up!

Programme of Study link

Writing

- Amending the vocabulary, grammar and structure of their writing to improve its coherence and overall effectiveness
- Summarising and organising material
- Applying their growing knowledge of vocabulary, grammar and text structure to their writing and selecting the correct form

Description

Ask students to summarise the editorial in no more than 50 words.

Explain that summarising is a means of shortening a piece, highlighting the main points. This can be done by making notes of the main events; placing them in order; and rewriting them in their own words, perhaps using short sentences or bullet points. Remind students to read through their response and check spelling and punctuation. Build the lesson up by doing these steps in turn until the 50-word limit is reached.

Learning outcomes

- Students will be able to identify key points from the article in 50 words. Full stops and capital letters will be used correctly.
- Students should be able to reduce the article to 50 words encompassing the main points of the original article. Punctuation will be used accurately to enhance meaning.
- Students may be able to reduce the article to 50 words, demonstrating well-controlled structuring of subject matter. Punctuation will be consistently accurate in a variety of sentence structures.

Differentiation

Lower ability students should work in pairs or small groups. They can be given a section of the article to reduce before joining with another pair who have reduced a different section.

Higher ability students can be instructed to use a variety of connectives.

Assessment opportunities

- Writing: form and structure; grammatical range and accuracy
- **WAF 6, WAF 3**

Activity 3

Language analysis

Programme of Study link

Reading

- Making inferences and referring to evidence in the text
- Knowing how figurative language features provide meaning

Spoken English

- Speaking confidently and effectively through giving a presentation, expressing their own ideas and keeping to the point

Description

Select an example of imagery from the article and model an explanation of its effect for students. Imagery uses linguistic devices to bring writing to life, conjuring up pictures of what is being written about. For example, 'the patter of little paws' to describe the prospect of offspring is more descriptive than simply hoping that offspring follow; 'performance anxiety' makes the pandas seem like performers rather than acting as nature intended.

Ask students to draw a table with three columns. The first column names the linguistic device such as metaphor, whilst the second column gives the example from the text. In the third column, students explain the effect of that imagery on the reader. The table is then used to produce a piece of writing that explains and comments upon the writer's use of language.

Learning outcomes

- Students will be able to select basic features of imagery from the text and attempt to explain the effect on readers.

Linguistic devices	Example	Effect
Metaphor	'Sweetie is girlishly watching her figure'	The panda is described like a girl wanting to look attractive for her first date. This humanises the panda and relates the story to real life.

- Students should be able to select various features of imagery from the text and demonstrate an understanding of their effect on readers.
- Students may be able to select a range of features of imagery from the text and develop a precise, perceptive analysis of how language is used.

Differentiation

Lower ability students might need some sections of the chart completed for them and the opening paragraph of the extended explanation modelled.

Higher ability students can be asked to give a spoken appreciation of how the writer's language choices contribute to the overall effect on the reader. They can use PowerPoint or other supporting resources and can be assessed.

Assessment opportunities

- Reading: comprehension; critical analysis
- Spoken English: presentation and communication
- **RAF 3, RAF 5, SLAF 1**

Activity 4

The zookeeper's report

Programme of Study link

Writing

- Writing for a range of purposes and audiences

Description

The article is light-hearted and humanises the pandas through figurative language – language that relies on devices such as metaphors and similes, as opposed to formal language which is more strictly accurate, using literal language. Ask students to identify all of the facts in this article and use these to write the 'Zookeeper's factual report' of the situation. They should imagine they are writing a formal report for the manager of the zoo. Students will need reminding that formal language avoids contractions (can't, won't) and slang, and establishes facts. This activity can be built through establishing a word bank of suitable vocabulary with reference to formality and tone in school reports which students will have experience of. Students should be reminded to use third-person narrative and avoid emotive language.

Learning outcomes

- Students will be able to write the zookeeper's report using facts from the editorial.
- Students should be able to adopt a suitable tone, vocabulary and format for the report.
- Students may be able to demonstrate consistent control of the appropriate level of formality and a varied range of stylistic conventions.

Differentiation

Lower ability students should be given topic sentences to structure their reports and can be given a writing frame or pro forma with selected facts to include. For example:

Pandas, Tian Tian and Yang Guang were placed together at … (time/place)

During their second meeting …

Higher ability students can undertake independent research to obtain additional information on this story to include in their report. Students can be extended through creating the zookeeper's report from a negative standpoint that is critical of the zoo's approach to the pandas.

Assessment opportunities

- Reading: comprehension; critical analysis
- Writing: from and structure; style and vocabulary
- **WAF 1, WAF 2**

Activity 5

Zoos – right or wrong?

Programme of Study link

Spoken English

- Participating in structured discussions, summarising and/or building on what has been said

Description

Using Worksheet 1.2, ask students to individually diamond rank statements about zoos for further discussion and debate. A diamond rank is a visible stimulus that enables students to order points according to given criteria such as 'most to least' important.

By putting students into groups, this can be developed into oral debate whereby students justify their preferences and extend their thinking to consider alternative views. Ask students to agree and justify a diamond ranking for their group. Students can also be asked to produce a written justification of their own diamond ranking, either without the group discussion or following a group discussion, which may cause them to amend their individual diamond ranking.

Learning outcomes

- Students will be able to rank the statements provided.
- Students should be able to rank the statements and explain their selection to another student.
- Students may be able to rank the statements, evaluate their choices and add to the statement bank.

Differentiation

Lower ability students might need you to remove some of the statements so that they have less information to read and rank.

Higher ability students can provide further statements for their peers to rank.

Assessment opportunities

- Spoken English: discussion and knowledge of language
- **SLAF 2**

SPAG focus

Homophones are different words that sound the same – for example, weak and week.

A Which is the correct homophone for the following definitions:

• The feet of an animal	Paws/Pause
• Popular with chips	Stake/Steak
• Two	Pair/Pear
• Between three and five	For/Four

B To, too or two?

- Edinburgh Zoo's _____ pandas.
- I am planning to go ____ the zoo.
- ___ foster a romantic atmosphere.
- The pandas are looking forward _____ mating _____.

C There, their or they're?

- Pandas will be given some privacy while they use _______ brief fertility window.
- _______ will be no candles and chocolates.
- _______ hoping that the patter of little paws will follow.

4: Should kids work for their pocket money?

Context

Bella magazine is a women's weekly publication featuring an opinion column consisting of two opposing views. Two writers argue 'yes' and 'no' in response to a topical question. An opinion column differs from an editorial in that it only reflects the view of that particular writer rather than presenting the standpoint of the entire publication. Therefore, the writer of an opinion column can be more controversial and outspoken. This text consists of just the 'yes' argument.

This text is suitable for Year 7s of middle and high ability.

Getting started

Students should carry out research prior to reading the article. They should ask parents/carers how much pocket money, if any, they received at the student's age and what was expected of them in return.

Starter 1

Ask students to provide feedback on homework research where they have asked their parents/carers how much pocket money, if any, they received as a child and what they had to do in return. Calculate a class average.

Starter 2

Groups of students can discuss what, if anything, they receive as pocket money and calculate an average for their group. These can be shared with the whole class and a class average can be calculated and discussed. Ask students what they have to do, if anything, in return for pocket money. Compare this with the results from the homework research.

Activity 1

Role play

Programme of Study link

Spoken English

- Improvising, rehearsing and performing play scripts using role, intonation, tone, volume, mood, silence, stillness and action to add impact

Description

Ask students to role play a parent/carer and child where the child requests pocket money. Remind them to think about their choice of words, and also gestures and movements, which help to make the scenario realistic and make their viewpoint convincing. In pairs, they should think about how a parent/carer might be expected to react as well as how the child may behave. They should think about words, gestures and movements. For example, in the first scenario the words might be kind and reassuring, with smiles and perhaps a hug. Three different scenarios can be created in the classroom. Scenario one is a role play with a parent/carer who hands over money without expectations. Scenario two is a parent/carer who wants jobs completed in return for giving pocket money, and scenario three is a parent/carer who refuses to give any pocket money at all. Students should present their role play to the rest of the class.

Learning outcomes

- Students will be able to convey straightforward ideas about characters and situations.
- Students should be able to show insight through deliberate choices of speech, gesture and movement.
- Students may be able to demonstrate empathy and understanding through insightful choice of speech, gesture and movement.

Differentiation

Lower ability students might benefit if you model one of the scenarios to support and provide a bank of stock phrases.

Higher ability students can be extended by recreating the role play in the era when their parents/ carers were children.

Assessment opportunities

- Spoken English: reading aloud and drama
- **SLAF 3**

Activity 2

Identifying the writer's argument

Programme of Study link

Reading

- Making inferences and referring to evidence in the text
- Knowing the purpose, audience for and context of the writing, and drawing on this knowledge to support comprehension

Description

Students should identify how many arguments the writer puts forward to support the view that children should not have pocket money without working for it. Bullet point these arguments. This is in preparation for the following activities, which build towards writing the counter argument to the text.

Students can use the bullet-point list from above. You should model embedding one of the bullet-point arguments in an explanation that identifies and comments on the writer's purpose and viewpoint. For example:

> The writer argues that children who work for their pocket money are more confident and have a better understanding of the value of money than those that do not work. The writer is implying that paid jobs are educational in teaching children that labour equals a wage and

that money from parents is not limitless. The suggestion is that children will feel they have earned the things that they can buy with the money they have worked for.

Students can continue this, working through their bullet-point list.

Learning outcomes

- Students will be able to identify the main purpose and viewpoint of the writer and make some simple comments about this.
- Students should be able to clearly identify the purpose and viewpoint of the writer and offer explanation with reference to the text.
- Students may be able to begin to develop some analytical or evaluative comment on how viewpoint is established.

Differentiation

Lower ability students can work in pairs or groups or complete guided writing with you.

Higher ability students should critically evaluate the effectiveness of the points made in the writer's argument.

Assessment opportunities

- Reading: comprehension; forms, conventions and language
- **RAF 2, RAF 3, RAF 6**

Activity 3

Counter arguments

Programme of Study link

Writing

- Organising material, and supporting ideas and arguments with any necessary factual detail
- Applying their growing knowledge of vocabulary, grammar and text structure to their writing and selecting the correct form

Description

Ask students to list arguments *against* children working for pocket money and place them in order of importance. Worksheet 1.3 supports this activity. If they have completed Activity 2 they could suggest counter arguments to each point they picked out. This can be carried out as a class or group discussion to collate information from Activity 2. Students can use Worksheet 1.4 to research the legal ages and hours for working children. They can then use what they have learned in an opinion column that supports the 'no' argument.

Ask students to write a column that supports the 'no' argument. The opinion column should consist of the counter argument to Text 4 and it should be in the same format as the 'Yes' opinion column in Text 4. They should deploy a range of stylistic features (alliteration, assonance, metaphors, puns, etc.), and structure their argument appropriately using connectives. Using the headings below, have a class discussion to produce a range of connectives that could be used in the 'No' opinion column.

Connectives to be used in argument writing:

- cause and effect: for example, consequently, as a result, thus, therefore, because
- contrasting: for example, on the other hand, on the contrary, an opposite view, whereas, alternatively, in comparison
- comparing: for example, equally, in the same way, similarly, as with
- emphasising: for example, above all, in particular, significantly, especially.

Learning outcomes

- Students will be able to organise ideas by clustering related points. The main purpose of the writing is clear.
- Students should be able to structure their material clearly with overall direction of the text supported by clear links between paragraphs. The main purpose of the writing is clear and consistently maintained.
- Students may be able to clearly control the material and sequence, taking account of the reader's likely reaction and adapting conventions to suit purpose and audience.

Differentiation

Lower ability students can be supported by a writing frame and topic sentences such as:

- Having children work for their pocket money exploits them because …
- Furthermore, children are not young for long and should be … rather than …
- Moreover, it is up to parents to provide their children with …

Higher ability students can be asked to select an appropriate illustration and create an alternative headline with a subheading. They can adapt layout to suit the form.

Assessment opportunities

- Writing: style and vocabulary; form and structure
- **WAF 3, WAF 2**

5: We don't need Asbos for yobs, we need police

Context

The *Sun* newspaper features television host Jeremy Kyle in this guest opinion column. A guest writer is chosen based on specialist knowledge, experience or reputation. As Jeremy Kyle is well known for his outspoken attitude and no-nonsense approach towards the public, the editor and reader may expect contentious issues to be discussed. It allows a newspaper to be controversial by proxy, through the voice of the guest writer, whilst remaining neutral itself.

This text is suitable for Year 8s of high ability.

Getting started

Students will probably have heard of ASBOs and may have their own anecdotes to tell. This can be introduced through examples of local news reports on ASBOs.

Starter 1

Ask students what they think an ASBO is (Antisocial Behaviour Order). They should discuss this in pairs and feed back what they think it means, how it works, and who might receive an ASBO and why.

Starter 2

Introduce the term 'stereotype'. Develop students' understanding of stereotypes through the role play of two stereotypical characters meeting in a doctor's waiting room – such as a policeman, teacher, tearaway teenager or granny, or more imaginative stereotypes like a cowboy, princess, villain or footballer. Go on to discuss what the stereotype of a person receiving an ASBO is.

Activity 1

Using synonyms

Programme of Study link

Grammar and vocabulary

- Consolidating and building on their knowledge of grammar and vocabulary

Description

Read the headline 'We don't need Asbos for yobs, we need police'. Students should focus on the word 'yobs' and suggest synonyms (words with the same or similar meanings) for this word: thugs, tearaways, louts. They can use a thesaurus or dictionary to help them. They can then choose one of these synonyms to replace the word 'yobs' in the headline and comment on the effectiveness of that choice.

Discuss how these synonyms compare with the stereotype of an ASBO recipient as established in Starter 2.

Learning outcomes

- Students will be able to find a synonym for the word 'yob' and make a simple comment on their choice.
- Students should be able to find up to 10 synonyms for the word 'yob' and show awareness of the effect of language choices.
- Students may be able to find 10 synonyms for the word 'yob' and show appreciation of how language choices contribute to the overall effect on the reader.

Differentiation

Lower ability students can work in groups using a copy of the appropriate page from a thesaurus. They can cross-reference their choices with a dictionary to ensure they understand the meaning of new words.

Higher ability students can work together and synthesise comments in a group to produce shared writing that analyses the writer's choice of headline and their own alternative.

Assessment opportunities

- Reading: critical analysis
- Writing: style and vocabulary
- Spoken English: discussion and knowledge of language
- **RAF 5, WAF 7, SLAF 2**

Activity 2

Linking presentation to meaning

Programme of Study link

Reading

- Making inference and referring to evidence in text

Spoken English

- Participating in structured discussion

Description

Read the article and study the picture. Pictures are important in news articles because, as is said, a picture is worth a thousand words – it can convey a message quickly and succinctly.

Pairs should discuss the presentation of the article, focusing on the picture and using the points below as a guide:

- What is the setting of this picture? Where might it be?
- What has been used to write on the wall? What is being suggested by this?
- Describe the style of writing in the picture and comment on its effectiveness
- Are the bricks new or old? Where might you see bricks like this?
- What is being 'let' in this mock advertisement?
- How does the picture link with the article?
- What is the overall effect of the picture?

Learning outcomes

- Students will be able to discuss the picture, making simple inferences when answering the questions.
- Students should be able to develop their comments about the picture, making inferences and deductions when answering the questions.
- Students may be able to begin to develop an interpretation of the picture, making connections between insights and weighing up evidence.

Differentiation

Lower ability students can use more detailed prompts for their discussion and be given key words such as 'graffiti' and 'humour' with explanations to support their commentaries.

Higher ability students can define 'satire' and discuss how this picture is satirical. They can discuss the caption under the picture.

Assessment opportunities

- Reading: comprehension
- Spoken English: discussion and knowledge of language
- **RAF 3, SLAF 2**

Activity 3

Emotive language and factual report

Programme of Study link

Reading

- Knowing how language, including figurative language and vocabulary choice, presents meaning

Writing

- Amending the vocabulary of their writing to improve coherence and overall effectiveness
- Selecting the appropriate form
- Summarising and organising material and supporting ideas and arguments with any necessary factual detail

Description

Using Text 5 and Worksheet 1.5, students can complete the activities on emotive language to promote their understanding of the writer's purpose and use of language. Emotive language is the use of words and phrases that create an emotional response and appeal to the reader's feelings. Emotive language is designed to make the reader feel a certain way – such as sorry for someone, or sadness, shock or relief. For example, yobs, tearaways or louts.

Having identified Jeremy Kyle's use of emotive language, students can recreate this article in a factual style for a police report. This should not contain any emotive language or ambiguous statements, but should clearly argue why ASBOs should be replaced with alternative sanctions. This will involve looking at Jeremy Kyle's opinions and writing them as fact, perhaps through the addition of a statistic or reference to an expert. Students may not find all the facts they require in the article so should be prepared to understand the style of a factual report and add material accordingly. Factual language is strictly accurate, using literal language rather than imagery and figurative language.

Learning outcomes

- Students will be able to produce a text in a suitable form for the purpose and audience.
- Students should be able to produce a text where purpose and audience are consistently maintained.
- Students may be able to produce a convincing text where purpose and audience are consistently maintained through individual voice or point of view.

Differentiation

Lower ability students can use Worksheet 1.6: an edited version of Worksheet 1.5 so that they have fewer emotive words to rank. A dictionary can also be used to support this task. Support lower ability students with a role play prior to writing where they role play two police officers discussing the pros and cons of ASBOs. Topic sentences can be provided with appropriate connectives to structure the argument. They may also need support in adding statistics and expert references.

Higher ability students can comment on the cumulative effect of emotive language by tracing key words and their use through the article. They can also create a factual report arguing the opposite point of view.

Assessment opportunities

- Reading: critical analysis; form, conventions and language
- Writing: style and vocabulary; form and structure
- Spoken English: reading aloud and drama
- **RAF 5, RAF 6, WAF 7, WAF 3, WAF 2**

SPAG focus

Speaking figuratively means the speech is not literal but uses a figure of speech, such as a simile or metaphor. For each of the following examples from the text, ask the students to explain the literal meaning. This can be done individually at first and then discussed in pairs and fours, comparing and building on others' thoughts.

- A tearaway whose life was turned round
- Without anyone ever feeling like they will be properly brought to book
- Those who delight in sticking two fingers up at the law
- Families where individuals had gone off the rails
- Nothing but cobwebs in the country's coffers
- Pull some lever in Whitehall
- Just as bad as the toothless ASBOs

6: Fallout from a photograph that shocked London

Context

Oli Scarff, a professional news photographer took this photograph at the Notting Hill Carnival in London on 29 August 2011. Scarff reacted to an incident occurring in the street, though at the time he did not know a stabbing had taken place. He took a series of photographs on seeing police rushing towards the crowd and only later realised he had captured both the victim and his attacker on film. The next day, Scarff's image featured in newspapers and on television across the UK and was a significant piece of evidence in bringing the attacker to justice.

This text is suitable for Year 9s of high ability.

Getting started

This topic can be introduced through some practical work selecting photographs from a range of broadsheets and red tops and looking at the different subjects chosen for pictures. Students might want to look at the percentage of space taken up by a photograph on the front page of different types of newspapers and consider what they can learn about the readers as well as the writers.

Starter 1

Make a spotlight tool by cutting a 2–3 cm diameter circle out of a piece of A3 card. Place the tool over a photograph so students can only view a selected area of the whole picture. Students should discuss what the whole picture might show and how they come to that conclusion. If an interactive whiteboard is available you could project an image and use the spotlight tool to explore it.

Starter 2

Provide a variety of photographs from newspapers to groups of students to match to a list of adjectives or to rank on a scale such as positive to negative. Vary the adjectives and criteria according to the vocabulary of the students.

Activity 1 

Deducing information from a photograph

Programme of Study link

Reading

- Making inference and referring to evidence in the text

Spoken English

- Participating in formal discussion

Description

Use the jigsaw technique. Firstly, each group must contain five students who all represent the same choice from the list of five Ws (who, what, where, when, why). For example, one table discusses 'Why?' whereas another table discusses 'Who?', and so on.

Then, after a short time discussing the prompt, the groups are rearranged so that each contains one student from each of the original groups. So each of the five different prompts (who/what/where/when/why) is represented in each group and students can share their ideas from the first discussion. Once everyone has fed back, students should spend 10 minutes writing down their personal responses to all five prompts and justifying this by drawing on evidence from the text.

Learning outcomes

- Students will be able to make inferences based on evidence from different points in the text.
- Students should be able to develop explanations of inferred meanings drawing on evidence from across the text.
- Students may be able to consider the wider implications or significance of information, teasing out meanings and weighing up evidence.

Differentiation

Lower ability students can be supported by offering some statements relating to the photograph and asking them to select the most likely scenario and find evidence from the text to support their selection. Statements could include:

- The man running away has stolen a knife.
- The scene is part of a drama presentation within the carnival.
- The stabbed man is a wanted criminal who threatened the public.
- This is a family dispute between relations.
- Both men have escaped from prison and are running from the police.

Higher ability students can further their responses by considering the time and place of the photograph then discussing how their responses may change if they were to place the photograph in a completely different time and place such as 50 years ago in a different country.

Assessment opportunities

- Reading: comprehension
- Spoken English: presentation and communication; discussion and knowledge of language
- **RAF 2, RAF 3, SLAF 1, SLAF 2**

Activity 2

Role play based on a photograph

Programme of Study link

Spoken English

- Improvising, rehearsing and performing play scripts using role, intonation, tone, volume and action to add impact

Description

Assign labels to the people in the photograph such as witness, bystander, victim, perpetrator or policeman. Students in pairs choose one of these people to interview in a role play. This could be a police interview with the perpetrator for example. Students should try to elicit as much information about the event and its circumstances as possible with a view to creating a written report in Activity 3. Questions might be:

- 'Where were you standing?'
- 'What did you see?'
- 'Did you see a knife?'
- 'How would you describe the people involved?'
- 'What were they wearing?'
- 'What did you hear?'

Learning outcomes

- Students will be able to convey straightforward ideas through deliberate choices of speech, movement and gesture.
- Students should be able to sustain and adapt different roles through flexible choices of speech, movement and gesture.
- Students may be able to give a more detailed response to ideas and issues by exploiting dramatic approaches and techniques creatively and experimenting with complex roles and scenarios.

Differentiation

Lower ability students can be supported through modelling different types of questions that a police officer might ask, for example, 'Where were you at the time of the incident?'. Ask for class suggestions of questions before beginning the task.

Higher ability students can be stretched by asking them to complete an additional role play changing the situation to a different time and place, such as a journalist interviewing a witness. They can discuss how the content and structure of the talk may vary according to time, place and context, and they can experiment with varying contexts.

Assessment opportunities

- Spoken English: reading aloud and drama
- **SLAF 3, SLAF 4**

Activity 3

Writing a witness statement

Programme of Study link

Writing

- Summarising and organising material with necessary factual detail
- Applying their growing knowledge of text structure to their writing and selecting the appropriate form

Description

Students follow the role play with a written witness statement from either the perpetrator, victim, a bystander or a witness. The witness statement should include evidence gained from the questions and answers in the role play, but it should be written in a formal, non-emotive, informative style as an official police document. The witness statement should be in chronological order detailing a sequence of events leading to the moment this picture was taken. More information on writing factual reports can be found in Text 3, Activity 4.

Learning outcomes

- Students will be able to organise their ideas into paragraphs, following a logical sequence.
- Students should be able to structure the material clearly using a range of features to signal overall direction to the reader.
- Students may be able to skilfully manage and shape text providing textual coherence and cohesion.

Differentiation

Lower ability students may be supported by providing them with a writing template with topic sentences or connectives to help them in linking ideas across the whole text (see Worksheet 1.7).

Higher ability students can be extended through transforming their text for a different purpose, such as the victim's blog or the witness's diary.

Assessment opportunities

- Writing: form and structure; style and vocabulary
- **WAF 2, WAF 3, WAF 4**

Activity 4

Analysing emotive headlines

Programme of Study link

Writing

- Applying their growing knowledge of vocabulary, grammar and text structure and selecting appropriate form

Description

Through discussion, analyse the emotive language in the headline accompanying the photograph 'Fallout from a photograph that shocked London' paying specific attention to the inferences of using the word 'fallout' and 'shocked'. Ask students to think of alternative scenarios which that headline could be describing, either in today's world or in history.

Remind students of the different types of newspapers, and the sorting exercise (Text 2, Starter 1) using the categories of broadsheet, red top, local, international. Ask students to select three emotive photographs either through research or from newspapers provided. For each photograph, students should write two headlines that demonstrate two entirely different scenarios to accompany that photograph. One headline should be for a broadsheet newspaper and the other for a red top newspaper and both are to be linked to the photograph. They should aim to use varied punctuation, emotive language and exaggeration as well as the features of headlines they have studied such as alliteration, rhyme, puns, etc.

Learning outcomes

- Students will be able to demonstrate some evidence of deliberate vocabulary choices.
- Students should be able to demonstrate a wide vocabulary chosen for effect.
- Students may be able to demonstrate imaginative, well-matched vocabulary that is ambitious and judiciously chosen.

Differentiation

Lower ability students may need to use a thesaurus. You can provide example headlines from newspapers to support them or give them words on card to accompany a selection of photographs. The words can be rearranged to form various headlines through manipulation of syntax.

Higher ability students can be extended by writing a 100-word report to accompany the headline they have created for a broadsheet and for a red top.

Assessment opportunities

- Writing: style and vocabulary; grammatical range and accuracy
- **WAF 6, WAF 7**

SPAG focus

Some words have a silent 'gh', like 'sight', but in others the 'gh' sounds like 'f', as in 'photograph'.

Sometimes the 'h' is silent and 'gh' just sounds like 'g', as in 'ghost'.

Ask students to use Worksheet 1.8 to write down a selection of these 'gh' words under the correct heading.

They can then use each word in a sentence of their own.

7: Bob Marley, the eloquent ambassador of reggae

Context

An obituary is a news article reporting a person's death, which includes an account of their life. While a local newspaper will print obituaries for any local resident, national newspapers like *The Times* and the *Guardian* only write obituaries for well-known people. Bob Marley, who features in this obituary in a national newspaper, was a famous Jamaican singer and political activist.

This text is suitable for Year 8s of lower and middle ability.

Getting started

As a starting point, ask students whether they have heard of reggae music and the Rastafari faith. They probably have, and may have heard of Bob Marley. This could lead to discussions and research into other reggae singers, what the features of reggae music are and whether they have listened to that type of music. Students will probably have lots of opinions about music that can prompt a discussion about internationally known singers and musicians and what their appeal is.

Starter 1

Research the word 'obituary' to ensure students understand what this type of news report is. Extend this to include false or premature obituaries and look at some famous obituaries such as Michael Jackson or Marilyn Monroe. These can be found through a search engine online or in the back of national newspapers.

Students can take turns to read out obituaries of famous people without revealing their name. Other students have to guess who is being referred to by focusing on the key details of the obituary.

Starter 2

Discussion: If you could have asked this person one thing, what would you have asked him/her? Why?

Discussion: If this person was to come back to life today, what do you think he/she would say about the headlines following his/her death? What would he/she think about the obituary?

Activity 1

Understanding obituaries

Programme of Study link

Reading

- Making inferences and referring to evidence in the text
- Knowing the purpose, audience for and context of the writing, and drawing on this knowledge to support comprehension

Description

Ask students to read the obituary and select key words and phrases that suggest to them what Bob Marley was like as a person. For example, the word 'conscientious' suggests that Marley was dedicated in what he did. This can be done as a mind map.

Ask the question: What impression is the reader given of Bob Marley? Select words and phrases to support your answer.

Students should be guided towards identifying facts and deducing further information from what is written or deliberately not written. For example, the article mentions he was a spokesman for young blacks but does not elaborate on what form this took and what his views were. No mention is made of his marriage or his numerous children. Why might this information have been omitted and is it important?

Learning outcomes

- Students will be able to select factual information supported by relevant textual reference.
- Students should be able to summarise and synthesise factual information from different places in the text incorporating apt textual reference, making inferences with regard to ambiguous information.
- Students may be able to precisely select and apply textual reference and identify subtle inferences in support of an interpretation of the text.

Differentiation

Lower ability students can be supported by using group mind maps with some preselected points already added. These could include Marley's importance in bringing reggae music to a worldwide audience, his links to politics and how he distanced himself from his musical success. Provide relevant textual references to be matched to aspects of the person such as 'has been almost single-handedly responsible for introducing reggae music to an international audience'. Students can consider aspects of the person such as 'dedication to work' and mark on a scale of 1–10 where they perceive the person to be. They can then add key words from the text indicating this.

Higher ability students can use this textual evidence to create a short speech that Bob Marley could give explaining his passion for his music and politics, and his vision for the future. Students will need to use first-person narrative and include the information they deduced about Bob Marley as a person so that they present him through his own words.

Assessment opportunities

- Reading: comprehension
- **RAF 2, RAF 3**

Activity 2

Writing a newspaper obituary

Programme of Study link

Writing

- Summarising and organising material
- Applying their growing knowledge of text structure

Description

Using Worksheet 1.9, students can research then write the newspaper obituary of a famous person.

Students should focus on their writing skills in presenting factual information in an accessible and interesting way using a chronological style to guide the reader through the main points. Encourage them to use appropriate connectives in their obituary to provide order and sequence.

Learning outcomes

- Students will be able to cluster related points and include relevant material.
- Students should be able to effectively manage material across the text, developing ideas and material for the selected form.
- Students may be able to skilfully manage and shape information to achieve the intended purpose using a style and convention matched to the intended effect.

Differentiation

Lower ability students will find Worksheet 1.9 supportive as a writing template. They can choose a celebrity for their obituary and look at some examples before writing.

Higher ability students can be challenged through their choice of person, such as a literary or mythological hero, which will involve greater research. This can be related to texts studied in class.

Assessment opportunities

- Writing: style and vocabulary; form and structure
- **WAF 1, WAF 2, WAF 3, WAF 4**

SPAG focus

Introduce different types of connective such as causal (because, so), adding (also, furthermore), temporal (then, later) and exemplifying (for example). Following this, discuss the different purposes of connectives with a focus on temporal or time connectives to provide order.

Students can decide where to add connectives to the text and discuss how they can create a better structure in the obituary through these connectives. This can be completed with coloured pens on a whiteboard projection or by adding sticky notes to the text. The discussion should lead to the identification of chronological order and its purpose in information writing of this type.

8: Twitter news stories

Context

Twitter is an online social networking site where users send and read texts of up to 140 characters that are called 'tweets'. Twitter was created by Jack Dorsey in 2006 and is based in San Francisco in the United States. It now has over 140 million users worldwide with up to 340 million tweets being posted every day making it one of the top 10 internet sites. Users can upload their tweets from their mobile phones or other devices and the service is a bit like texting except it is over the internet so reaches a wider audience more quickly. It is easy to see why some users have landed themselves in trouble through using Twitter. An example is the revelation of model Imogen Thomas's affair with footballer Ryan Giggs, which was revealed through Twitter despite his High Court injunction preventing newspapers from naming him. Other celebrity stories include 'rants' and arguments played out through Twitter by stars like Rihanna or Katie Price (aka Jordan).

This text is suitable for Year 9s of middle and high ability.

Getting started

Students will need to understand the difference between counting words, counting letters and counting characters since Twitter is limited to 140 characters per tweet. Some discussion can be generated regarding why this limit may be in place and the advantages/disadvantages of it. Students may have their own anecdotes to share and might want to look at the different Twitter names that celebrities choose.

Starter 1
Ask students to name all of the ways they communicate with their friends and family. Collate the ideas and draw up a tally chart to see which are the most popular methods. This should lead to a discussion of modern technology and its role in communication and spreading information.

Starter 2
Return to the list of communication methods from Starter 1 and label them as usually involving either formal language (not using slang words, using correct grammar and spelling, e.g. school essays, business documents) or informal language (a casual, familiar and generally colloquial use of language, such as talking to friends, Facebook posts, etc.).

Activity 1

Advantages and disadvantages of Twitter

Programme of Study link

Writing

- Writing for a range of purposes and audiences
- Considering how their writing reflects the audience and purposes for which it is intended

Description

Discuss with students how the instantaneous and far-reaching nature of tweets can be both a disadvantage and an advantage. The discussion may cover advantages such as: it is instant, short, often emotional and reactive so engaging to the reader, and it can reach a large number of readers quickly. Disadvantages may include the fact that although a remark can be removed, it may have been read by many already or 're-tweeted' so it will continue to exist in someone else's profile. Also, it may be created in the heat of the moment, and the voicing of certain emotions may be regretted later.

Students should discuss how best to advise a Twitter user so as to avoid the pitfalls. Then they can design 'Etiquette for Tweeting'. This can be written as an advisory piece. The tone should be advisory and helpful, and advice can include a cooling off or waiting time before 'going live' with tweets or avoiding unpleasant, nasty, mean or clever insults. Further advice can be not naming others, consideration of possible readers, use of photographs, and how to include lots of information in 140 characters using abbreviations that can be understood.

Learning outcomes

- Students will be able to discuss the nature of tweeting and write advice for users.
- Students should be able to recognise the arguments and their counter arguments and use these to offer clear, helpful advice.
- Students may be able to develop precise, perceptive advice in a sophisticated style.

Differentiation

Lower ability students can look at some further examples of tweets. These can be found through a search engine. Offer sentence starters such as 'To avoid upsetting others, make sure you …' and 'Use abbreviations that can be understood, like …'.

Higher ability students can be stretched by changing the audience at which their advice is directed, such as aiming it at a celebrity rather than a member of the public.

Assessment opportunities

- Writing: style and vocabulary
- **WAF 2, WAF 7**

Activity 2

Using de Bono thinking hats

Programme of Study link

Spoken English

- Speaking confidently and effectively using Standard English
- Participating in structured discussions, summarising and building on what has been said

Description

Ask students to read the first story about the man who used Twitter to travel around the world and then the third story about a party that becomes uncontrollable. Some might argue that whilst story one gives a positive use of social media, the third story is a good reason not to use social media networking sites. Students should draw a chart of positive (P) negative (N) and interesting (I) points relating to social networking sites and their place in modern society as a whole. This can be furthered through additional research.

Using the chart, groups of six can debate the role of social networking sites in modern society. Groups can use the de Bono thinking hats so that each person has a defined role in the discussion as follows:

- Blue hat – planning – How will we tackle this topic?
- White hat – facts – What do we know about social networking?
- Red hat – emotions – How do we feel about social networking?
- Black hat – problems – Are there any weaknesses in these arguments regarding social networking sites?
- Yellow hat – benefits – What are the advantages of social networking sites?
- Green hat – ideas – Are there any alternative or unusual solutions to social networking?

Students should reflect on their performance after the task.

Learning outcomes

- Students will be able to take a defined active role and contribute to the discussion.
- Students should be able to develop discussions in different ways and understand implicit meanings.
- Students may be able to interrogate and respond to what is said, showing perceptive understanding of complex, varied speech.

Differentiation

Lower ability students might need to have roles assigned with de Bono hats according to strengths and confidences of each student. Provide key points about social networking sites to support lower ability students, or complete whole class discussion and mind mapping first. Key points may include advantages such as easy accessibility from mobile phones, PCs and internet cafes, keeping in touch, promoting a product or service and publicity, and the disadvantages such as risks of cyber bullying, viruses, identity theft and addiction.

Higher ability students can work in larger groups with additional students assigned to the role of marking the speaking of the main six students using the Key Stage 3 speaking and listening criteria. Extend higher ability students further through analytical reflection on their own performances using the Key Stage 3 speaking and listening criteria.

Assessment opportunities

- Spoken English: discussion and knowledge of language
- **SLAF 2, SLAF 4**

Activity 3

Creating a leaflet

Programme of Study link

Writing

- Writing for a wide range of purposes and audiences
- Drawing on knowledge of literary and rhetorical devices to enhance the impact of their writing
- Using Standard English confidently in their own writing

Description

Students should complete Starter 1 and identify which methods use the most modern technology. In pairs, ask students to discuss the issues linked with modern communication, such as how the elderly may cope with texting or emailing and the problems that may occur when trying to teach someone how to use these methods. Students should be made aware of predictive text and its advantages (it is quick, it may help spelling) and disadvantages (wrong words chosen).

Ask students to plan then create a leaflet called 'Teaching Your Granny to Tweet' or 'Teaching Your Granny to Use Facebook'. Students need to be familiar with writing to advise and instruct as well as demonstrate understanding of the features of non-fiction. This should include providing reasons for a course of action, several suggestions about what to do, building the confidence of the reader, using imperatives, and it should lead to a clear conclusion about actions to be taken. The leaflet should use formal and informal styles as appropriate. (A reminder of key features of leaflets can be found in Text 3, Activity 6.)

Learning outcomes

- Students will be able to demonstrate clear purpose in their writing, with ideas that are relevant to the chosen content.
- Students should be able to demonstrate consistently maintained purpose in their writing, development of ideas and material with some imaginative detail.
- Students may be able to demonstrate adaptation of form and convention with distinctive style matched to intended effect.

Differentiation

Lower ability students can be supported by receiving a selection of non-fiction leaflets as examples so that they can discuss key features such as eye-catching presentation, clear layout, not too much text, catchy slogans. A template can be designed from a sample leaflet and appropriate vocabulary can be written as a class.

Higher ability students can create a YouTube-style 'How To' video using filming techniques or still images. This can be accompanied by the student's explanation of their techniques and intended effects.

Assessment opportunities

- Writing: style and vocabulary; form and structure
- **WAF 3, WAF 1, WAF 2**

Activity 4

Writing transformation

Programme of Study link

Writing

- Summarising and organising material
- Drawing on grammatical constructions and using these consciously in their writing to achieve particular effects

Description

Using any of the Twitter stories from this text, students are to transform the full report into a 140-character tweet that captures the essence of the original story. Groups of students should first discuss the abbreviations they themselves use when messaging others, then compile a list of the common ones. The discussion should move on to personal abbreviations suggested by students that others do not use and consideration of the confusion this may cause. An example is 'lol' which used to mean 'lots of love' but has come to mean 'laugh out loud'.

Learning outcomes

- Students will be able to transform the text for a new purpose and audience showing some awareness of the reader.
- Students should be able to transform the text for a new purpose and audience and maintain the reader's interest throughout.
- Students may be able to transform the text for a new purpose and audience, directly addressing the reader and taking them into their confidence.

Differentiation

Lower ability students can work in small groups highlighting key information on the reports before deciding what should be in the final tweet. They may need to see further examples of tweets.

Higher ability students can use one of the other texts in the book, which are much longer, and transform that into a 140-character tweet.

Assessment opportunities

- Writing: style and vocabulary
- **WAF 2**

SPAG focus

When you add 'ed' or 'ing' to verbs of one syllable that end with 't', the following rules apply:

- Double the 't' if it is preceded by a single vowel – for example, jot and jotted.
- Do not double the 't' if it is preceded by a double vowel – for example, Tweet and Tweeted.

Using these rules, combine the following words with the suffixes given in brackets:

- bat (ing)
- pet (ed)
- greet (ing)
- fit (ing)
- root (ed)
- pot (ed)
- net (ed)
- flirt (ing)
- float (ing)

9–10: Fuel crisis articles

Context

Panic gripped Britain when the workers' union Unite called for oil-tanker drivers to strike over pay and working conditions. Government minister, Francis Maude, made the situation worse by suggesting drivers fill cans with petrol in case of a strike and, though no strike actually occurred, drivers hurried to the petrol pumps fearing a fuel shortage. These two stories demonstrate the power of the media in influencing public behaviour and attitudes, and illustrate the wit of the red top.

In Text 10 the same story is reported in a red top on the same day as Text 9, which was in a broadsheet. Notably, the headline in the broadsheet story (Text 9) is much more serious than in text 10, the *Daily Mirror*, though it is interesting to note the two newspapers have used the same image of a man carrying cans of fuel. This sort of approach is good preparation for the non-fiction element of the GCSE examination where both layout and language features are always asked about.

This text is suitable for Year 9s of middle and high ability.

Getting started

This topic can be introduced through general discussion about strikes. Should people have the right to strike? Or should certain occupations not be permitted to strike? Once students consider which services they perceive as essential for life, they may have strong views about striking. It is worth considering the way society has evolved in the last 100 years and how reliant we are on cars, for example.

Starter 1

After reading the front page, in pairs students should discuss who is the intended audience for the two newspapers (the *Daily Mirror* and *The Times*). They can also think about the titles of these two newspapers and discuss connotations. This can be extended to include other broadsheets and red tops with consideration of intended audience.

Starter 2

Ask students to identify alliteration in the main story headline and experiment with alliteration using their own names. They can also consider the meaning of the pun in Text 9 and the effect this has.

Activity 1 

Denotation and connotation

Programme of Study link

Reading

- Making reference and referring to evidence in the text
- Reading critically knowing how language presents meaning
- Discussing reading with precise and confident use of literary terminology

Description

Begin with a class discussion of denotation (literal meaning) and connotation (associated meaning) to ensure that students understand both terms. A starting point could be the colour red, where denotation would state it is a primary colour but the connotations may include danger, blood and passion. Small groups can mind map the denotations and connotations of the headline in Text 9.

Students can move on to mind map the denotations and connotations of the headline in Text 10. They can produce a written analysis comparing the headlines, using their mind map to help them. Remind students how to structure a piece of comparative writing using comparative connectives like: similarly, in comparison and however. Students should focus on purpose and audience with consideration of the differences between a broadsheet and a red top as well as on the language choices made to suit purpose and audience.

Learning outcomes

- Students will be able to identify and make simple comments about structure and language.
- Students should be able to draw together comments on structure and language with explanation.
- Students may be able to show clear appreciation and understanding of how structure and language support the writers' purpose and contribute to meaning.

Differentiation

Lower ability students can be supported with analytical labels to link to the correct part of the headline: 'alliteration creates sharp, crisp sounds to mirror sharp, crisp movements of martial arts' and 'the word "crisis" implies a serious situation that will not be solved easily'.

Higher ability students can repeat the activity with other headlines from the texts in this unit. They can research other headlines from 30 March 2012 that relate to this story and rank them according to their effectiveness.

Assessment opportunities

- Reading: comprehension; critical analysis
- **RAF 3, RAF 4, RAF 5**

Activity 2

Comparing syntax in broadsheets with red tops

Programme of Study link

Reading

- Making critical comparisons across texts
- Knowing how language, including figurative language, vocabulary choice and grammar present meaning

Description

Using Text 9 and Text 10, or one broadsheet and one red-top newspaper from a range offered in the classroom, ask students to work through the tasks below:

- Count the number of words in the first five sentences of each story on the front page.
- Count and make a tally chart to show the number of syllables per word in these sentences.
- Highlight the different punctuation marks used by each paper and show findings in a tally chart.
- Present findings as a written analysis comparing the syntax, punctuation and vocabulary favoured by each type of newspaper.

If the provided texts are not used, make sure that the examples offered have been carefully selected to ensure there are significant differences that can be identified. You should include a political or financial story from a broadsheet and a story about a celebrity from a red top for the best results. You can guide students to particular paragraphs of increasing/ diminishing complexity.

Learning outcomes

- Students will be able to identify and comment on structure, language and punctuation, and make simple comparisons.
- Students should be able to identify and explain writers' use of syntax, vocabulary and punctuation, making connections between texts.
- Students may be able to evaluate and compare the extent to which syntax, vocabulary and punctuation choices support the writer's theme or purpose.

Differentiation

Lower ability students can be supported by providing them with a writing frame that contains topic sentences and key words.

Higher ability students can be asked to repeat the tasks using a local newspaper and to include this third type of paper in the written analysis.

Assessment opportunities

- Reading: critical analysis; forms, conventions and language
- **RAF 4, RAF 5**

Activity 3

Comparing use of pictures in broadsheets and red tops

Programme of Study link

Reading

- Knowing the purpose, audience for and context of the writing and drawing on this knowledge to support comprehension

Description

Both *The Times* and the *Daily Mirror* use the same picture of a man carrying six metal petrol cans, but the pictures are used for different purposes and have different effects on the reader.

Compare and evaluate the effectiveness of the caption used with the picture in each newspaper, commenting on how it contributes to overall meaning:

Daily Mirror: 'HOARD filling up jerry cans'.

The Times: 'The owner of a shop in Bournemouth carries his six jerry cans to sell to panicked motorists'.

Learning outcomes

- Students will be able to make simple comments on language and structure.
- Students should be able to begin to develop detailed exploration of language and structure.
- Students may be able to evaluate the use of language and structure with appropriate terminology.

Differentiation

Lower ability students can evaluate the effectiveness of just one photograph with its caption. A writing frame is provided on Worksheet 1.10.

Higher ability students can relate this picture to the other pictures used in the story and evaluate the effectiveness of the pictures together.

Assessment opportunities

- Reading: critical analysis; forms, conventions and language
- **RAF 4, RAF 5**

Activity 4

The qualities of a broadsheet and a red top

Programme of Study link

Reading

- Making critical comparisons across texts
- Reading critically knowing how language, including figurative language, vocabulary choice, grammar, text structure and organisational features, presents meaning
- Knowing the purpose, audience for and context of the writing, and drawing on this knowledge to support comprehension

Spoken English

- Participating in structured discussions, summarising and building on what has been said

Description

Using their analysis from Activities 1–4, students in pairs can compile a list of the qualities of each newspaper to include picture captions, use of linguistic devices in the headline, sentence length and word choices, for example. They can compare lists in groups and feed back to the whole class so that you can extract the main points and draw the information together, pointing out the ways in which the newspapers are similar and/or different.

Learning outcomes

- Students will be able to make simple comparisons of language, structure, audience and purpose.
- Students should be able to provide detailed explanations of language, structure, audience and purpose.
- Students may be able to show clear appreciation and understanding of how text structure and language supports the writers' purposes and contributes to meaning.

Differentiation

Lower ability students may need a writing frame or they could draw up a chart of comparative points before writing. The opening section can be modelled by you or created through guided writing in small groups according to ability.

Higher ability students can conduct research into the topic and how it was presented in the media, and this can be included as part of their analysis. They can develop their list of newspaper qualities into a full written comparison, using the information from the previous activities on the texts.

Assessment opportunities

- Reading: critical analysis; forms, conventions and language
- Spoken English: discussion and knowledge of language
- **RAF 4, RAF 5, RAF 6, RAF 7, SLAF 2**

11: Teenagers: they don't drink, they don't smoke. What do they do?

Context

The report is a light-hearted but positive look at teenagers and offers a different point of view to Text 5 which is negative towards teenagers. The article includes several interviews with teenagers so a variety of voices is heard though they seem to support the same point of view.

This text is suitable for Year 8s of high ability.

Getting started

This is a subject that will be close to students' hearts so it is worth setting a homework task for them to collect newspaper reports about teenagers. The stories can be sorted into negative and positive views to spark discussions about how teenagers are presented in the media and whether presentations are neutral or biased.

Starter 1

Discussion: at what age do students think they are adults? Students should consider the legal changes that occur when they turn 18 and are officially adults. It becomes legal for them to participate in certain activities. Discuss why such age-related laws are in place and whether students think they are necessary.

Starter 2

Role play a teenager attempting to persuade an adult to allow him or her to do something such as staying out at a late-night party, living with a boy/girlfriend or going on holiday with friends. Students in the role of teenagers should offer reasons to support their request, whilst students playing the role of adults should offer valid reasons against the request.

Activity 1

Age-of-consent laws

Programme of Study link

Spoken English

- Using Standard English confidently in a formal classroom discussion
- Participating in structured discussions, summarising and/or building on what has been said

Description

Students should work in groups of three or four. Give each group one statement or all four of the statements shown below that relate to child consent laws in the UK. They should discuss the age at which they think a person is legally allowed to:

1. have their own mobile phone contract
2. be asked to give their fingerprints at a police station in relation to a crime
3. buy alcohol
4. have their own bank account in their own name.

This will lead to discussions of child consent laws together with students' knowledge of these and misconceptions. It may be interesting to note where any student finds they are breaking the law themselves.

The answers are 1: 18; 2: 10; 3: 18; 4: 5.

Ask students to consider whether they comply with these and whether they think the age limits are appropriate.

Learning outcomes

- Students will be able to develop their ideas within a structured discussion.
- Students should be able to shape speech in deliberate ways for clarity and effect.
- Students may be able to manage and manipulate speech with precision and effect.

Differentiation

Lower ability students can be supported with easier statements such as the legal age for buying alcohol, which is more widely known than the legal age for fingerprinting.

Higher ability students can be given additional statements to discuss with regard to whether the age limits are appropriate and why, such as:

- Car passengers are responsible themselves for wearing their own seatbelt from the age of 14.
- From 2015, all young people have to be in job training or full-time education until they are 18.
- You must be 18 to have a mortgage or rent a property in your own name, but you can leave home at 16.

Assessment opportunities

- Spoken English: presentation and communication
- **SLAF 1**

Activity 2

Who? What? Where? When? Why?

Programme of Study link

Reading

- Making inferences and referring to evidence in the text
- Reading critically

Description

Pairs should read the text and identify the key points using the prompts: Who? What? Where? When? Why?

This links back to Text 6, Activity 1 and can be followed by highlighting the projected text on the whiteboard in five colours to correspond with these five prompts. Alternatively, students can use sticky notes in five colours to identify sections of the text. These five prompts are being looked at to identify the balance of information in the article and identify the facts presented. This also reiterates to students the requirement to provide this basic information in a newspaper article.

Learning outcomes

- Students will be able to identify relevant points from the text.
- Students should be able to identify clearly the relevant points and incorporate some textual evidence.
- Students may be able to select detailed points that are well supported by textual reference.

Differentiation

Lower ability students may need more detailed prompts or preselected information to sort into the correct categories given above.

Higher ability students can be asked to apply the who, what, where, when, why approach to an article they select from some sample newspapers or from other texts in this unit. Again they should look at the balance of information by highlighting a projected picture or using coloured sticky notes as before. They should write a commentary on the balance of the information.

Assessment opportunities

- Reading: comprehension; critical analysis
- **RAF 2, RAF 3**

Activity 3

Using Socratic circles

Programme of Study link

Spoken English

- Participating in structured discussions, summarising and/or building on what has been said

Description

Read the article and draw attention to the passage 'At worst, they're hoodie-wearing, gang members – smashing up shop fronts, not out of political motivation, but for free trainers. At best, they're monosyllabic airheads obsessed with Facebook.' Discuss as a class what is meant by these sentences and draw out the negative points such as teenagers are unintelligent vandals who do not speak clearly.

Students should work on a Spoken English task using Socratic circles. The class is organised into two concentric circles facing one another. Those in the inner circle talk to those in the outer circle about the extent to which they think teenagers deserve such labels. Students in the outer circle just listen to the speaker and do not comment.

It is important to swap students over at some point so that everyone has an opportunity to speak and to listen on the same topic.

Once completed, place students into groups of four to discuss what they have heard and said so each group can feed back the main ideas to the whole class. This feedback should also include comments on how others spoke during the activity.

Learning outcomes

- Students will be able to contribute to the discussion and listen to another speaker.
- Students should be able to draw ideas together and move a discussion forward as well as demonstrate focused listening skills.
- Students may be able to show perceptive understanding of varied, complex speech sustaining concentrated listening.

Differentiation

Lower ability students may need to be listeners first to gather ideas that they can use when they are speakers.

Higher ability students can research examples of news stories featuring teenagers that counteract this quotation. These can be presented back to the rest of the class.

Assessment opportunities

- Spoken English: presentation and communication; discussion and knowledge of language; reading aloud and drama
- **SLAF 1, SLAF 2, SLAF 3**

UNIT 2 Language out loud

Overview of unit

This unit aims to make explicit the differences between informal and formal spoken language. The texts represent a range of speech styles, and students will have the opportunity to speak in formal and less formal ways as well as to complete some analytical work on spoken source texts.

Key words

Compressed grammar
Formality
Multimodality
Phonetic spelling
Standard English

Assessing learning prior to this unit

1 How confident are students about adapting their speech for more formal contexts?
2 How familiar are students with the differences between spoken and written language?
3 Have students worked with transcripts of spoken language before?

Key questions for this unit

1 Can I make relevant contributions to discussions by listening to others and adding my ideas?
2 Can I use my speech to create effective performances in improvisation, poetry and drama?
3 Can I give a short speech or presentation to convey information or ideas?
4 Can I explain why being able to speak in Standard English is important?
5 Can I understand and explain different views about spoken language?

Example scheme of work

A six-week overview of how the texts and activities could be put together to form a teaching sequence.

Week 1	Week 2	Week 3
• Explore Texts 1 and 2. Include activities on vocabulary and a discussion activity allowing assessment of students' discussion skills. • Text 3 moves the focus on to how speech is presented in writing, allowing students to explore a novel extract and complete some narrative writing. This can be assessed for any writing objectives, or it can be used to assess how students have presented speech and created a spoken-style voice.	• Text message language can be explored using Text 4. This text offers linguistically focused activities that are likely to be new to the students. This can be extended by exploring messages on their own phones to broaden the introduction of linguistic methods if desired. • There is also a creative writing task on this text, asking students to adapt their language and write in a particular way.	• Texts 5 and 6 explore the question of language in schools. • Both texts can be studied together, or students can complete the activities in Text 5 first to ensure they understand the 'slang' arguments before moving on to Text 6, which focuses on dialect. • The activities include a formal debate, writing a formal letter, a presentation and writing a report, offering a range of assessment outcomes.

Week 4	Week 5	Week 6
• Text 7 and Text 8 (two poems) set up a project on performing poetry aloud. • Students can practise and try out different ways of speaking on the poems provided, and then research to find a poem they would like to present. This is assessed as a Spoken English task.	• Speaking for information and instruction can be explored through the how-to video transcribed as Text 9. This offers students the opportunity for some more Spoken English work when they prepare an informative or instructive talk of their own. • There is also some more analytical work on structure (through the SPAG focus activity). • Another type of speech is explored through Text 11, an extract from Malorie Blackman's Children's Laureate acceptance speech, with activities analysing it structurally (looking at discourse markers) and an imaginative writing task.	• More poetry can be explored in Text 10 (Six O'Clock News), but the focus of the activities here is more on the meanings conveyed in the poem, asking students to think about people's attitudes to accents. • This can be usefully linked with Text 12 (an extract from *Pygmalion*) with Activity 1 focusing on attitudes to language and subsequent activities focusing more on the play (performance – again to potentially assess for Spoken English – and guessing what happens later).

Assessing the learning outcomes of this unit

Reading tasks in this unit mostly focus on audience or introduce analytical skills in studying spoken language.

Writing tasks in this unit include narrative writing, letters, reports and imaginative personal writing.

Grammar and vocabulary tasks in this unit focus mainly on the differences between spoken and written English, with some attention also to different varieties of English.

Spoken English tasks in this unit include discussion of language, formal presentation and poetry performance.

Links between the texts

Texts 1 and 2 show experts offering feedback to the public, varying in their depth of detail.

Texts 4 and 10 could be examined together for technical linguistic analysis, as both use non-standard features.

Texts 5, 6, 10 and 12 all deal with attitudes to language in different ways. Texts 10 and 12 are more challenging texts and could build upon work done from Texts 5 and 6 to enable progression.

Online resources

There are editable PowerPoint versions of all activities and Word versions of all worksheets available in Kerboodle.

In addition, there are exemplar student outcomes plus teacher notes and additional activities for the following activities from the Teacher's Book:

- Text 1: Activity 2 (video)
- Text 10: Activity 2
- Unit assessment task

1: Emma Hearts LA

Context

This is the opening of a novel that follows the story of a teenage girl struggling with the upheaval of her life when her family decide they are moving to LA.

Using the first person and the present tense, the text has a very immediate style of narration that also mimics speech is some specific ways (e.g. 'She's a drama dork, my sister.'). The text also features dialogue, allowing for activities based on using direct speech effectively in narrative writing.

The book is marketed at 12+-year-olds and is accessible to Year 7 students while also being of interest to Year 8 and 9 pupils. The activities here are pitched more towards the Year 7 level, but can also be productively enjoyed by older students (with less support).

Getting started

What kinds of stories do students enjoy? Has anyone read any books by this author before? A brief discussion about the kind of book that this is (or could be) might be a useful starting point.

Starter 1

Students discuss their reading (and perhaps viewing) habits in pairs. Which genres do they particularly like or dislike, e.g. crime, horror, romance, adventure, real-life, etc.? Is this novel the kind of thing they would usually choose?

Starter 2

Hold a vote in class to see where in the world students would choose to live. They can choose by continent, you can give a short list to select from (e.g. the US, Australia, Spain, the United Arab Emirates, South Africa), or they can simply write a place on a slip of paper. Some students can then be asked to explain their choice.

Further resources

Here are some popular recent novels. All titles are by UK-based authors (no US dialect) and are worth exploring in terms of narrative voice.

First-person narratives:

- *Acid* by Emma Pass
- *Fifteen Days without a Head* by Dave Cousins
- *When I Was Joe* by Keren David

Third-person narratives:

- *Hollow Pike* by James Dawson
- *Mortal Chaos* by Matt Dickinson
- *Monkey Wars* by Richard Kurti

Activity 1

Analysing the presentation of spoken language

Programme of Study link

Grammar and vocabulary

- Studying the effectiveness and impact of the grammatical features of the texts they read

Description

Students think/pair/share how the text creates a spoken voice and what the effect on the reader is. Firstly allow students time to work on their own to come up with ideas in response to the task. They can then get into pairs to share and collate their ideas before feeding back to a larger group or the whole class. Some will be able to do this unaided, while others will benefit from being directed (see the prompts below under differentiation).

Learning outcomes

- Students will be able to recognise differences between spoken style and written style and consider how this affects the reader.
- Students should be able to identify first-person narrative and informal vocabulary choices and consider how these contribute to a relationship between the writer and the reader.
- Students may be able to recognise syntactical choices to create a spoken voice style and link these to an effect on the reader.

Differentiation

Lower ability students may benefit from more direction in the form of prompts such as:

- Find three words or phrases that you think sound more like things people say than things people write.
- Do you think this book opening sounds more like a modern story or a traditional story? Give reasons for your answer.
- Would you agree that a stereotypical story style would start something like 'Once upon a time, there was a young girl who …'? In how many ways does the style of this story differ from that model?

Higher ability students would benefit from being asked: 'How does this text create a spoken voice? Find and identify as many techniques used as possible.'

Assessment opportunities

- Reading: critical analysis; forms, conventions and language
- **RAF 5, RAF 6**

Activity 2

Acting and reacting

Programme of Study link

Spoken English

- Improvising, rehearsing and performing play scripts and poetry in order to discuss language use and meaning, using role, intonation, tone, volume, mood, silence, stillness and action to add impact

Description

How would you feel if it was announced that you had to move abroad? Why might a parent make that choice?

Students role play a scene in which a family deals with the idea of moving overseas. Students can work in threes (to give a parent and two children, as in the text) or in larger groups with a different family structure. The aim is for students to react to one another and interact realistically, thinking carefully about how to express their views appropriately. Students should be encouraged to use gesture and tone of voice effectively to create the most realistic performance they can.

Learning outcomes

- Students will be able to express ideas creatively using language and action.
- Students should be able to make use of movement, gesture and posture to convey ideas.
- Students may be able to express complexity and ambivalence using drama.

Differentiation

Lower ability students should work on the scenario in a straightforward way, selecting roles to represent a family group and the likely discussion they would have in this situation.

Higher ability students can be challenged to try out different reactions before deciding which one to role play.

Assessment opportunities

- Spoken English: reading aloud and drama
- **SLAF 3**

Activity 3

Writing creatively in the first person

Programme of Study link

Grammar and vocabulary

- Drawing on new vocabulary and grammatical constructions from their reading and listening, and using these consciously in their writing and speech to achieve particular effects

Description

Students imagine a scenario that they would feel strongly about (such as the family moving overseas, as in the text, or changing schools, a new baby in the family, no more pocket money due to family budget tightening, a grandparent moving in because they need care, etc.). They produce a piece of creative first-person writing expressing their feelings and showing a reaction. They can be encouraged to fictionalise themselves (e.g. exaggerate their own traits or give their narrator characteristics that they do not share). Some students can also be challenged to include dialogue and to show discussion with other characters about the scenario.

Learning outcomes

- Students will be able to write consistently in the first person and show some emotional reactions to an imagined situation.
- Students should be able to create a spoken tone convincingly in their writing.
- Students may be able to produce convincing dialogue and vary their voice for different characters.

Differentiation

Lower ability students may benefit from support given through examining the source text in more detail. How do we know that Emma is not happy about the move? (She does not exactly say so.) A planning session with guidance on what to think about might help students who lack confidence in their ideas (e.g. What arguments can you use to protest against this idea? What questions would you have about it? How might your family respond?). Worksheet 2.3 may be used to support this task.

Higher ability students can be explicitly challenged to include two characters besides the narrator and to show the narrator's emotional response without using emotional vocabulary (i.e. showing anger and not telling the reader 'I am angry.').

Assessment opportunities

- Writing: style and vocabulary
- **WAF 1**

SPAG focus

The focus on how speech is represented here presents an ideal opportunity to discuss and explicitly draw up rules for writing direct speech. Worksheet 2.4 can be used to support core and lower ability students. Students can:

- explain and/or demonstrate how direct speech is punctuated
- produce explanatory posters for display in the classroom.

The task on creative writing (and any exploration of narrative voice or comparisons with other novels) also provides an opportunity to talk about tense consistency in writing. Students can:

- check their writing specifically for tense consistency
- continue the narrative extract
- convert the narrative extract to the past tense
- convert their own writing to experiment with different tenses.

2: The Great British Bake Off

Context

The Great British Bake Off is a televised baking competition which uses expert judges and focuses on the specific skill of baking. The programme is enormously popular, appealing to a somewhat specialist audience who have an interest in food and baking.

The transcript shows the judges giving feedback to two contestants. The activities on this text are aimed at the Year 7 level. This text could be a useful introduction to transcripts, as it is quite straightforward with little in the way of hesitancy and simultaneous speech.

Getting started

Who has watched *The Great British Bake* off or other talent-based television programmes? Many students will have watched this or similar programmes and will be quite happy to discuss and explain the format to those who are less familiar with it. Opening with a broader field (e.g. *The Voice*) may be more accessible for students unfamiliar with this programme.

Starter 1

Students role play being television judges. This can be left quite open, or it can follow the text quite closely with students giving feedback based on baking. Students could be asked specifically to role play commenting on a singing act. How can they describe good singing, for example, tuneful, melodic, beautiful, uplifting?

Starter 2

Why do people watch talent-type television programmes? For example, do they want to be entertained, or inspired, or encouraged? Audience is a key contextual factor in this text, so it is a good idea to encourage students to think about audience from the start.

Further resources

Clips from further similar programmes can be examined and considered in terms of audience and how the vocabulary is pitched for them. For a broad range, programmes like *The Apprentice* and *Dragon's Den* can be compared alongside more arts-based shows such as *Strictly Come Dancing* or *The X Factor.*

Activity 3 asks students to compare the language used here with another clip (which they watch, rather than studying a transcript). Suitable programmes include *Britain's Got Talent*, which allows a comparison of broad versus specific feedback, *The Voice*, which also offers specific feedback but in a different field, or *MasterChef* for very specific feedback in a related field.

Activity 1

Vocabulary to describe performances

Programme of Study link

Grammar and vocabulary

- Consolidating and building on their knowledge of grammar and vocabulary

Description

Using a thesaurus, gather positive and negative vocabulary to describe performances or skills (this can focus on food to match the text, but it does not have to). All students should be encouraged to use a dictionary to double-check the suitability of words found in a thesaurus. Students should present their favourite vocabulary finds in the form of three short 'judge's comments'.

Learning outcomes

- Students will be able to use a thesaurus to find new vocabulary, using a dictionary to check its suitability.
- Students should be able to produce varied 'judges' comments' by selecting appropriate new vocabulary.
- Students may be able to find and use a range of descriptive vocabulary, including adjectives, verbs and adverbs.

Differentiation

Lower ability students can be given a frame to complete at the finding stage (e.g. 'That was ...'; 'In my opinion that was ...'; 'I have to say that ...'; or 'You are a ... cook/baker.', etc.). They may also use frames to present their favourite found words.

Higher ability students can be challenged to find and include verbs and/or adverbs as well as adjectives.

Assessment opportunities

- Writing: style and vocabulary
- **WAF 7**

Activity 2

Commenting on vocabulary in the texts

Programme of Study link

Grammar and vocabulary

- Consolidating and building on their knowledge of grammar and vocabulary
- Discussing reading, writing and spoken language with precise and confident use of linguistic and literary terminology

Description

Students draw out the vocabulary used in the text to describe Janet's and Jason's macaroons, either by being asked simply to find words and phrases describing them, or by being instructed more specifically to identify adjectives, verbs and phrases used to give the contestants feedback. For example, adjectives: 'chewy', 'dry'; verbs: 'coming through', 'tastes'; phrases: 'makes you smile'.

Having listed words and phrases that describe contestants' food, they then select three words or phrases to analyse by explaining their likely effect on the contestants, for example, to praise or instruct (and perhaps also their broader effect, for example, to evoke physical sensations as in 'makes you smile').

Learning outcomes

- Students will be able to explain the intended effect of vocabulary choices, e.g. in terms of praising Jason.
- Students should be able to explain the effect of vocabulary choices in terms of expressing positive opinions.
- Students may be able to explain the effect of figurative uses of vocabulary.

Differentiation

Lower ability students can use Worksheet 2.1 to help them.

Higher ability students may be able to work from the instruction 'Find adjectives, verbs and phrases that give the contestants feedback'. They can also be challenged to provide completely separate explanations for their three examples (ideally referring both to more abstract effects of language and to the personal effect on contestants).

Assessment opportunities

- Reading: critical analysis
- **RAF 5**

Activity 3

Comparing the transcripts – audience and purpose

Programme of Study link

Grammar and vocabulary

- Discussing reading, writing and spoken language with precise and confident use of linguistic and literary terminology

Description

Students consider the differences between this text and another clip, in terms of the concepts of audience and purpose.

Suitable programmes to use include *Britain's Got Talent*, *The Voice* and *MasterChef*.

To do this, they work in pairs or small groups and decide between them what is different about the audiences for each of these two programmes. You may need to encourage them to think in terms of why each audience watches and what each audience is expected to know already. For example, the *Britain's Got Talent* viewers might be watching because they want to be entertained by a variety of acts. *The Great British Bake Off* viewers might also want to be entertained, but already have an interest in food and might be hoping to pick up some baking ideas.

Then they identify three features of the two programmes (this can be three quotations or three more abstract features such as specialist vocabulary, specific versus non-specific adjectives – amazing/gooey, and formality) which support their ideas about the audiences.

Learning outcomes

- Students will be able to consider different audience needs and interests and recognise that these have an impact on language use.
- Students should be able to connect vocabulary choices to audience, e.g. to explain that specialist vocabulary is used to appeal to a specialist audience.
- Students may be able to discuss differences in formality based on different audience expectations.

Differentiation

Lower ability students can be supported towards the idea that a *Great British Bake Off* audience is expected to understand a range of concepts relating to food, whereas *Britain's Got Talent* does not make any expectations in terms of specialist knowledge of singing (perhaps because it accepts acts of any type and not just singers). They can be asked to find quotations that demonstrate this without conceptualising it any further, for example *The Great British Bake Off* transcript includes descriptions of the macaroons' specific qualities such as 'dry' or 'gooey'.

Higher ability students may be expected to compare the audiences and language without assistance, and to use more terminology (e.g. adjectives) to describe the language they select as evidence.

Assessment opportunities

- Spoken English: discussion and knowledge about language
- **SLAF 4**

Activity 4

Discussing 'talent show' television

Programme of Study link

Spoken English

- Participating in formal debates and structured discussions, summarising and/or building on what has been said

Description

Students work in small groups to discuss views about talent shows on television. They should discuss in a formal and structured way, addressing set viewpoints and considering how they feel about these different ideas. Each group is given a set of viewpoints (perhaps 3–5) and told that they must consider the pros and cons of each viewpoint and then, as a group, rank them in terms of how far they agree with these views.

Set viewpoints to consider can include:

- Talent television shows are a good way of providing family entertainment.
- Talent shows focusing on specific skills such as cooking are useful for people to learn from.
- People who are humiliated on talent television shows set themselves up for it.
- Talented people can be discovered and develop a career in entertainment.
- The judges on talent television shows are chosen because they are expected to be controversial.
- Talent television shows encourage bullying by making it acceptable to criticise and laugh at people.

Learning outcomes

- Students will be able to express their own views and make them clear to others.
- Students should be able to listen to other views and build upon them.
- Students may be able to take a leading role in discussion and support others to contribute.

Differentiation

Lower ability students can be given fewer viewpoints to discuss.

Higher ability students can be challenged to also add to the viewpoints they are given – perhaps adding two opposing or contrasting views to the list.

Assessment opportunities

- Spoken English: discussion and knowledge about language
- **SLAF 2**

SPAG focus

How do we form comparatives and superlatives? Students may remember from KS1–2, but some may need reminding of the -er/more and -est/most patterns. The focus here on giving people feedback and commenting on performance provides an opportunity to practise forming comparatives and superlatives.

Students can role play giving feedback that focuses on how to improve, perhaps returning to adjectives found in Activity 1 and converting them to comparatives, for example, delicious to more delicious or chewy to chewier.

An additional task to reinforce the concept of comparatives and superlatives is to produce a written newspaper-style review on an imaginary episode of a talent show, making comparisons between the acts and ideally using superlatives as well. Students can examine some newspaper reviews first to help them with the format. A challenge to include three comparatives and three superlatives can also be given. Worksheet 2.2 provides a Cloze-style exercise to support lower ability students by focusing on comparatives and superlatives as the main learning aim.

3: Text messages

Context

The text message has exploded into a popular medium of communication. Students will be familiar with text messages but may not have considered them as things to be studied. In linguistic studies, text messages are seen as being multimodal as they are neither fully written texts (due to the fact that they are informal, conversational and not intended to be fixed or permanent) nor are they fully spoken (since they are received and interpreted visually rather than aurally and can therefore use symbols and non-letter characters as part of their communication).

This collection of text messages allows some initial exploration linguistically and provides an opportunity to open up debate about register and using different forms of language in different contexts.

The activities here are all quite linguistic in focus and are geared towards the later end of Year 7 or Year 8, but the data set could also be explored productively with Year 9 students (see the differentiation notes for ideas on appropriate terminology and concepts to introduce for more challenge).

Getting started

Who uses text messaging? Students are likely to be able to readily discuss what text messages are for and to be able to start to describe the specific vocabulary of texting.

Starter 1

In pairs or small groups ask students to share their opinions about text messaging. Do they use text? Who do they text with? What purpose do text messages serve?

Starter 2

How would you explain the language of text messaging? In pairs, students can write 3–5 rules about how you can write in a text, imagining that they are writing for someone who has never used it.

Further resources

Other multimodal texts such as forum posts or tweets can be explored in a similar way. It is a good idea to stick to relatively monologic texts (single-voiced rather than interactions between two or more participants) to start with so that issues of turn taking and response can be considered separately at a later time.

Activity 1

Identifying the features of text messages

Programme of Study link

Grammar and vocabulary

- Discussing reading, writing and spoken language with precise and confident use of linguistic and literary terminology

Description

Students explore the collection of texts in order to identify ways in which 'text message language' is distinct from other kinds of language. This can be introduced before students even see the messages with the straightforward question: 'What is text message language?'

The aim of the task is for students to produce a set of ideas about what makes text language special and distinct, which they will then be given the appropriate labels for. This way, they are engaging with the data and working to classify and categorise its features without getting bogged down in looking for examples of particular things. They can also be encouraged to include their own existing knowledge of text messaging, not just examples from Text 3. This works well as a paired activity (in matched-ability pairs), so that students can share and develop ideas together.

The feedback phase can also include class discussion about why these features are used. Some features are used to save space, but not all. It is also worth discussing why some people use text forms and some do not – predictive text and smartphone tendencies to correct may play a role, but also some types of people avoid using text message style reductions. With more able students, this may serve to introduce the idea of our language use linking to our identity. For example, when we speak, our vocabulary choices and expressions can reveal something of our personality or background, and the choices we make about how we use text language can do the same.

Some students will enjoy beginning to work with terminology relating to multimodal texts, for example:

- number homophones (both on their own and as part of words), e.g. 4, 18r
- letter homophones, e.g. u, b
- clipped letters from the end of words, e.g. seein
- phonetic spelling, e.g. evryone
- deleted letters (especially vowels), e.g. tmrw, hlp
- slang and colloquial words, e.g. gonna
- initialisms (where the letter names are said), e.g. idk, h/w, and acronyms (where the letters can be said as a word), e.g. lol
- informal greetings, e.g. hey, hey hun
- exaggerated phonetic spelling/elongated words, e.g. pleeease
- non-standard use of punctuation for effect, e.g. ?!?!?
- compressed grammar (missing out non-essential words), e.g. Hey u ready? U ok?
- symbols and emoticons, e.g. xxx :-)

Learning outcomes

- Students will be able to explain key features of text messaging such as deleted or clipped letters, homophones and initialisms.
- Students should be able to explain and label features that are used for brevity and those that are used for expression.
- Students may be able to express ideas about language as an aspect of personal identity.

Differentiation

Lower ability students can be asked to seek out patterns (such as missing letters or use of non-letter symbols) and then list these, with examples, according to whether the feature saves space in a text or is used for some other reason (to then be discussed). They can be led to notice that some texts show changes to spelling while others miss out words but avoid using any non-standard spellings.

Higher ability students can seek out patterns and then be provided with labels from the list above to apply to their findings. This can be completed as a Q&A feedback session, in which students explain something they've noticed and are then given the appropriate label before the class discusses why a writer may choose to use that feature, perhaps referring back to the texts in the source or using their own experience.

Assessment opportunities

- Spoken English: discussion and knowledge about language
- **SLAF 4**

Activity 2

Introducing multimodality

Programme of Study link

Grammar and vocabulary

- Discussing reading, writing and spoken language with precise and confident use of linguistic and literary terminology

Description

Students identify ways that text messages and other blended or multimodal forms of communication are like speech, and ways in which they are written.

In pairs or small groups, students use a large piece of paper and create a spectrum by writing 'Written' at one end and 'Spoken' at the other. They can initially discuss ways in which written language is different to spoken language (e.g. more formal, more visual, more likely to be addressed to a large unknown audience, etc.). The idea of 'channel' can be introduced in this initial discussion, i.e. that written language is a visual phenomenon (received by the eyes) and written texts can use layout, images and symbols as part of their meaning, while spoken language is aural (received via the ears), meaning that spoken texts can make more use of sound.

They can then plot different aspects or features of the language (identified and discussed in Activity 1) onto this written/spoken spectrum to show the modal range in this blended form. They are likely to produce more detailed, analytical work if it is modelled for them first, for example by placing 'Hey' as a greeting in the spoken half of the scale (not all the way at the spoken end, but partway between the centre and 'Spoken'), and labelling it 'Informal greetings'.

Worksheet 2.5 also explains and models this for students and can be used to support weaker students once the basic idea has been introduced.

Clearly, the extent to which students can label features in detail depends on the depth achieved in Activity 1, but all should be able to think about whether a feature is more typical of speech or writing. The trickiest ones are things like acronyms, as they only work as written features in that they depend on being seen, but they are too informal for traditional written texts. However, many KS3 students will not yet be able to see this complexity, and making decisions based on a feature's formality is perfectly acceptable at this stage.

Learning outcomes

- Students will be able to think about the degree to which key features are 'written' or 'spoken'.
- Students should be able to recognise that there is a link between formality and mode.
- Students may be able to begin to consider the impact of 'channel' (i.e. to realise that written = visual, and spoken = aural, and what impact this has on the text).

Differentiation

Lower ability students will need to rely more heavily on Worksheet 2.5 to prompt them. Then they will be discussing the various features in terms of how 'written' or 'spoken' they are, perhaps by thinking about other kinds of text that use the same features.

Higher ability students can be challenged to think of further examples of multimodal communication (e.g. Facebook chat, tweets, online forums). Can they think of any features or conventions from these types of communication that are not included in this set of text messages?

Assessment opportunities

- Reading: critical analysis; forms, conventions and language
- **RAF 4, RAF 5, RAF 6**

Activity 3

How do we use language in text messages?

Programme of Study link

Grammar and vocabulary

- Discussing reading, writing and spoken language with precise and confident use of linguistic and literary terminology

Description

Students develop from labelling features and plotting them on a mode continuum to writing analytically about how language is used in this medium. This is essentially an activity to 'write up' the previous two activities.

Students practise producing PEE (point, evidence, explanation) chains or analytical paragraphs by explaining how the features of text messages relate to their purpose, context and intended meaning.

Following an introduction to PEE chains (or other models used such as TEPE – technique, evidence, purpose, effect), students select three aspects of the text messages to produce PEE chains about. They should identify (i.e. label) features, give evidence (i.e. provide examples of quotations) and explain how each feature is typical of text messages and/or what its intended effect is.

Learning outcomes

- Students will be able to make connections between the way language is used and context, for example in commenting on the level of formality appropriate in a text message.
- Students should be able to link language choices to mode, for example by explaining features as typical of multimodal talk.
- Students may be able to link language choices to intended effect, for example in terms of conveying friendliness.

Differentiation

Lower ability students will benefit from creating a chain as a class first, or from having one modelled for them.

Higher ability students can be challenged to ensure that their comments on effect or explanations are as different as possible for each of the three chosen features.

Assessment opportunities

- Reading: forms, conventions and language
- **RAF 6**

Activity 4

Creative writing in different modes

Programme of Study link

Writing

- Considering how their writing reflects the audiences and purposes for which it was intended

Grammar and vocabulary

- Drawing on new vocabulary and grammatical constructions from their reading and listening, and using these consciously in their writing and speech to achieve particular effects
- Knowing and understanding the differences between spoken and written language, including differences associated with formal and informal registers, and between Standard English and other varieties of English

Description

Students work on writing basic stories using different styles based on different modes. Students can invent a story which they then tell in different ways, or present a familiar story such as a fairy tale or a class text in different ways. Students can be told particular formats to use, with some initial class discussion about appropriate language for different formats, or they can be asked to choose an alternative format to produce alongside a more typical written story.

Possible formats include:

- a series of tweets (140 characters each)
- a series of Facebook entries (length not so controlled)
- a story using text message language.

For example, a series of tweets for Snow White could include:

- Stepmother acting v strangely today – keeps talking to a mirror! #weird
- Going for a walk in the forest with the huntsman today.
- Grumpy in a really bad mood today. Must keep smiling ☺

Plenary discussion can usefully focus on the idea of appropriacy – students can explain why writing in this form is not usually recommended, or why it is useful to be able to adapt writing style in this way.

Learning outcomes

- Students will be able to adapt their writing to different contexts, clearly writing in more- and less-formal ways as is appropriate for the context.
- Students should be able to make choices about both vocabulary and the form of words, e.g. using text message abbreviations as appropriate.
- Students may be able to vary syntax as well as vocabulary, for example by using compressed grammar in less-formal writing.

Differentiation

Lower ability students may require a more structured approach, for example by being instructed to write a story in a standard way first and then being asked to adapt it into text language. A particularly weak group may do well in creating (or recalling) a story as a group which they then adapt into text language independently.

Higher ability students are likely to benefit from more freedom of choice in the exercise. They can be asked to list all of the ways they communicate multimodally on a regular basis (e.g. Facebook, Twitter, texts, etc.) and then asked to create a series of short texts from the point of view of a character from a well-known story or a class reader. Can other students guess who they are writing as?

Assessment opportunities

- Writing: style and vocabulary
- **WAF 2, WAF 7**

4: Hiya pupils, please avoid slang, ta

Context

This is an interesting text on one school's decision to ban all slang from the school grounds. This raises interesting questions in relation to identity, language, life chances and language use. The school clearly feels, as others have in the past, that enforcing a particular kind of language will help to prepare their pupils for adult life and success in the workplace. However, there seems to be a lack of recognition that slang is an important part of how pupils express themselves, that spoken language is different from written language, and that the whole of the school grounds may not really be considered a formal space.

The activities here are focused around Year 8 in terms of level.

Getting started

A fairly simple 'what do you think of this?' discussion is a reasonable starter for this text. Students are likely to have opinions about the ideas presented, and the text does provide different perspectives that will help students to consider all angles.

Starter 1

How should we talk in school? In pairs, students try to list three reasons why language in school should be controlled and three reasons why it does not need to be controlled.

Starter 2

Individually at first, students should write down three to five words or phrases that they regularly use which are considered slang. Have they ever been told not to use them in certain contexts? How did that feel?

Further resources

This text links well with the next one, which focuses specifically on dialect and its exclusion from a school. The *Pygmalion* extract at the end of the unit can also be brought in here for a mini-unit on attitudes to non-standard language use.

Activity 1

Structured discussion – language in schools

Programme of Study link

Spoken English

- Participating in formal debates and structured discussions, summarising and/or building on what has been said

Description

Students use de Bono thinking hats to carry out a structured discussion on the topic of how language should be used in schools. This discussion can be constructed as one hat (or two hats) per group, or you can ask students to work through the whole series. If using two hats per group, these can be doubled up so that each colour is tackled by two different groups, perhaps combining them differently so no two groups have everything the same (e.g. white + blue, blue + black, etc.). This can lead to a jigsaw group scenario if time allows (e.g. group A is white and blue, group B is blue and black, group F is yellow and white, so group A splits and joins with pupils from B to discuss blue and F to discuss white).

Here are some suggested focuses/questions for the different hats:

- White – what information are we given?
- Blue – what was the school governors' thought process?
- Black – how is this idea likely to work in practice?
- Red – how do we feel about this plan?
- Green – can we come up with another way of achieving the same thing?
- Yellow – what could be the benefits of doing this in a school?

Learning outcomes

- Students will be able to share opinions about language use in a school context.
- Students should be able to successfully convey opinions and ideas about language use in a school context.
- Students may be able to successfully present points of view that they do not personally hold.

Differentiation

Lower ability students are likely to have more chance for success with the questions suggested for the white, black, red or yellow hats.

Higher ability students can be challenged to apply the hats themselves rather than being given the questions above.

Assessment opportunities

- Spoken English: presentation and communication
- **SLAF 1**

Activity 2

Writing a formal letter

Programme of Study link

Writing

- Writing a range of other narrative and non-narrative texts, including arguments and personal and formal letters

Grammar and vocabulary

- Knowing and understanding the differences between spoken and written language, including differences associated with formal and informal registers, and between Standard English and other varieties of English

Description

Students either:

- imagine their school wants to bring in the same rules prohibiting the use of slang in school, and write a letter to the head teacher or head of governors to express their views

or:

- write to a newspaper expressing their views about the rules.

They should demonstrate an awareness of the reasons for this ruling, and express their own views about the importance and relevance of Standard English and how it can be taught/encouraged in school.

Learning outcomes

- Students will be able to convey opinions and express ideas in a formal context.
- Students should be able to argue convincingly for a particular point of view.
- Students may be able to recognise and counter-argue against other points of view.

Differentiation

Lower ability students may welcome the support of a suggested structure:

- polite and formal opening
- paragraph one: overview of your reaction to the idea (i.e. do you agree) and brief statement of who you are (i.e. why this is relevant to you)
- paragraphs two to four (or five): main points of your argument, with reasons for your claims
- polite and formal closing.

It may also be helpful to elicit or provide sentence starters to support students in expressing opinions in a formal context, such as:

- I support this view because …
- I feel this would be unhelpful because …
- Although I accept that …, I believe that …

Worksheet 2.6 may help those students.

Higher ability students can be challenged by suggesting that they offer a real context for their writing – perhaps the best example(s) in the class can be published in a school newsletter or forwarded to the local paper.

Assessment opportunities

- Writing: style and vocabulary
- **WAF 2**

SPAG focus

Ask students to spell words focusing on whether they have an *-able* or *-ible* ending. Having written two lists, they can then decide which words have associated nouns ending in *-ability/-ibility*. Some also have associated nouns ending in *-ation* (e.g. application) which have a different meaning to the *-ability* noun (e.g. applicability). A more able group may be able to explore how these different forms work and what patterns emerge.

Suggested words to use:

applicable, changeable, comfortable, considerable, dependable, employable, enjoyable, forcible, horrible, incredible, legible, noticeable, possible, reasonable, reliable, sensible, terrible, tolerable, visible.

Note that this list includes some with spelling changes to preserve a soft 'c' or 'g' (changeable, noticeable).

5: Middlesbrough primary school issues list of 'incorrect' words

Context

This newspaper article is similar to Text 5 – both are about language in school, but where Text 5 focused on slang, this article is about accent and dialect, and therefore tackles broader identity issues, dealing with the language spoken across a geographical area rather than by a social group. Again, a school is struggling with issues of life chances and trying to help students maximise these, but it seems likely that this school would gain less support from parents than the last. While many families will notice and want to correct children's and teens' slang usage, picked up from their peers, if a child does speak in dialect, they will have learned it at home. This letter from school could therefore feel like a criticism of the family. With dialect (as opposed to slang) also, concepts and values such as heritage come into play, as dialects are often old and well established and tied up with a region's sense of identity.

The activities here are pitched at Year 8, but the concept of language and identity can easily engage older students too.

Getting started

A useful introduction to this text, especially to follow on from the Sheffield school piece, is to consider the differences between slang and dialect.

Starter 1

What kinds of non-standard English do you use? (You may wish to ban swear words clearly from the start.) Students work in pairs to think about words and phrases that they say but know would not be appropriate to write in a formal piece of classwork. The follow-up session can begin to separate out slang from dialect under teacher guidance.

Starter 2

Provide students with a definition of slang (words and phrases that are very informal and more common in speech than writing) and a definition of dialect (language specific to a particular geographical area) and ask them to discuss the differences in pairs. Do both feature in their use of language? Why might a school want to ban either slang or dialect?

Further resources

To discuss accent/dialect and identity further, clips from soap operas such as *Coronation Street*, *Emmerdale* and *Eastenders* could be used.

David Almond has written an interesting comment on this story about schools and dialect (and the North East dialect specifically): www.guardian.co.uk/commentisfree/2013/feb/08/taalk-proper.

Activity 1

Presentation on own use of language

Programme of Study link

Writing

- Writing notes and polished scripts for talks and presentations

Grammar and vocabulary

- Knowing and understanding the differences between spoken and written language, including differences associated with formal and informal registers, and between Standard English and other varieties of English

Spoken English

- Giving short speeches and presentations, expressing their own ideas and keeping to the point

Description

Students prepare and give a short talk or presentation about their own use of language. They could include:

- regional influences, including parents' background, places they have lived, etc.
- peer influence, including specific in-group words and phrases (often these have interesting stories behind them)
- media influence, including words and phrases drawn from TV, films, gaming or music
- specialist vocabularies relating to hobbies or interests (e.g. technical terms from a sport, craft or other hobby or interest).

This can be prepared as an individual talk, perhaps discussing in a group first to help ideas to flow. Alternatively, groups can prepare together and divide the work up, perhaps with each member of the group introducing and talking about another member of the group, or with each student taking responsibility for a topic (e.g. family influences, how TV influences our language, etc.).

This project can be particularly powerful with EAL and multilingual students, who can explain the different languages they use and in what contexts. This is often fascinating to monolingual students and can be a great way to increase interaction within a class.

Students can produce notes and visual aids to support their presentation, or they can script their talks fully. Worksheet 2.7 supports this task.

Learning outcomes

- Students will be able to identify and explain how their background and interests affect their use of language.
- Students should be able to discuss how they use language in different contexts.
- Students may be able to explore a range of influences on their own language use.

Differentiation

Lower ability students may find the group version of this task more accessible. The less confident will benefit if they are tasked with explaining about each other's use of language, removing the embarrassment of talking about themselves.

Higher ability students can be encouraged to research and/or discuss the topic at home to enhance their material.

Assessment opportunities

- Spoken English: presentation and communication
- **SLAF 1**

Activity 2

A local dialect display board

Programme of Study link

Writing

- Summarising and organising material, and supporting ideas and arguments with any necessary factual detail

Grammar and vocabulary

- Knowing and understanding the differences between spoken and written language, including differences associated with formal and informal registers, and between Standard English and other varieties of English

Description

Students explore the dialect in their local area and contribute to a display covering a range of material. Firstly, they discuss in pairs/groups (or as a whole class, if appropriate) special ways that people speak locally. What is the local accent? What special local words are they aware of (e.g. perhaps words for 'bread roll' or 'alleyway')? It may help to visit the BBC Voices project for ideas to prompt students (www.bbc.co.uk/voices/). The 'Where I Live' section provides recordings of people from your area. The British Library's Sounds Familiar project (www.bl.uk/learning/langlit/sounds/index.html) may also have relevant recordings for your region.

In terms of explaining accent and dialect features, it is probably best to encourage students to focus on dialect lexis, i.e. words and phrases specific to the region, and dialect grammar, i.e. aspects such as verb agreements (e.g. we was) or irregular pronouns (e.g. hisself, yous). Some pronunciation features can also be explored, but these are far more difficult to explain in writing. Students can work together to suggest and try out different ways of expressing pronunciation differences in writing (i.e. through spelling). There is no need to try to introduce the International Phonemic Alphabet at this stage. If students become very interested in the sounds of the local dialect, the project can be presented as a webpage with students making recordings of pronunciation differences.

Next, the work is divided among the students, who work individually, in pairs or in groups, as appropriate, to present ideas for the display. Most will also need to do a bit more research at this stage. Students can work on:

- particular words used locally, compared to Standard English and other regions
- dialect grammar and the equivalent Standard English (perhaps in the form of 'we may say x but we must write y').

There can be a large group working on particular usages whose members will need to divide up the features between themselves:

- historical information, e.g. about invasions into the area and the influence this has had on place names (e.g. many 'thwaite' places in Yorkshire, showing a Norse influence)
- discussion pieces about whether dialects are important or whether they should be discouraged.

There is also scope for visits or visiting speakers here, such as:

- Dialect preservation or heritage society representatives can be invited to the school (this works best if situated in an area that has such a group).
- Older people from the community who use traditional dialect can be invited in.
- A visit to an older people's community can be arranged so that students can interview people who have been in the region a long time.

Learning outcomes

- Students will be able to present information about their local dialect clearly.

- Students should be able to explore a range of different features of their local dialect.
- Students may be able to discuss influences on the local dialect (e.g. historical factors).

Differentiation

Lower ability students can produce work explaining particular examples of local dialect (e.g. specific words), perhaps comparing them to other regions and/or to Standard English (by exploring BBC Voices or a similar resource).

Higher ability students can tackle the pros and cons of dialect usage.

Assessment opportunities

- Spoken English: discussion and knowledge about language
- **WAF 2, SLAF 4**

Activity 3

Reporting on local dialect

Programme of Study link

Writing

- Summarising and organising material, and supporting ideas and arguments with any necessary factual detail

Grammar and vocabulary

- Knowing and understanding the differences between spoken and written language, including differences associated with formal and informal registers, and between Standard English and other varieties of English

Description

Students consolidate a range of material from the display work activity into a report format. They use the information on their local dialect as a case study and this leads to a recommendation about whether dialect usage should be discouraged in schools. They should:

- use subheadings to divide up the content
- write clearly and formally
- use features of argument writing (e.g. rhetorical questions, statistics, opinions, etc.)
- introduce and conclude clearly, presenting a clear argument (i.e. reach a conclusion).

Learning outcomes

- Students will be able to present information clearly.
- Students should be able to use features of their local dialect to illustrate their case.
- Students may be able to write in a sophisticated style.

Differentiation

This is an extension task for the most able.

Assessment opportunities

- Extension Writing: form and structure
- **WAF 3**

SPAG focus

Text 5 offers the opportunity to explore relative clauses, both those with relative pronouns and those without. Students can be reminded of how these are used, and the text can be used as an exemplar for how they add information and detail. This can usefully be done before completing the report-writing task, allowing students to put this into practice in their writing.

6–7: Two poems to perform

Context

These two short and well-loved poems have been chosen so that students can develop their skills in rehearsing and performing poetry.

Christina Rossetti's 'Remember' was written when she was only 19, in 1850. Although young, she was already writing about death and loss, perhaps influenced by the fact that her father had been seriously ill for several years at that point. The poem is popular and widely known and can be considered canonical as well as somewhat representative of the Romantic tradition.

William Henry Davies' 'Leisure' is also well known and is often cited. Davies' life was complex and included periods of living rough in both the UK and the US. His book, *Autobiography of a Super-tramp* is mostly concerned with his time as a hobo in the US and features a preface by George Bernard Shaw (who also negotiated on Davies' behalf to get him better terms from his publisher). The poem included here was first published in 1911, when he was 40 years old, by which point he was living in a cottage in Kent (paid for by the poet Edward Thomas).

Both poems offer a relatively straightforward message suitable for Year 8 students, as well as interesting rhythms that benefit from reading aloud.

Getting started

Students' previous experiences of poetry can be discussed to start this topic, or poetry can be discussed in fairly broad terms. Many students will be able to recall some aspects of poems studied previously, and can begin to appreciate poetry as a spoken and heard medium.

Starter 1

Students can be given a short time to discuss in pairs the questions: What can you remember about poems that you have studied previously? Do you recall names of particular poems you have encountered or any details about them (e.g. what they were about or who wrote them)?

Starter 2

Poetry is not meant to be read silently. It is supposed to be heard rather than seen. What do students think of this claim? Challenge them to come up with at least one argument for and one argument against this. They can also compare their arguments with a partner: which do they find most persuasive?

Further resources

Any other poems can be offered for preparation and performance. There are also many great recordings of poetry available on the internet, for example at the Poetry Station (www.thepoetrychannel.org.uk/).

Activity 1

Practising to perform poetry

Programme of Study link

Spoken English

- Improvising, rehearsing and performing play scripts and poetry in order to discuss language use and meaning, using role, intonation, tone, volume, mood, silence, stillness and action to add impact

Description

Students work in pairs to practise different ways of reading the poems. They can focus on just one, or they can try both. The emphasis should be on experimentation rather than practising for a polished performance. They should be encouraged to try out variations in rhythm, intonation, pausing, speed, etc. For example, they can try:

- reading at a steady pace versus speeding up and slowing down as they see fit
- reading to punctuation rather than to the end of each line
- pausing on rhyme words to help emphasise them
- pausing consciously at full stops and at stanza ends
- thinking about acting and being dramatic in their reading.

It will be helpful for students to make notes as they try out different ways of reading and some students might like to consider the impact of the different readings. These notes will help in the next activity. They can also consider whether the discoveries they make work for both poems (and therefore perhaps for poems generally) or specifically for one of the poems (and therefore probably for certain poems).

Learning outcomes

- Students will be able to vary tone, pace and volume to contribute to a performance.
- Students should be able to explain which variations have the most impact.
- Students may be able to consider why a different way of reading may or may not be helpful.

Differentiation

Lower ability students may welcome more guidance in terms of variations to try. Some groups may benefit more from a whole class approach, with volunteers making a particular kind of performance and then the class discussing it, rather than all students being expected to perform.

Higher ability students will be able to work from a list of different factors that can be varied: speed, volume, intonation, emphasis on different words, the impact of pauses and silences, varying the rhythm, acting out the poem, etc.

Assessment opportunities

- Spoken English: reading aloud and drama
- **SLAF 3**

Activity 2

Performing a poetry reading

Programme of Study link

Spoken English

- Improvising, rehearsing and performing play scripts and poetry in order to discuss language use and meaning, using role, intonation, tone, volume, mood, silence, stillness and action to add impact

Description

Students choose a poem to practise and then perform to the class. They should be asked to focus on making their reading/performance convey their poem's meaning to the class.

Students might choose from a selection put together for them, or they can be given access to a range of books and internet sources to choose from. They should be given sufficient preparation time to learn about their poem's meaning and practise their delivery to convey an appropriate tone etc.

This can be an individual, paired or group activity. Pairs and groups should perform in a way that enables all to take part.

Learning outcomes

- Students will be able to read their poem aloud convincingly.
- Students should be able to make sensible choices regarding delivery style.
- Students may be able to perform in an entertaining and/or illuminating way.

Differentiation

Lower ability students may benefit if they are given a selection of poems to choose from, and then perhaps asked to 'claim' one poem each/per group. It is then relatively simple to also provide guidance on the core meanings of the poems.

Higher ability students can be given a freer rein (or a selection of poems usually set for older students), and should also benefit from research time to learn about their poem in order to deliver it well.

Assessment opportunities

- Spoken English: reading aloud and drama
- **SLAF 3**

SPAG focus

The poem 'Remember' contains many imperatives (direct commands). Students could be encouraged to notice how they are formed (i.e. verb first, no pronoun). They could practise writing different kinds of requests/commands by varying the structure and the verb used (e.g. 'You should remember me'; 'You could remember me'; 'I would like you to remember me'.) Students could try to produce as many different versions of the same request/command as possible, and order them according to how definite or authoritative they seem. This could also lead into a discussion of modal verbs (e.g. would, could, should).

8: Six O'Clock News

Context

Tom Leonard is a Glaswegian poet who writes extensively about issues of language and identity. This poem was written in 1976 and is numbered 3 in a cycle entitled 'Unrelated incidents', all of which centre on language/dialect and identity issues. The poem presents an imagined news broadcast in which the presenter talks explicitly about language. It is written using a phonetic approximation of Glaswegian.

The activities here are aimed at Year 9 students.

Getting started

Students may be familiar with television news and can discuss how news should be delivered to convey its seriousness. A brief class discussion (perhaps opened as think/pair/share) can open up the subject.

Starter 1

Are you familiar with the news? Take a quick poll of how often students see the television news or hear the radio news. How else do students find out about the news, e.g. through websites, on Twitter? What methods do they use most frequently? As a class or in groups, ask students to identify the most and least popular means of accessing news.

Starter 2

Students individually write a brief summary of the most interesting news story that they have seen/heard about recently.

Further resources

Tom Leonard reading this poem and talking about its message can be found on the BBC Learning Zone website at www.bbc.co.uk/learningzone/clips/tom-leonard-the-six-o-clock-news/10301.html.

This text can be explored alongside Texts 5 and 6, the news stories about controls on language within schools.

Depending on your region, you may be able to find dialect literature specific to your area online, which could support Activity 3.

Activity 1

Reading for meaning

Programme of Study link

Reading

- Checking their understanding to make sure that what they have read makes sense

Description

Students read through the poem in pairs and note down ideas about what the poem is trying to say (in terms of attitudes that people have towards different accents), making links where possible to other ideas about spoken language that they have encountered (e.g. in this unit), for example, Text 6 on the use of dialects in schools.

A follow-up feedback session brings together students' ideas into a class discussion.

Learning outcomes

- Students will be able to identify that the poem is about accents and how people feel about them.
- Students should be able to discuss attitudes to accents as a key theme of the poem.
- Students may be able to explore how other ideas about language link to those in this poem.

Differentiation

Lower ability students may benefit from hearing the poem and following it on the page before being asked to consider meanings. A selection of prompts can be provided for less able students to select from, discussing their relevance to the poem rather than working solely from the poem and their own ideas. Suitable positions that can be tested for relevance to the text include:

- The poem suggests that speaking in an accent is better than using plain or 'standard' language.
- The poem is written using unusual spelling to make it difficult to read.
- The poem points out that people do not take others seriously if they have an accent.
- The poem implies that people with an accent are less important than those who use 'standard' language.

Higher ability students may enjoy the opportunity to read the poem aloud in their pairs and experiment with it as a spoken piece before discussing meaning.

Assessment opportunities

- Reading: forms, conventions and language
- **RAF 6**

Activity 2

Analysing the poem, carousel style

Programme of Study link

Reading

- Knowing how language, including figurative language, vocabulary choice, grammar, text structure and organisational features, presents meaning

Grammar and vocabulary

- Knowing and understanding the differences between spoken and written language, including differences associated with formal and informal registers, and between Standard English and other varieties of English
- Discussing reading, writing and spoken language with precise and confident use of linguistic and literary terminology

Description

Students work towards a full analysis of the poem through focused group (or paired) work on different aspects, conducted in a carousel of activities. Students move around the tasks, adding to their notes at each stop. Having completed all tasks, students can then organise and develop their notes and write up a formal analysis of the poem, or this can serve as preparation for a class discussion on Leonard's methods and intentions.

Carousel station prompts include:

- The voice in this poem is that of a newsreader using a 'BBC accent', and yet the poem is not written in Standard English. Which do you think are the most interesting examples of this non-standard language? Why do you think Leonard has done this? How would the impact of the poem be different if it was written in Standard English?

- Think about features that you expect to find in poetry (e.g. rhyme, rhythm, similes, etc.). Which of those features do you find in this poem? What about it makes it a poem?
- This poem is said to express Leonard's anger at the way people with accents are treated or thought of. What evidence of anger can you find in the poem?
- The poem talks to us directly, seeming to assume that we speak with an accent. Find at least one example for this and discuss what the effect of this could be. How do you feel, reading this poem?

These prompts are provided as cue cards on Worksheet 2.8.

Learning outcomes

- Students will be able to identify some features of the poem and begin to explain how they create meanings.
- Students should be able to discuss a range of ideas and provide some evidence from the text.
- Students may be able to link language use successfully to effects.

Differentiation

Lower ability students may need support to produce a written analysis, perhaps in the form of a suggested structure, some sentence starters, or a refresher of analytical techniques such as point, evidence, explanation (PEE) etc.

Higher ability students should be encouraged to discuss the effects of features of the writing beyond meaning.

If there is a wide range of abilities, responsibilities can be allocated within groups (e.g. students A and B are responsible for selecting examples while C and D are in charge of organising discussions on meaning and making notes).

Assessment opportunities

- Reading: critical analysis; forms, conventions and language
- **RAF 3, RAF 5**

9: University of Oxford 'How to Apply' video

Context

This video is one of several advice clips on the Oxford University website (others focus on aspects such as finance and the college system). Its approach is friendly, direct and simple, making it a good model for this sort of instructional clip, intended to inform and instruct its audience in making their application.

The activities here are pitched at Year 8 level. Note that the SPAG focus is a useful task to complete before the role play and/or scriptwriting, as it helps students to break down the text and see how it works, allowing them then to apply this to their own speech and writing.

Getting started

Students may have sought out 'how-to' or advice videos online for various things and can easily engage with the genre.

Starter 1

In pairs and in two minutes, students come up with the longest list possible of things that people need instructions or 'how-to' advice for.

Starter 2

Think/pair/share: what are the advantages and disadvantages of putting online advice and information in video form rather than in writing?

Further resources

The clip can be watched at: www.ox.ac.uk/about_the_university/introducing_oxford/an_oxford_education/applying/application_videos.html.

Activity 1

Role-playing a 'how to' video

Programme of Study link

Spoken English

- Improvising, rehearsing and performing play scripts and poetry in order to discuss language use and meaning, using role, intonation, tone, volume, mood, silence, stillness and action to add impact

Description

Students briefly plan and then act out an instructional or advisory video. They should work independently, choosing something that they can do but others may not be able to do. This can be anything and should be drawn from their own interests, for example, a sports-related skill, a craft, something technological. It should be a small and specific skill, so rather than 'how to play netball' it could be 'how to line up a scoring shot' for example.

Their preparation should consist of breaking their knowledge down into steps and making brief notes (not a script). They should examine the video transcript for ideas on structuring and appropriate vocabulary.

They should then perform their role play in small groups and give each other feedback on how easy their 'video' was to follow. Working in a small group is likely to be more beneficial for the next task of scripting, as they will gain from seeing and commenting on more presentations.

Controlled groupings (similar abilities) will be useful for this task as it will enable students to give each other valuable feedback and to provide sufficient opportunities for all to feel confident in participating.

Learning outcomes

- Students will be able to organise their ideas into a logical structure.
- Students should be able to control their vocabulary and pace to allow their audience to follow.
- Students may be able to also make their 'video' interesting and engaging for their audience.

Differentiation

Lower ability students should be encouraged to focus on how they structure their information and how they convey their information to an audience that does not already know about their topic. These students may also need more support initially in deciding on their topic (or they may be asked to select from a list); this can be a brief group discussion before switching to individual work to prepare their notes.

Higher ability students can be stretched by suggesting that they also aim to engage and interest their audience: how can they be entertaining without losing the ability to inform and instruct?

Assessment opportunities

- Spoken English: presentation and communication
- **SLAF 1**

Activity 2

Writing a script for a 'how to' video

Programme of Study link

Writing

- Writing notes and polished scripts for talks and presentations

Description

Having experimented with speaking for information and advice, students now produce scripts for instructional videos. They may like to watch the clip again (or to watch others) for ideas. The simplest model is to imagine a single voice with helpful visuals that support the information, but students can produce scripts for two or more actors.

Students should consider the advice they received in the last activity, and what they learned both from role playing their own ideas and from watching others.

Learning outcomes

- Students will be able to produce a script that would clearly inform or advise an audience.
- Students should be able to indicate clearly the different steps or a progression in their script.
- Students may be able to use language to create a lively and engaging script.

Differentiation

Lower ability students may find it helpful to focus on the structure of their script, using discourse markers (from simple markers such as 'firstly' to phrases such as 'it is important to …') to indicate the steps for an audience to follow.

Higher ability students should be challenged to produce an entertaining script that also informs/advises. The additional challenge of not being allowed to produce a script for the same task as in the role play above may also engage these students.

Assessment opportunities

- Writing: form and structure
- **WAF 3**

SPAG focus

Students can identify the way the text uses headings, subheadings and other discourse markers (or signposting) to help the audience to understand its messages. It is effective to do this with the text first, and then to show the clip, helping students to see how the slide transitions and animations also work as structuring devices in this case.

10: Malorie Blackman, Children's Laureate acceptance speech

Context

Malorie Blackman took up the children's laureateship in 2013, in recognition of her superb body of work for teenagers in particular. Known for relatively hard-hitting fiction which does not shy away from realities in teens' lives, her acceptance speech clearly sets out her love of books and her intended championing of libraries.

The activities here are intended for Year 9 students.

Getting started

Students may already be familiar with some of Malorie Blackman's work, so an introductory discussion on this topic is an appropriate way in. Alternatively, an opening discussion can focus more on the nature of speeches.

Starter 1

Who has read any of Malorie Blackman's books? A quick classroom poll can be taken, perhaps initiated with a list of some of her more popular works on the board (e.g. *Noughts and Crosses, Pig Heart Boy, Boys Don't Cry, Noble Conflict*).

Starter 2

In what contexts do people give speeches? In one minute, jot down as many different types and purposes of speeches as you can think of.

Further resources

A video of Malorie Blackman delivering her speech can be found at: www.youtube.com/watch?v=4M_AR8aKBQY.

Videos of Nobel Prize acceptance speeches can be found by searching for 'acceptance speech' in the media player at the Nobel Prize website: www.nobelprize.org/mediaplayer/.

Activity 1

Analysing the structure of the text

Programme of Study link

Grammar and vocabulary

- Studying the effectiveness and impact of the grammatical features of the texts they read

Description

Students work in pairs to find words and phrases that help to structure the text.

They can also conduct focused analysis on the types and length of sentences used, exploring how structure (at sentence and paragraph level) is helpful in a text that is written to be spoken.

Students can be asked to collect:

- words and phrases that act as signposts through the text (e.g. 'so' 'and')
- examples of topic sentences
- examples of repetition (of ideas, of phrases and of patterns).

This can be presented as an exercise in collecting ideas from a successful text to use in future writing (and can be linked directly to Activity 2). Worksheet 2.9 leads students through this activity.

Learning outcomes

- Students will be able to select words and phrases that lead the audience through the speech.
- Students should be able to identify ways in which the text's cohesion is created.
- Students may be able to identify different sentence types in the text and give some consideration to the needs of a listening rather than a reading audience.

Differentiation

Lower ability students can be directed to look for examples of repetition and to explain the link between the first sentence of each paragraph and the rest of the paragraph.

Higher ability students can be asked simply to examine aspects of the text that relate to its structure and cohesion as a whole text, and to its effectiveness as a speech

Assessment opportunities

- Reading: critical analysis
- **RAF 4**

Activity 2

Imaginative/personal writing: what would you like to be recognised for?

Programme of Study link

Writing

- Writing for a wide range of purposes and audiences, including:
- well-structured formal expository and narrative essays
- stories, scripts, poetry and other imaginative writing

Description

Students imagine what they could be known for in the future and produce a piece of writing based on this idea, creating their own acceptance speech accepting an award and explaining why and how this achievement came about.

Other acceptance speeches can also be watched or listened to. This will help students to select appropriate content for their speeches. Alternatively, news articles can be studied to see how a person's 'story' can be constructed. There are several acceptance speeches on the Nobel website, for example, although many of these are suited to the most able – more popular awards such as movie and music awards may not provide such useful models.

Learning outcomes

- Students will be able to convey their own ideas clearly and largely appropriately for a speech.
- Students should be able to use some features of effective speech writing in exploring their ideas.
- Students may be able to use a range of features of speeches effectively when expressing their imagined future.

Differentiation

Lower ability students can be invited to write in a different format, to suit individual students' abilities and skills, for example, a newspaper piece celebrating their achievement, their Wikipedia page, a personal essay explaining what they would like to achieve and why.

Higher ability students can be challenged to produce two contrasting forms using some of the same ideas (e.g. a formal acceptance speech and a Wikipedia bio page or a personal essay and a local newspaper piece celebrating their achievement as a local).

Assessment opportunities

- Writing: style and vocabulary; form and structure
- **WAF 1, WAF 3**

SPAG focus

Students select the phrases in the text which introduce Malorie Blackman's intentions as laureate (e.g. I particularly want to; I intend to). Attention can also be drawn to adverbs such as 'particularly'. This activity can be extended by asking students to write a few statements outlining their plans as head girl/boy.

11: Pygmalion

Context

George Bernard Shaw wrote the play *Pygmalion* to express some of his views about language, famously commenting on how judgemental people are of each other based on accent. In the play, the Note Taker, keen to prove his prowess as an elocution tutor, teaches the Flower Girl to speak 'properly' (i.e. using Received Pronunciation and Standard English) with the aim of passing off a common girl as a duchess. This key extract from early in the play introduces students to the Note Taker's extreme attitude towards the Flower Girl's language.

The ideas and language it uses make this a challenging text for Year 9 students.

Getting started

A useful opener for this is to share George Bernard Shaw's comment from the original published introduction to *Pygmalion*: 'It is impossible for an Englishman to open his mouth without making some other Englishman hate or despise him.'

Starter 1

Students can list 5–10 things they would be likely to judge someone by when first meeting them. (Language may not feature in students' thoughts at all initially, but they are likely to recognise the tendency for people to judge by accent or language choices.)

Starter 2

Students are shown Shaw's comment and asked to think about it and/or discuss it in pairs. What did he mean? Was he right? Are there things they do not like hearing people say?

Further resources

This text can usefully be explored alongside the two newspaper texts earlier in the unit, about language use in schools, as all three are essentially about attitudes to language.

Students can also be shown a clip of *My Fair Lady*.

Activity 1

Ranking attitudes to language

Programme of Study link

Grammar and vocabulary

- Knowing and understanding the differences between spoken and written language, including differences associated with formal and informal registers, and between Standard English and other varieties of English

Spoken English

- Participating in formal debates and structured discussions, summarising and/or building on what has been said

Description

Students work with statements from Worksheet 2.10, which offer a range of views about accents. There are different possibilities in how this is managed.

The simplest version asks students to sort the statements into two piles: those that they agree with and those they do not agree with. They then work with a partner to compare their ideas, choosing one thing they agree about and one thing they disagree about to report back to the class.

There is an alternative (more challenging) version. Students organise statements about language according to how far they agree with them. They then compare with a partner and discuss the ideas, aiming ultimately to persuade each other so that they have one version which they both believe. If they happen to agree on everything to start with, their discussion should focus on the reasons for their selections.

Students are each given two statements (at random, or carefully chosen) and are asked to choose the one they most agree with (see Worksheet 2.10 for statements). They then speed date with a range of other students, with the aim of discussing the various statements, presenting both of those given to them, and arriving at a hierarchy ranking them by how true students feel them to be. Each student then ends up with their own list expressing their personal agreement with the statements.

Learning outcomes

- Students will be able to discuss whether they agree with a set of views about language.
- Students should be able to explain why they feel a given view is wrong or right.
- Students may be able to rank a range of statements according to how far they agree with them.

Differentiation

Lower ability students can be asked to simply sort statements into two piles, and to compare their ideas with a partner.

Higher ability students might be expected to produce a rank order and to try to persuade a partner to adopt their hierarchy.

Assessment opportunities

- Spoken English: discussion and knowledge about language
- **SLAF 2, SLAF 4**

Activity 2

Dramatic performance

Programme of Study link

Spoken English

- Improvising, rehearsing and performing play scripts and poetry in order to discuss language use and meaning, using role, intonation, tone, volume, mood, silence, stillness and action to add impact

Description

Students work in threes (or fours with a director role) to prepare a performance of the text. Directors will be held responsible for the performance and will comment on their actors' use of gesture, intonation, movement, etc. to create an effective performance. Students can be told that they may be asked to perform their version of the scene, or to comment on the activity in a more reflective way (so that they are prepared to comment).

A feedback session can:

- run through all student performances
- take a select few volunteers or conscripts to perform

- ask students to give feedback by commenting on the task (difficulties they encountered, parts they enjoyed or found easiest to perform, etc.).

Learning outcomes

- Students will be able to make simple decisions about how to perform the scene (e.g. in terms of action/gesture to accompany lines, or mood of particular lines).
- Students should be able to use intonation, tone and volume to contribute to their performance.
- Students may be able to produce a convincing performance.

Differentiation

Lower ability students or those who are less confident with drama activities may be able to get more out of the exercise if feedback focuses on commentary rather than performance. How the feedback is managed is important to this task. Less-confident drama students can therefore be asked to give feedback on what they learned about the extract by performing it, or to describe some of the process they went through to perfect their performance.

Higher ability students or those who are keen drama students may well want to perform and demonstrate their work.

Assessment opportunities

- Spoken English: reading aloud and drama
- **SLAF 3**

Activity 3

Predicting the story

Programme of Study link

Reading

- Making inferences and referring to evidence in the text

Description

In pairs, students guess possible outcomes for the plot of the play, making reference to evidence in the text that they have. Students should consider characterisation and likely theme in their discussions. They are given a brief time (perhaps four or five minutes) to discuss and prepare suggestions for possible directions that the plot could go in.

Learning outcomes

- Students will be able to make informed guesses, referring to lines from the text.
- Students should be able to create sensible suggestions, referring to what they can tell of the characters.
- Students may be able to posit directions that the plot could go in by drawing on the attitudes shown in the text.

Differentiation

Lower ability students may need some support to come up with ideas related to the text. Pairing by ability is productive for this activity, to enable all to contribute.

Higher ability students should be able to provide evidence for their deductions.

Assessment opportunities

- Reading: critical analysis
- **RAF 3**

SPAG focus

Words ending in *-ous, -plus, -ious* and *-eous*

Students can initially be asked to think of as many words as possible in a minute that end in *-ous*. They can then be asked to compare their lists and to see how many of these words have a root word (e.g. danger – dangerous). Of those with a root word, do any change their spelling to add the *-ous* ending? If not, prompt students with the following: humour – humorous. Can students think of more? (E.g. glamour, vigour.) They can also be directed to think about what happens to the final 'e' (e.g. fame – famous, but a soft 'g' needs to keep the 'e', e.g. courageous).

The word from the text (bilious: nauseous, sickly) can be focused on to mention that most words with an 'e' sound before the 'ous' are spelt with 'ious', but a few exceptions have 'eous'. Can students think of any? (E.g. hideous, courteous, spontaneous).

Unit assessment task

Description

Students write an essay explaining what they have learned about spoken language. They should include at least some of the following:

- explanation of key ways that speech is different from writing
- exploration of different kinds of spoken language (e.g. in different contexts)
- discussion of the importance of Standard English

- explanation and discussion of different attitudes that people have to different kinds of spoken language.

Learning outcomes

- Students will be able to make their views clear.
- Students should be able to explain others' viewpoints, perhaps also arguing with them.
- Students may be able to make connections between different views and produce evaluative writing.

Differentiation

Lower ability students may need the support of collaborative planning in a teacher-supported small group with discussion about what could go in such an essay. For some students a reduced scope would be appropriate, such as:

People have different views about how language should be used. What are some of these views, and what is your opinion?

Students can be directed back to the newspaper texts explored earlier in the unit to support this, and given the suggested structure:

- Describe the two schools' initiatives to change/ control pupils' language.
- Explain why the schools think this will be helpful to pupils.
- Explain why some people may not like this idea.
- Give your own view on what is good/bad about different kinds of language.

Higher ability students can be given an opportunity to research and conduct some wider reading, for example on attitudes to language. Some of the resources referenced earlier in the unit, such as BBC Voices or British Library Sounds Familiar, could be a good starting point for specific varieties. An interesting poll was conducted by *Newsnight* in August 2013, and reports of the results (e.g. www.itv.com/news/2013-09-25/28-of-britons-feel-discriminated-against-due-to-accent) make accessible reading for most Year 9 students.

Assessment opportunities

- Writing: form and structure
- **WAF 3, WAF 4**

UNIT 3 The power of persuasion

Overview of unit

This unit aims to introduce students to a range of persuasive texts, both written and spoken, and to provide them with opportunities to write and speak persuasively.

Key words

Address
Balance
Repetition
Rhetorical questions
Structure
Tone

Assessing learning prior to this unit

1. How familiar are students with key features of persuasive language?
2. How confident are students in discussing the intended audience of a text?
3. How confident are students when speaking persuasively in a formal setting such as a debate or making a speech?

Key questions for this unit

1. Can I explain how a text tries to persuade its audience?
2. Can I write persuasively in different contexts?
3. Can I speak persuasively in different contexts?

Example scheme of work

A six-week overview of how the texts and activities could be put together to form a teaching sequence.

Week 1	Week 2	Week 3
• Explore a collection of advertising slogans (Text 1) and a government health advice leaflet (Text 2), leading up to students producing analytical work on audience, by considering the audiences of the various slogans and looking at how the leaflet uses tone to engage its audience. • Students may then put their analysis to productive use by planning and preparing an advertising campaign of their own and write an advisory leaflet using a similarly friendly tone.	• Different kinds of text are introduced: an email asking for support for a petition (Text 3) and a rousing Shakespeare extract (Text 4). Again, these are initially approached analytically, enabling students to practise analysing persuasive texts. • More assessment opportunities include writing a petition-promoting email of their own and rehearsing a performance of the St Crispin's Day speech from *Henry V*, focusing on delivery.	• Commercial texts are the focus of this week. Students first use a print advertisement (Text 5) to revisit the concept of audience, and then explore some book blurbs (Text 6). The books blurbs lead to a structured role-play activity in which students act as publishers championing a book for which they have written the blurb.

Week 4	Week 5	Week 6
• This week focuses on political persuasion using Text 7 (an open letter) and Text 9 (a political speech). Again, there are opportunities to assess students' analytical and productive skills in writing. • They may also look at selling via social media in Text 8, which provides a small sample of promotional tweets.	• The idea of context can be broadened and explored using the interesting vintage advert in Text 10. Activities from this text also allow students to prepare presentations on topics from advertising, exploring a theme in advertising and reporting back on it to the class. • The concept of formal debating can then be introduced using Text 11 and students discuss the importance of speaking and listening skills.	• Students have the opportunity to prepare for and hold a full formal debate about celebrities as role models using ideas introduced in Text 12 as the basis for their arguments, and building on the ideas about debating introduced via Text 11.

Assessing the learning outcomes of this unit

Reading tasks in this unit focus primarily on exploring issues of audience and purpose, and in analysing the effect of features of persuasion.

Writing tasks in this unit include writing letters, speeches and articles to persuade others.

Grammar and vocabulary tasks in this unit focus largely on features used to persuade, such as imperatives and syntactical patterning.

Spoken English tasks in this unit include a formal debate and smaller tasks such as discussion, negotiation and presentation.

Links between the texts

Texts 1, 5, 8 and 10 can be explored together as a mini-unit on advertising.

Texts 3 and 7 can be compared as examples of letter/email form.

Online resources

There are editable PowerPoint versions of all activities and Word versions of all worksheets available in Kerboodle.

In addition, there are exemplar student outcomes plus teacher notes and additional activities for the following activities from the Teacher's Book:

- Text 3: Activity 1
- Text 6: Activity 2
- Text 12: Activity 2 (video)

1: Advertising slogans

Context

This small collection of advertising slogans, drawn from a range of sources, represents mostly recent and current examples that students are likely to be familiar with. It provides an opportunity for thinking about how advertising texts target an audience and provides a focus for an interesting group discussion and presentation task.

This text is suitable for Year 7 students.

Getting started

Students will be familiar with a range of advertising slogans and are likely to have talked about them in KS2, so an opening activity simply asking them to think of some slogans is a comfortable way in to this type of text.

Starter 1

Quickly recap what a slogan is (perhaps by sharing an example or eliciting a definition). How many slogans can the class think of in one minute?

Starter 2

What makes a great slogan? Students can work in pairs to list features that make a slogan memorable – write down as many as possible in one minute.

Further resources

Further slogans can be considered, or the work on audience and/or advertising more generally can be expanded to look at whole adverts. Alternatively, connecting with the SPAG focus on this text, a selection of headlines would also be interesting as a comparison point in terms of condensed or elliptical sentences.

Activity 1

Commenting on audience

Programme of Study link

Reading

- Knowing the purpose, audience for and context of the writing and drawing on this knowledge to support comprehension

Description

Using Worksheet 3.1, students explore the comments about audience and match them to the appropriate slogan. They can then add in evidence to support these ideas so that they produce full analytical comments about the likely audiences for a selection of the slogans in the text.

Learning outcomes

- Students will be able to make deductions about the audience of a text.
- Students should be able to identify specific audiences based on content and features choices.
- Students may be able to produce analytical comments describing the audience of the text and linking their claims to the language used.

Differentiation

Lower ability students may need more support with thinking about audience. If the whole class is lower ability, this can be a think/pair/share activity to build confidence (see the explanation on p33 in Unit 2). For some students, it may be appropriate to indicate which five of the slogans they are working with initially – this can be added to the editable version of the worksheet, making the matching part of the activity slightly simpler and allowing them to see the sentences as models for commenting on texts.

Higher ability students can quickly move on to writing their own comments about the slogans they are left with.

Assessment opportunities

- Reading: forms, conventions and language
- **RAF 6**

Activity 2

Inventing and marketing a product

Programme of Study link

Spoken English

- Using Standard English confidently in a range of formal and informal contexts, including classroom discussion
- Improvising, rehearsing and performing play scripts and poetry in order to discuss language use and meaning, using role, intonation, tone, volume, mood, silence, stillness and action to add impact

Description

Students work in teams to invent a new product, create a slogan for it and develop an advert, which they then present to the class. (Note: this can be a time-consuming project requiring two weeks of English lessons, depending on the timetable.)

They can be given free rein to invent their product, or one or more types of product can be specified. Effective ideas include: a snack food, a range of toys, a magazine/comic.

Students must discuss and plan their work in groups, deciding on the details of their product, the audience they are targeting and some specific details for their advert. They must all have a slogan and a name for their product.

Initial teaching might include some features of slogans and persuasive language such as puns, alliteration, rhyme, imperatives, repetition.

Once students have planned some aspects of their product and its marketing, some teaching on presentation skills can be included, emphasising clear delivery and instructing groups to decide how to divide up their presentations (e.g. one student presents and the others hold up posters/ storyboards, take questions, etc., or each member of the group explains a different aspect). Effective pitches from the TV series, *Junior Apprentice,* can be shown at this point as exemplars.

The advert produced can be:

- a completed print advert (which the group would then show and explain to the class)
- a storyboarded television advert (which the group can act out or explain to the class).

The presentation to the class must explain the product and state the audience for it, and then present the advertising campaign.

Learning outcomes

- Students will be able to produce a slogan that has some features of existing slogans and present their ideas clearly to the class.
- Students should be able to create an advertisement that clearly matches the audience and purpose and explain this fully to the class.
- Students may be able to show flair and creativity in their work and present in an engaging way.

Differentiation

Lower ability students can be instructed to create a product of a certain type (e.g. a snack food), and part of the preparation can include looking at advertising campaigns for this kind of product to help them focus on typical features.

Higher ability students can be given more choice about the product they invent – perhaps by suggesting possible categories (snack food, toys, magazine) but ultimately allowing them to choose something else if they wish. They can also be instructed to produce an *Apprentice*-style pitch.

Assessment opportunities

- Spoken English: presentation and communication; discussion and knowledge about spoken language
- **SLAF 2, SLAF 1**

SPAG focus

Slogans offer an opportunity to talk about ellipsis for effect. Some of the slogans included here are grammatically complete sentences, but not all of them are. Students can explore which are which and think of further examples for each category.

You might also like to flag up to students that headlines and headings/subheadings are forms that often use technically incomplete sentences, for example by omitting pronouns or whole clauses.

Students can complete SPAG work by identifying which elements of full sentences are present in the slogans in Text 1 and which are missed, e.g. pronouns. They can also discuss the effect of missing words out (informality, a friendly tone, etc.). They might be able to discuss implied parts of sentences and perhaps expand into spoken language, where we often use incomplete sentences to reply and avoid repeating elements (e.g. Who did that? James (did)).

2: Don't Let Drink Sneak Up on You

Context

This is part of a government health advice leaflet featuring a set of cartoon characters that have been used in a range of different health advice messages under the broad heading of 'Change 4 life'. These campaigns are aimed at families, and previous messages have focused on aspects such as being active (getting 60 minutes healthy movement every day for children) and eating healthily (swapping unhealthy snacks for more nutritious ones). This leaflet focuses on alcohol, with the message that it is easy to inadvertently drink an unhealthy amount.

The activities here are aimed at Year 7 students.

Getting started

Students may well be familiar with these characters and the style of advice from TV advertising or other leaflets (there have been several aimed at families on topics such as eating '5 a day' and getting children to be more active).

Starter 1
Have you seen this kind of advert or leaflet before? If so, what other advice have you seen these characters giving? If not, who do you think the advert might be aimed at? Why? Write down who you think the audience is and give your reasons.

Starter 2
Are you familiar with other kinds of health advice leaflet or television adverts (e.g. anti-smoking)? How do texts like this try to convince the audience to take their advice? Discuss with a partner and write down three things that they do to make their point.

Further resources

Other health advice leaflets (easily found in hospitals and GP surgeries) can be compared for style and content. Something more traditional and shocking in its style would make an effective contrast. For example, there are some quite hard-hitting adverts that promote the dangers of smoking, or that highlight the work of cancer charities or that encourage people to give blood. Students can be encouraged to think of television as well as print advertising as these can often have a powerful impact.

Activity 1

Analysing tone/address to audience

Programme of Study link

Reading
- Knowing the purpose, audience for and context of the writing and drawing on this knowledge to support comprehension

Description
Ask students to find examples of particular features in the text and to discuss how these features affect the audience.

Firstly, the audience is identified for them as 'normal' people, not those considered to be particularly heavy drinkers.

Students should be aware that the leaflet aims to persuade people by playing down the issue and making it seem like something everyone should think about.

Working in pairs or small groups, students are given a particular aspect to explore in the text: finding examples of it, deciding which are the best examples to share with the class, and discussing how this aspect helps to persuade the audience.

Aspects worth exploring include:

- ways that alcohol itself is presented as being to blame
- ways that drinking too much is presented as an easy mistake to make
- how cutting down on drinking is shown to be simple
- how they try to present serious information (such as warnings about health risks) in a way that is not too frightening
- how the health benefits of drinking less are emphasised more than the dangers of drinking too much
- how the audience is addressed.

Worksheet 3.2 lists these for students.

Students can also be asked to identify aspects for themselves, particularly once they have discussed their allocated aspect.

Groups can be given two aspects each, so that more than one group will feed back on each aspect. This can then be a jigsaw group activity, with groups splitting in half to share on one of their two aspects each before regrouping to consolidate what they have discussed. This technique is good for building confidence.

Learning outcomes
- Students will be able to identify how an aspect of the text could be persuasive to the intended audience.
- Students should be able to select effective evidence from the text to support their point.
- Students may be able to also identify further persuasive aspects of the text for themselves.

Differentiation
Lower ability students may find it easier to tackle the first five points above. If the whole class is lower ability, it may be best to use the 'jigsaw' approach.

Higher ability students can be given one aspect to consider (perhaps as a think/pair/share task) before completing their own work identifying persuasive approaches for themselves.

Assessment opportunities
- Reading: comprehension
- **RAF 2**

Activity 2

Producing an advice leaflet

Programme of Study link

Writing

- Drawing on knowledge of literary and rhetorical devices from their reading and listening to enhance the impact of their writing

Description

Students produce their own advice leaflet for an audience of their peers, taking a similar approach in terms of tone and writing.

They can write advice on topics such as:

- cutting back on 'screen time' (i.e. television, computer games, social media)
- getting enough sleep
- being a 'positive bystander' and combating bullying.

Or they might have other ideas of their own.

Firstly, students will need to identify (or be given) their topic. They should work in pairs or groups to produce the leaflet. Depending on the time available they can either just write the text or produce a full-colour, professionally laid out leaflet.

The initial teaching for this task can discuss aspects such as:

- the layout of the leaflet and its structure in sections with bullet points, the use of subheadings, the positioning of any texts and images, etc.
- the tone, as discussed in the last activity.

Learning outcomes

- Students will be able to use different sections in their leaflet to present different ideas.
- Students should be able to create a friendly and encouraging tone.
- Students may be able to write with flair and precision.

Differentiation

Lower ability students will need a clear structure and should be allowed to use the source text as a model. It will help these students if they are given a topic that is discussed as a class first as this will provide them with some ideas for content. For example, the class could discuss different sections of the leaflet addressing various questions such as why or how. In a 'cut back on screen time' leaflet, for example, students may need help to find ideas such as why it is a good idea (protecting eyesight, avoiding overstimulation, increasing real-world interaction, developing good habits of self and time management, etc.) and how to achieve it (replace with healthy outdoor activity, meeting with friends face to face, reading books/magazines, etc.).

Higher ability students can be encouraged to copy the leaflet's friendly and encouraging tone while perhaps varying the structure. This group can also be given more freedom when choosing a topic.

Assessment opportunities

- Writing: style and vocabulary
- **WAF 2**

3: Petition email

Context

This email originates from one of the petition websites (Care2) and is focused on the badger cull of 2013. The badger cull was introduced as a way of protecting cattle from TB, which can be spread by badgers. The issue is a very contentious one as the cull proposed killing badgers indiscriminately, so some who are no threat to cattle would inevitably be killed, and the alternative of vaccinating cattle was not seen as being given serious consideration.

The tasks here are aimed at Year 7 students.

Getting started

Students may not be familiar with the idea of online petitions, so they could start by looking at some online examples (see the Further resources box that follows).

Starter 1

Individually or in pairs, students come up with an idea for something they would launch a petition for. Why would they support that cause? Suggest two or three arguments that they could use to persuade people to sign up. It could be something national (like teenagers should be allowed to drive from the age of 15) or local (such as campaigning for new sports facilities at school).

Starter 2
Online petitions are a rapidly growing area. Look at the front page of a petition site and discuss with a partner what the most popular types of issue seem to be.

Further resources

You might also like to explore these websites with your students:

- Government petition site: http://epetitions.direct.gov.uk
- Change.org: www.change.org/en-GB
- 38 degrees: www.38degrees.org.uk

Activity 1

Focus on audience/purpose/context

Programme of Study link

Reading

- Discussing reading, writing and spoken language with precise and confident use of linguistic and literary terminology
- Knowing how language, including figurative language, vocabulary choice, grammar, text structure and organisational features, presents meaning

Description
In pairs or in groups, whichever is most appropriate for them, students use the persuasive language glossary on Worksheet 3.3 to identify features used in this text. They then write brief analytical points (perhaps using a PEE structure – point, evidence, explanation) to demonstrate their learning.

Effects can be suggested first (to avoid all being simply described as 'to make it persuasive'), so it effectively becomes a matching task and more like writing in a frame.

Possible effects include:

- to provoke an emotional reaction (students should specify what kind, e.g. angry, sympathetic, etc.)
- to make a phrase memorable
- to emphasise/highlight a key idea
- to make the audience question something
- to mock an idea.

A PEE template or other desired analytical structure can be modelled and the students can use this to construct their own analytical points about the text. It is best if students choose up to three features to write out to avoid excessively repetitive explanations. This stage can also be collaborative if appropriate.

A suitable model might include phrases such as:

The writer of the email uses (the phrase/image/adjective/emotive language/named feature) '____' in order to (make the audience feel/question/understand, highlight the point, make the phrase memorable).

Learning outcomes

- Students will be able to explain simple effects of persuasive features.
- Students should be able to discuss how an audience may react to features used in a text.
- Students may be able to explore the effects of features with sensitivity and insight.

Differentiation
Lower ability students can complete this more as a matching activity, working from a list of possible or suggested effects of features in order to help them select appropriate ideas to slot into a PEE (or similar) frame.

Higher ability students may enjoy making this a competitive task: how many different features can you identify and explain in terms of effects (using varied explanations) within 15 minutes?

Assessment opportunities

- Reading: critical analysis
- **RAF 5**

Activity 2

Planning and writing a petition email

Programme of Study link

Writing

- Drawing on knowledge of literary and rhetorical devices from their reading and listening to enhance the impact of their writing

Description
Students work in small groups to plan a petition for an issue they are concerned about, and they produce text for an email to encourage people to sign their petition, using effective features of persuasion.

It might be helpful to recap some of the features of a petition email from Activity 1, for example, using direct language, a mix of fact and opinion. See Worksheet 3.3 for more features.

Initial teaching for this task can also focus on the structure of the email. Students can sum up each paragraph of the text, which is then drawn together as a class to create a kind of overview of how the email works to create an argument.

Then, as the first stage of the productive work, students discuss in groups and negotiate to arrive at an agreed issue to base the petition on.

Next, students plan the content of an email requesting support for their petition. They should remember to include features to persuade their audience (referring to the glossary on Worksheet 3.3 and/or their own notes on the email from Care2) and should follow a similar structure in order to be persuasive.

Learning outcomes

- Students will be able to use some features of persuasion.
- Students should be able to use a range of features to persuade an audience.
- Students may be able to produce an effective and persuasive text.

Differentiation

Lower ability students can be given a choice from specific issues (e.g. school-specific matters such as a new uniform or canteen provision, or something very well known from current affairs). This will ensure they do not spend too long on this phase of the task and it will help them to focus.

Higher ability students can be encouraged to take on a more difficult issue of their own choice.

Assessment opportunities

- Writing: style and vocabulary
- **WAF 2**

SPAG focus

The text features several passive constructions ('aren't being monitored'; 'will be overseen'; 'will be monitored'), so there is an opportunity to talk about passive structures with students. They may notice (or be shown) that all include some version of the verb 'to be' (this also enables discussion of the fact that verbs are not only 'doing words') and a past participle. It is also worthwhile discussing the effect of the passive voice. In this text, for example, what is the implication in terms of who would 'monitor' or 'oversee' the cull?

A simpler approach is to ask students to rewrite the passive constructions into active ones (perhaps as a group task – what would 'aren't being monitored' become?). This activity will reveal the issue of missing agents and enable you to discuss the effect/purpose of passive constructions and perhaps also their grammatical construction.

4: Henry V

Context

This well-known extract from *Henry V* offers a brilliant example of classic rhetoric as well as showing where several phrases that are now clichés were first used. This speech occurs before a major battle and is designed to make the men feel ready and well equipped to fight, even though they are relatively few in number.

The activities here are likely to challenge Year 8 students or would be suitable for older students.

Getting started

What do you need soldiers to feel and think when they are going into battle, especially when the odds are against them? The most productive way to enable students to 'perform' the scene and discuss it in terms of literary qualities will be to start off with a sense of the purpose and context of the text.

Starter 1

Ask students to rank the following comments from the most to least encouraging and ask them to justify their order. Why do they think their top choice is the most encouraging?

- You can do it!
- Remember when you [did a similar difficult thing ...]
- Don't worry, it'll be fine.

Students can then add their own encouraging comments to the list.

Starter 2

How could you encourage a small group of soldiers facing what you know will be a difficult battle? What is likely to help them to feel ready and able to fight? Discuss and make notes with a partner/group.

Further resources

Performances of this speech can be found online. Those by Kenneth Branagh and Richard Burton are easy to find and effective to listen to as models.

Activity 1

Understanding the speech

Programme of Study link

Reading

- Checking their understanding to make sure that what they have read makes sense
- Making inferences and referring to evidence in the text

Description

Guide students through the speech's meaning by providing a summary/paraphrase and working to find and rephrase examples. Students use Worksheet 3.4 to help them understand the text and find examples in it.

Learning outcomes

- Students will be able to find evidence for simple points such as the repetition of the date and the more obvious references to bravery.
- Students should be able to identify implications of camaraderie.
- Students may be able to explain the effects of aspects of the text.

Differentiation

Lower ability students can be given the very specific instructions above to find evidence in the speech. This can then lead into a mini-plenary discussing what this evidence tells us about the intended overall effect of the speech. An analytical paragraph can be produced as a class on the board as a summary activity, or students can be asked to select the quotation or feature that they think is most persuasive and write a couple of sentences about it (e.g. by stressing the date through repeating it, Henry emphasises how they will be able to look back on this day).

Higher ability students may be able to extend this activity by talking about the effect of some of the aspects they have gathered. This can be written up analytically, or presented diagrammatically (perhaps for display), clustering pieces of evidence together and showing their effect.

Assessment opportunities

- Reading: comprehension
- **RAF 2**

Activity 2

What kind of a king is Henry V?

Programme of Study link

Reading

- Studying setting, plot and characterisation, and the effects of these

Description

Students generate as many adjectives/descriptive phrases as possible to describe Henry's character based on this speech. Having generated a mass of descriptors, they then rank them (perhaps using diamond ranking) to decide which are most important.

Helpful prompts to get started include:

- What does he seem to think is important?
- What skills or abilities does he show in this speech?
- How do you think his men feel about him?

Having addressed these prompts, students then come up with an adjective or descriptive phrase that answers the question 'What is Henry like?', thinking about each point in turn. For example, if a student decides that Henry thinks pride is important, he or she may feel that this shows Henry is a proud man.

Once a list of descriptors has been produced (individually or as a group), students can rank (or diamond or pyramid rank) these ideas to decide which they feel are the most important. In diamond or pyramid ranking, students may have more than one concept at the same level. For example, they would identify the single most important thing, then at level two they might have two equally important concepts, then three at level three, and so on. The overall shape formed would be a diamond or triangle.

Learning outcomes

- Students will be able to identify a few aspects of character based on what Henry says in the speech.
- Students should be able to discuss which aspects of character appear most strongly in the speech.
- Students may be able to explore how other characters would react to Henry based on this speech.

Differentiation

Lower ability students will benefit from generating as many ideas as possible and then sifting through them, in quite a structured, brainstorm style, with initial ideas being simply recorded and not criticised or judged until the ranking stage. Worksheet 3.5 provides the structure for this activity, which may help these students.

Higher ability students can be asked to decide on Henry's top three qualities, perhaps for each of the prompts above. They may also be able to produce a short piece of analytical writing exploring Henry's character and providing quotations as evidence. The most able may enjoy a discussion about what they can tell of Henry's values from the speech.

Assessment opportunities

- Reading: comprehension
- **RAF 3**

Activity 3

Spoken performance of the extract

Programme of Study link

Spoken English

- Improvising, rehearsing and performing play scripts and poetry in order to discuss language use and meaning, using role, intonation, tone, volume, mood, silence, stillness and action to add impact

Description

Students collaborate to produce effective readings of the text, experimenting with aspects such as volume, intonation and pace. This could be a good point at which to listen to or watch performances of the speech.

Working in pairs, students take it in turns to read the text (or a portion of it) aloud, consciously performing (i.e. using intonation, gesture, stance, etc. in deliberate ways for effect). The other student then offers suggestions for improvements and incorporates these ideas into their own performance.

Learning outcomes

- Students will be able to use aspects of voice such as pace, volume and intonation to create an interesting performance.
- Students should be able to use gesture and perhaps action to enhance their performance.
- Students may be able to use creative and engaging dramatic techniques to present the speech.

Differentiation

Lower ability students can direct the teacher to perform the speech, perhaps being allowed discussion time in pairs before offering suggestions. They can then work in their pairs to practise performances of their own, but less publicly.

Higher ability students (or more able actors) can be encouraged to experiment more with movement and gesture. What if Henry walks around? At which points is he most likely to gesture? They can also be encouraged to experiment more with their voice. How long can/should pauses be? Which parts will be quietest/loudest?

Assessment opportunities

- Spoken English: reading aloud and drama
- **SLAF 3**

5: Clairol Nice 'n Easy

Context

This straightforward example of a print advertisement can be used to stimulate discussion on advertising in broad terms, as well as to conduct an analysis of this type of text.

The activities are aimed at Year 8 students.

Getting started

Students will be familiar with advertising and may have discussed its characteristics previously when studying Text 1 in this unit. Following up on the questions in the Student Book and thinking a little about the advertisement itself will be good starting points.

Starter 1

What does the slogan 'All they see is you' in this advertisement mean? Think/pair/share your responses to the questions in the textbook.

Starter 2

What moods or feelings does this advertisement convey? Discuss in pairs and make a list of feelings or moods that you think the advertisers want to provoke (e.g. happiness, fun, relaxation) with this text. Try to stretch your vocabulary and write down as many words as you can, even those with similar meanings (e.g. if you thought of happiness, you could also write pleasure and joy).

Further resources

Any other print advertisements can be explored in a similar way to Activity 1 below. Or, in an extension to Activity 2, students can bring in some magazines that they tend to read, and they can be analysed in terms of which sorts of products they advertise.

Activity 1

How features create meaning

Programme of Study link

Reading

- Knowing how language, including figurative language, vocabulary choice, grammar, text structure and organisational features, present meaning

Description

This simple analytical activity models analysis for the students by showing them how to put together comments on meaning with textual evidence. They fill in Worksheet 3.6 by finishing off the sentences and finding evidence in the text, completing an analysis of the advertisement. The second part of the worksheet prompts them to think more freely and produce some analytical comments of their own.

Learning outcomes

- Students will be able to select appropriate words to complete the analysis.
- Students should be able to also complete some analytical comments of their own.
- Students may be able to analyse with insight.

Differentiation

Lower ability students may need you to provide phrases to help them complete the task, so the worksheet can be edited slightly to make this a Cloze exercise. Suggested phrases to offer are:

in love   a good relationship   the woman's hair
have grey hairs that they   wish to cover
the emphasis on 'up to 100% grey coverage'

Higher ability students should be able to use the second part of the worksheet unaided to produce analysis of their own.

Assessment opportunities

- Reading: comprehension
- **RAF 3**

Activity 2

Discussion

Programme of Study link

Spoken English

- Participating in formal debates and structured discussions, summarising and/or building on what has been said

Description

Working in small groups, students discuss their views on advertising and the media in the format of a televised discussion (e.g. on a magazine show such as *This Morning, Loose Women* or *The One Show*). Each student has a role within the panel, for example, as show host, representative of a parenting charity/group, representative from a toy/snacks company. Students should be encouraged to work towards success criteria including: interacting effectively, demonstrating listening and responding to others, supporting and encouraging others in the discussion. They should also be encouraged to refer to specific examples of advertising campaigns in their discussions.

Possible titles for the discussion include:

- Has television and radio advertising gone too far in aiming at children?
- We hear and see so much advertising these days: are we becoming immune to it?
- Is the media making it harder to be a good parent?

Some groups may wish to perform their group work for the class.

Learning outcomes

- Students will be able to share their own ideas and listen to the views of others.
- Students should be able to encourage others to speak and respond to each other.
- Students may be able to lead a discussion effectively.

Differentiation
Lower ability students may find that the easiest question is 'Has television and radio advertising gone too far?'

Higher ability students may be able to consider the implications for parents in a more subtle way and can also consider the question of immunity to advertising more effectively.

Assessment opportunities

- Spoken English: discussion and knowledge about spoken language
- **SLAF 2**

6: Book blurbs

Context

These three blurbs all come from 2013 publications for older children/teens. Although they all come from quite different genres, they follow the conventions of the form.

Activities based on this text are intended for Year 8 students.

Getting started

A broad discussion about reading habits is an effective way into the activities here.

Starter 1
In pairs, list at least three things you look at when deciding which book to read. (Alternative version: rate these five aspects by importance in deciding what to read: blurb, cover image, author, title, genre.)

Starter 2
Who reads what in the class? Take a quick straw poll of the genres read (students can vote in more than one category).

Further resources

More blurbs can be explored, perhaps of books within the classroom or recent class reads. Alternatively, film trailers can also be compared, as many of the conventions are the same (present tense, focus on central character and his/her initial problem, frequent use of questions).

Activity 1

What is a book blurb?

Programme of Study link

Reading

- Knowing how language, including figurative language, vocabulary choice, grammar, text structure and organisational features, present meaning

Description
Working in pairs, students identify the features of a book blurb. They do this by working through the following questions:

- What is a book blurb aiming to achieve? (I.e. what is its purpose?)
- Who are these blurbs written for? (I.e. who is the audience?)
- What do these blurbs have in common, in terms of how they are written? Think about: the sorts of words and phrases used; the kind of information included; the order of information (i.e. the structure).
- This can be done as a 'magpie' activity, in which students have a limited time to complete the task (e.g. 10 minutes), with some pairs/groups instructed to start with different questions (this makes sure everything is covered somewhere). After the brief time, students are then asked to compare their answers with those of other pairs/ groups and to 'magpie' (i.e. steal!) good ideas to improve their initial notes.
- A mini plenary collates students' responses to produce a definition/set of 'rules' for book blurbs.

Learning outcomes

- Students will be able to explain the basic context of a book blurb (i.e. audience and purpose).
- Students should be able to explain some of the key features of book blurbs.
- Students may be able to explain how blurbs are structured and the features they use.

Differentiation
Lower ability students can be asked to start by discussing the purpose of a book blurb.

Higher ability students can be asked to start by considering how blurbs are written.

Assessment opportunities

- Reading: forms, conventions and language
- **RAF 6**

Activity 2

Designing a book blurb

Programme of Study link

Writing

- Drawing on knowledge of literary and rhetorical devices from their reading and listening to enhance the impact of their writing

Description

Students use the prompts on Worksheet 3.7 to help them plan a book (emphasise that they are not being asked to write it) and produce a blurb for it.

They can collaborate, particularly if fans of similar books can work together – students can be grouped according to their favourite genre to plan out a new title in that genre.

Learning outcomes

- Students will be able to write a blurb that introduces the main character and their problem/conflict.
- Students should be able to write consistently in the present tense and make the audience want to know what will happen.
- Students may be able to produce a blurb that is a convincing example of the genre.

Differentiation

Lower ability students can produce blurbs for books that already exist and which they know well, such as a recent class reader.

Higher ability students or quicker workers can be challenged to produce two blurbs for different books, perhaps in different genres or aimed at quite different audiences.

Assessment opportunities

- Writing: style and vocabulary; form and structure
- **WAF 2, WAF 3**

Activity 3

Role play (discussion)

Programme of Study link

Spoken English

- Improvising, rehearsing and performing play scripts and poetry in order to discuss language use and meaning, using role, intonation, tone, volume, mood, silence, stillness and action to add impact
- Participating in formal debates and structured discussions, summarising and/or building on what has been said

Description

Students work in groups of four or five to role play a meeting at a children's publishing house. Each student is a book editor who has discovered a manuscript that they want to publish (their planned book, for which they have written a blurb in Activity 2). The group task is to discuss all the suggested books, evaluating their strengths and weaknesses and thinking about the audience they would be best for. Ultimately, the publisher can only take two books forward from each group, so the students will need to negotiate and work to persuade the others that their book should go ahead, while also listening to the others to see which books they would vote for. At the end of the discussion, each student votes for two books to be published and the votes will be counted to see whose books were most successful.

Learning outcomes

- Students will be able to explain their point of view.
- Students should be able to demonstrate clear listening skills.
- Students may be able to convince others to publish their book.

Differentiation

Lower ability students with low confidence, or a mixed ability group, may need this task to be less competitive so that the discussion runs on the basis that each student's presented book will be taken forward. The task could be to decide which market (i.e. age group, gender, interests) to target each book at and/or to discuss associated merchandising or media (TV shows, kids' magazines, toys, etc.).

Higher ability students can be challenged by tighter restrictions on the voting. For example, they can be banned from voting for their own book and/or they can be limited to only having one winner.

Assessment opportunities

- Spoken English: presentation and communication; reading aloud and drama
- **SLAF 2, SLAF 3**

SPAG focus

All of the blurbs use the present tense (a convention of blurbs and cinema trailers). This might be an opportunity to remind students about the use of various tenses. Students can discuss/explore which tense is most commonly used in a range of forms (e.g. news articles in the past tense, novels in past or present, adverts in present, etc.). Students can also rewrite the blurbs putting them in the past tense, and discuss why the present is the convention for this form.

7: Amnesty International open letter

Context

This letter was written by Amnesty International on the one-year anniversary of the imprisonment of two members of the Russian band Pussy Riot. Their arrest was for disorder and blasphemy after protesting in a cathedral in Moscow. The letter is a great example of a dual-audience text seeking to reassure the addressees while also intending to persuade others to support them, not least through the long list of well-known music artists whose signatures appear on the letter.

This text will stretch and challenge more able Year 9 students.

Getting started

Students may not be familiar with the concept of an open letter, so introducing this first might be an effective way in to the text. Alternatively, introducing the idea of Amnesty International as an organisation may be a useful opener for some classes.

Starter 1

Brief recap of persuasive language terms: students have 30 seconds (or a minute) to write down as many as they can think of. Ideas are collected to the front and any gaps are filled in by the teacher. Ask students to explain the terms once they have been reminded of them.

Starter 2

Show students a letters page from the local newspaper and ask: Who are they writing to/for? How do we know?

Further resources

Amnesty's UK website has lots of information and there are also teaching resources available there that can be used to introduce the organisation and stimulate students' writing, see www.amnesty.org.uk/issues/Education.

Stephen Fry's open letter to the Olympics Committee in August 2013 is an excellent example of rhetoric and persuasive argument putting forward a case for moving the 2014 Winter Olympics from Russia because of the country's recent record on gay rights.

Activity 1

A game of analytical consequences

Programme of Study link

Reading

- Knowing how language, including figurative language, vocabulary choice, grammar, text structure and organisational features, present meaning

Grammar and vocabulary

- Discussing reading, writing and spoken language with precise and confident use of linguistic and literary terminology

Description

Students work in groups of at least three to produce interesting analytical comments about the letter.

First, the letter is read aloud and any misunderstandings are dealt with.

Working in silence and secretively, each student chooses one feature and writes a simple analytical sentence at the top of a piece of paper (e.g. Amnesty International uses ___ (feature), e.g. ___ (quotation) in order to ___ (explanation).

Next, each student passes their paper to the person on the left of them within their group.

Then, each student adds a comment to the sentence they have just received, either adding to it (a 'yes, and also ...' type comment), offering a counter-argument (a 'yes, but ...' response) or criticising the original comment (a 'no, because ...' response).

This can be repeated to add another comment (this is more demanding), or the third student to receive the paper can then read it out to the group so that all ideas are shared.

Learning outcomes

- Students will be able to identify a feature and explain its effect.
- Students should be able to comment on different aspects of the text.
- Students may be able to engage in dialogue about the relative importance of different features.

Differentiation

Lower ability students may manage better if they are given a more concrete starting point. For these students, working together to complete an analytical comment may be more productive. They can be given a feature to find in the text and then explain, working in a pair. Worksheet 3.8 offers a structure for lower ability students to follow.

Suggested features to be found include:

- emotive language (e.g. shockingly unjust; anguish at being separated from your children; harsh sentences)
- pronouns (second person you/your to directly address the prisoners and first-person plural we/our to show that many people feel the same)
- formal language, especially relating to the law/politics (e.g. imprisonment, democracy, dissent) to emphasise seriousness and that the issue relates to politics/legal issues of human rights
- patterns of three (e.g. fellow artists, musicians and citizens; your children, your families and your lives; strength, bravery and fearlessness) for impact (note how very similar these concepts are – clustering rather than just using one has emphatic effect)
- attempts to flatter or show understanding towards the Russian authorities who have imprisoned the women (e.g. wonderful Russian sense of humour; While understanding the sensitivities of protesting in a place of worship).

Higher ability students can follow up the activity by discussing the features they have identified and ranking them by importance (in creating the text's meaning/effects) or their impact on them as readers.

Assessment opportunities

- Reading: critical analysis
- **RAF 5**

Activity 2

Writing an open letter of protest

Programme of Study link

Writing

- Drawing on knowledge of literary and rhetorical devices from their reading and listening to enhance the impact of their writing

Description

Students imagine a scenario in which a student in a neighbouring school has been excessively punished (e.g. excluded) for something. For example, this could be:

- dyeing their hair or some other uniform/clothing infraction
- wearing or displaying a religious symbol that they have been told to remove
- performing a protest song, poem or sketch in assembly that criticised a teacher or the head.

Having been given a scenario to work with, students produce an open letter to be sent to the local newspaper, in which they express solidarity with this student and comment on the human rights of the child in question. This should be completed individually, and can be peer assessed before final drafting.

Students should:

- address the letter directly to the penalised child/student using a plural first-person position (we/us/our)
- include comments that show sympathy to the authorities
- use features of persuasive writing (e.g. patterns of three, emotive language)
- use formal tone and style.

Learning outcomes

- Students will be able to write using basic techniques of persuasion and in a mostly formal style.
- Students should be able to maintain a formal, balanced tone and use features of persuasive writing.
- Students may be able to produce a cohesive and convincing piece of writing.

Differentiation

Lower ability students can be given a structure to work to, for example:

- Paragraph one: brief introduction (we are writing to …)
- Paragraph two: main concerns (we hoped that … but …)
- Paragraph three: emotional appeal (describe feelings in the community)
- Paragraph four: closing statement praising the child or expressing hope.
- They may also benefit from pre-teaching gathering ideas for content in each paragraph, so that the main focus of their individual work is on using appropriate phrasing.

Higher ability students can be challenged to produce a brief commentary on their own writing, explaining how they have used features similar to those in Amnesty's open letter (e.g. 'I used pronouns "you" and "we" to address X directly and to show that there is a group of us who are concerned about his/her treatment').

Assessment opportunities

- Writing: style and vocabulary; form and structure
- **WAF 2, WAF 3**

SPAG focus

Many of the sentences in this text are complex, using subordinate clauses of different kinds. However, many commas are used to mark off items in a list, so students will not be able to simply look for commas to identify complex sentences. It may be useful to explore the first two sentences specifically in terms of their grammatical make-up to remind students of some clause types in forming complex sentences.

For example, the adverbials can be noted and discussed in terms of their usefulness in adding time or place references to the sentence: 'As the one-year anniversary of your trial approaches'; 'around the world'.

Discuss how comment clauses ('we are writing to assure you that'; 'we know that') draw attention to the writer(s) and can sometimes be used to show that something is an opinion and not being declared as fact.

Relative clauses can also be highlighted in terms of how they serve to describe or add detail about people who are otherwise quite briefly mentioned ('who were also involved in the protests'; 'about whom we are also very concerned'). Worksheet 3.9 presents these grammatical details for students.

8: Promotional tweets

Context

This collection of promotional tweets from different companies demonstrates various things about selling and promoting via social media. Twitter is fast overtaking Facebook as a social media platform and many people use it to follow brands that they like and in order to hear news about new products and promotions.

The tasks provided here are intended for Year 8 students and offer a more abstract view of audience, suitable for more able Year 8 students or even Year 9 students.

Getting started

Students are likely to be familiar with the 140-character tweet format and may well follow companies or brands on Twitter and/or receive similar messages via Facebook.

Starter 1

Which companies and other 'brands' are followed by students in the class? Students take two minutes to compare in pairs/small groups, then a quick straw poll is taken of the kinds of companies/brands followed within the class (e.g. food and drink, games, magazines, musicians, actors, sports personalities, authors, other celebrities, media companies).

Starter 2

In pairs, draw up a list of ways in which companies can successfully promote themselves on Twitter. Can you come up with a set of rules that companies/ brands could follow?

Further resources

Students can collect further promotional social media messages as homework for further exploration in class, perhaps presenting the features of these tweets/Facebook posts to the class or within their group

Activity 1

Group writing on audience and purpose

Programme of Study link

Reading

- Making inferences and referring to evidence in the text
- Knowing the purpose, audience for and context of the writing and drawing on this knowledge to support comprehension

Description

Students collaborate to produce a short analysis of the tweets. They should consider:

- audience factors: who is assumed to be reading these tweets and what does the company assume about them (e.g. the Costa example assumes that its audience would see coffee and cake as an effective antidote to the Monday morning blues; this also assumes that its audience works Monday–Friday and views Monday mornings negatively)
- language used to persuade this audience to buy or otherwise support the brand.

The analysis should be written in essay format, providing evidence for all ideas. All members of the group should have input into the essay and will all be graded the same based on that essay (unless it is clear that someone did not contribute).

Learning outcomes

- Students will be able to identify key assumptions made about the readers of each tweet.
- Students should be able to explain how words chosen reveal assumptions about audience.
- Students may be able to analyse the language of the tweets with insight.

Differentiation

Lower ability students can be supported by being given assumptions made about the audiences and asked to identify the evidence that reveals this, effectively giving them a part-completed frame to work with. (For example, using the Costa example above.)

Higher ability students can be challenged by being asked to work to a strict time limit: how many fully worked points can they produce in 15 minutes?

Assessment opportunities

- Reading: forms, conventions and language
- **RAF 6**

Activity 2

ABC DEF

Exploring mode and its impact on language

Programme of Study link

Vocabulary and grammar

- Knowing and understanding the differences between spoken and written language including differences associated with formal and informal registers, and between Standard English and other varieties of English

Description

Building on the questions in the Student Book, students can explore how the tweets use language in non-standard ways that are typical of online communication. Students can discuss elements such as:

- hashtags (#jobs) used as a sort of category label or to highlight a theme
- elliptical style (e.g. Fact of the day: …)
- hyperlinks.

Some of these elements are also used more broadly in advertising, in an attempt to seem friendly and approachable (itself a persuasive technique), so this can be noted in discussion.

Students might also discuss how their own online communication features non-standard usages that they would perhaps avoid in formal writing or at school.

Students can produce annotated posters highlighting features of online communication and explaining what they are used for.

Learning outcomes

- Students will be able to explain some key differences between online and offline communication.
- Students should be able to make links between formality and Standard English.
- Students may be able to explore how and why non-standard features can be effective in persuasive texts.

Differentiation

Lower ability students can be given more support in terms of being allocated features to discuss and explain. For example links, hashtags and images as being typical of online communication; or direct address, questions and imperatives as features of persuasion.

Higher ability students can be challenged to explore the idea of informality as a persuasive technique by identifying ways in which the texts use informality to attempt to engage and persuade the reader.

Assessment opportunities

- Reading: critical analysis
- **RAF 4**

SPAG focus

All of these tweets address the audience directly using the second person 'you', and use a plural first-person position (we/us/our) to represent the company in an official way without any sense of an individual speaking. This is worth exploring as a specific grammatical feature. It can be useful to highlight how sometimes the first-person plural can be used inclusively (often in political speeches, as in Text 9 – 'all our young people'), but it can also be used in a way that does not include the audience/reader but expresses a plural subject position, usually a company or 'official line' of some kind.

Students can look for examples of first-person pronouns in texts explored so far, categorising them as either:

- specific individuals using singular pronouns I, me
- grouped subjects such as companies using plural pronouns we, us
- collective or inclusive subjects connecting the writer and the reader using plural pronouns we, us.

9: Education manifesto

Context

This extract from Blair's famous 2001 speech is provided as an example of political rhetoric. This speech came as part of Labour's campaign to continue in office for a second term, and became well known as the 'education, education, education' speech.

The activities provided are intended for Year 9 students.

Getting started

What do students already know about political speeches? They may be familiar with particular examples such as Martin Luther King's 'I have a dream' speech or Winston Churchill's 'We shall fight on the beaches'.

Starter 1

When, where and why do people make speeches? In pairs, list as many different kinds of speech as you can.

Starter 2

Imagine you are campaigning to be prime minister. Note down three things you will include in your campaign (i.e. tell people what you are going to do so that they know why to choose you). Compare your list with that of a partner.

Further resources

If students have read Martin Luther King's speech before, listening to it might be useful. It is available in various places on the internet. Searching for Martin Luther King 'I have a dream' audio should produce results.

Activity 1

'Zooming in' on features

Programme of Study link

Reading

- Knowing how language, including figurative language, vocabulary choice, grammar, text structure and organisational features, present meaning

Description

Students analyse the text by using the 'zoom lens' technique: starting with a 'big picture' comment and then focusing in on a small detail.

This can be modelled for them first: The speech emphasises education above everything else. This begins with the triplet 'education, education, education' and continues through the repeated use of the word 'education' in further explaining exactly what this means.

Students then choose further aspects of the speech to comment on, pairing each fine detail comment with a broad, overview-type comment, as above. It does not matter which they notice first, as long as both are presented as part of their written analysis. Explain that this technique is useful for GCSE analysis, as it ensures that both overview and detail are present in their answers.

Learning outcomes

- Students will be able to link broad comments to specific details in a useful way.
- Students should be able to make a range of comments linking fine details and big-picture observations.
- Students may be able to produce original and insightful analytical comments.

Differentiation

Lower ability students may benefit from a prepared list of either specific features, broad-brush comments or both to combine and expand. Alternatively, the class may be able to generate ideas first that can then be combined and developed through individual work.

Higher ability students can be challenged to construct their analysis into a mini essay, focusing on structure and cohesion to make it work as a whole piece.

Assessment opportunities

- Reading: critical analysis
- **RAF 4, RAF 5**

Activity 2

Writing a speech

Programme of Study link

Writing

- Writing polished scripts for talks and presentations
- Drawing on knowledge of literary and rhetorical devices from their reading and listening to enhance the impact of their writing

Description

Students draft and refine a speech of their own. This can be on a topic they find, or they can be given a list to choose from (e.g. 'Schools should not have uniforms because …'; 'Animal testing is wrong/necessary'; 'The NHS should not waste funding on drug addicts'). Alternatively, this can be linked to a class reader and students can write as a character, making an argument in the text about something that has happened (or could happen).

The drafting and refining process is important here, so students should initially write on alternate lines to make improvements easier to add. Once the content is written, students should be encouraged to check through for persuasive techniques: have they missed any opportunities for figurative language, repetition, etc.?

Learning outcomes

- Students will be able to include some key features of persuasion.
- Students should be able to include a range of features and structure their speeches appropriately.
- Students may be able to produce effective and engaging texts.

Differentiation

Lower ability students may benefit from using this activity to support work on a class reader, allowing them to 'inhabit' a character or write as a generic character (e.g. a soldier for Private Peaceful, an inmate from Holes, etc.) to argue about a scenario or event in the text.

Higher ability students can tackle a current affairs type issue, which would have had less class input than an event already studied, and would therefore require more independent thought.

Assessment opportunities

- Writing: style and vocabulary; form and structure
- **WAF 2, WAF 3, WAF 7**

Activity 3

Performing a speech

Programme of Study link

Spoken English

- Giving short speeches and presentations, expressing their own ideas and keeping to the point

Description

Students perform the speeches written in Activity 2. Listening to (or ideally watching) some polished speeches would be useful preparation for this task. Students can be asked to note body language – gesture, posture, etc. – used by politicians when giving speeches. To encourage students to perform and not merely read, this can be framed as a drama activity.

Learning outcomes

- Students will be able to use their voices effectively, using appropriate pace and volume.
- Students should be able to use a range of appropriate intonation.
- Students may be able to use effective gesture.

Differentiation

Lower ability students can work in groups to practise and refine their delivery, ultimately 'performing' only within their small group.

Higher ability students can be given less preparation time and may be expected to deliver their speeches in front of the class.

Assessment opportunities

- Spoken English: presentation and communication
- **SLAF 1**

SPAG focus

Noun phrases can be explored through Blair's list 'the joy of life: the exhilaration of music, the excitement of sport, the beauty of art, the magic of science'. Each of these uses two nouns with the second serving only to give more definition to the first (e.g. not just any 'joy' but the 'joy of life'). These are good examples of noun phrases in a different format to 'the/a (adjective) (noun)'.

Students can be given the basic nouns (life, music, sport, art, science) and asked to build their own noun phrases describing these subjects before Blair's versions are highlighted and their structure explained (or elicited from an able group). If this is completed before the writing activity (Activity 2), students can be challenged to include a similar listing technique in their speeches.

10: Humber Hawk advertisement

Context

This 1954 advertisement offers an excellent opportunity to talk about how texts, even quite functional ones like adverts, exist in a specific context that has an impact on them. This advert aims to highlight the new and exciting style of the Humber Hawk's engine (having overhead valves rather than the 'flathead' style of valves at the side of the engine).

The activities here are intended for Year 9 students.

Getting started

What does advertising do? What do we mean by context? A snappy starter to think about advertising or context specifically is a good way to get started with this text.

Starter 1

What is advertising for? In one minute, jot down as many things as you can think of that advertising does.

Starter 2

What do we mean by 'context'? What are the factors that influence a text? In one minute, jot down as many things as you can think of that can influence a text. If it helps to narrow it down, think specifically about a print advertisement: what are the factors that would affect its language, layout and message?

Further resources

The Advertising Archives website (www.advertisingarchives.co.uk) has a massive collection of adverts that could be discussed with students. However, it includes some images that make it unsuitable for students to search alone.

Activity 1

Focus on purpose/audience/context

Programme of Study link

Reading

- Making inferences and referring to evidence in the text
- Knowing the purpose, audience for and context of the writing, and drawing on this knowledge to support comprehension

Description

Students discuss how various aspects of the advertisement relate to its context as a 1950s text. They can present their findings as an annotated display or write them up more formally.

Students may consider:

- the qualities of the car that are being promoted
- how advertisements generally are different now (e.g. less text, simpler phrasing)
- how the woman is presented (they may be surprised to see a car advert from this time that features a woman driving).

Learning outcomes

- Students will be able to identify some aspects of context by reference to the text's features.
- Students should be able to make some inferences about changes in society since this advert.
- Students may be able to construct an effective analysis of this advert in context.

Differentiation

Lower ability students may require more support and may work best if they focus only on one or two of the points above (perhaps focusing on how advertising generally has changed).

Higher ability students may be able to bring the post-war context in and think about how that affected factors such as women's position in society. They may also welcome the opportunity to produce an extended piece of writing that explores the contextual factors of this text.

Assessment opportunities

- Reading: forms, conventions and language
- **RAF 7**

Activity 2

Talks on an aspect of advertising

Programme of Study link

Spoken English

- Giving short speeches and presentations, expressing their own ideas and keeping to the point

Description

Students research, prepare and present formal talks on a topic related to advertising. They may conduct research as homework, or be given computer or library time in lessons, but the task requires individual work following up something related to advertising which interests them. This can be an individual task, or for a lower ability or less-confident group it could be a group presentation, as long as all contribute.

Possible areas to explore include:

- the advertising of a particular kind of product or service (e.g. perfume or cars) or a specific brand (such as Chanel or BMW). This will probably include a historical overview with examples from different periods
- particular features of advertising (e.g. television adverts that are deliberately annoying or not related to the product).

Learning outcomes

- Students will be able to use a mostly formal style to share information they have discovered.
- Students should be able to maintain a formal style in presenting information and ideas.
- Students may be able to create an engaging talk in an appropriate register.

Differentiation

Lower ability students may need the scope to be kept quite narrow and specific (e.g. choose a brand and talk about its advertising over time).

Higher ability students can be given the challenge of a more abstract theme, such as annoying adverts or those that are less about the product. (For example, how new a phenomenon are these? What kinds of products use obscure adverts?)

Assessment opportunities

- Spoken English: presentation and communication
- **SLAF 1**

11: Debating

Context

The English-Speaking Union organises debating competitions for schools and colleges in England, which enable teams of students to compete at local, national and eventually international level. This transcript is from a video on the Union's website that introduces the major schools competition.

The activities here are intended for Year 9 students and lead up to the debate activity using the final text in the book.

Getting started

Students may or may not be familiar with formal debating. The starter activities are planned to introduce the topic broadly.

Starter 1

Why do speaking skills matter? In pairs, make a list of:

- jobs that require you to speak to an audience and
- contexts in which people may be expected to speak to a group of people.

Starter 2

What does it mean to debate? Discuss with a partner what you already know about formal debating.

Further resources

The ESU website has other useful resources for debating: www.esu.org.

Activity 1

Exploring formal speech

Programme of Study link

Grammar and vocabulary

- Knowing and understanding the differences between spoken and written language, including differences associated with formal and informal registers, and between Standard English and other varieties of English

Description

What do students already know about spoken language and how it differs from written language? Using this transcript as a basis, students explore how debating requires a high degree of formality and a fully standard variety of English. (The transcripts also enable them to clearly see that the debate style is not necessarily the student speakers' 'natural' way of talking, as we also see them talking less formally to the camera about their experience.)

Students briefly study the transcript for familiar features of spoken language (there are very few), and for features of persuasive language. They should notice that the persuasive features are mainly in the 'competing' turns of speech and the few spoken features occur mostly in the language of the competing teenagers in their non-competition turns.

Students then construct a continuum of six different kinds of talk, from most to least formal. They put the six genres of speech in order according to how formal they are, and discuss in their groups what decides on the formality levels (e.g. context factors such as audience or predetermined rules). The genres are: conversation with a friend about a personal problem, medical appointment, 'reality' television programme, television soap, debate competition, the Queen's speech at Christmas.

This can also be repeated for written forms (perhaps including forms such as a shopping list, an email asking a colleague for a favour, a magazine article, a textbook, etc.).

Learning outcomes

- Students will be able to explain that some forms of speech require a level of formality similar to that of written language.
- Students should be able to begin to explain the reasons that some forms of speech are formal.
- Students may be able to explore the influence of context on formality.

Differentiation

Lower ability students may find this more approachable the other way round, with the sequencing activity first. These students can use Worksheet 3.10 to help them.

Higher ability students can be challenged to compare the students' speech in the two parts of the transcript, allowing them to arrive at conclusions about formality and context.

Assessment opportunities

- Spoken English: discussion and knowledge about spoken language
- **SLAF 4**

Activity 2

Debates and discussions

Programme of Study link

Spoken English

- Participating in formal debates and structured discussions, summarising and/or building on what has been said

Description

This activity can follow on from and develop Activity 1. In mixed ability groups, students discuss whether spoken skills should be part of the school curriculum. They should consider and discuss factors such as:

- how likely it is that everyone will need to be able to speak in public
- whether electronic forms of communication and carrying out business make a difference to the need for speaking skills
- the pros and cons of making shy people talk in front of others
- the class time taken up (e.g. in having every student 'do a talk').
- The discussions should result in a clear list of responses to these questions. A successful discussion will have involved everyone in the group and will have remained on topic throughout whilst still exploring the topic in depth and detail.

Learning outcomes

- Students will be able to explain their views and listen to others.
- Students should be able to respond to the ideas of others.
- Students may be able to take a leading role, sharing their own ideas and encouraging others to speak.

Differentiation

Lower ability students can be given the task of recording the group's ideas, perhaps with several students being responsible for recording conclusions about one idea each. With a uniform lower ability class, the factors given above for inclusion can be used to scaffold the discussion, perhaps by creating a more structured discussion and giving students a fixed amount of time to consider each point.

Higher ability students should be spread around the groups to give them the opportunity to act as group leaders, driving the discussion, keeping it on task and making sure everyone participates.

Assessment opportunities

- Spoken English: discussion and knowledge about spoken language
- **SLAF 2**

12: Celebrity role models articles

Context

These two texts offer different angles on the topic of celebrity role models and are included here as supporting material for students to hold a formal debate on the topic. The articles are taken from the *Daily Mail* and the *Guardian* and provide different perspectives. The *Mail* piece criticises specific celebrities for being poor role models, while the *Guardian* piece presents research findings that children do not actually look to celebrities for models of behaviour.

This series of activities is intended for Year 9 students.

Getting started

The question of whether celebrities are appropriate role models is likely to be something that students will have opinions about.

Starter 1

Who are your role models? Discuss with a partner who you admire or would choose to be like and why. You can pick several people who you admire for different reasons.

Starter 2

Show students a series of images of popular celebrities (perhaps five) and ask them to state who is the best/worst role model of the group and why. They could prepare briefly in pairs before reporting back.

Further resources

Similar articles to these run fairly regularly: an internet search for the celebrity of the moment and the phrase 'role model' is likely to be fruitful.

Activity 1

Analysis of features

Programme of Study link

Reading

- Knowing how language, including figurative language, vocabulary choice, grammar, text structure and organisational features, present meaning

Description

Students work in three (or six) groups, in which they read the first article and analyse it by focusing on one of the following:

- How does the text address its audience? What does it assume about its audience? Which words and phrases are most relevant to quote for this aspect?
- What is the tone of this text? What attitudes is it sharing? Which words and phrases are most relevant to quote for this aspect?
- How is this text structured? How does it use sentences and paragraphs to present its argument?

Following this, the three (or six) groups break up and form new jigsaw groups, which include representatives from all three topics covered. They then share their findings to build a complete picture of how the text works.

Learning outcomes

- Students will be able to discuss ideas about the text and share these within new groups.
- Students should be able to explain how the text's features create meaning.
- Students may be able to teach each other effectively.

Differentiation

Lower ability students will benefit from clear structuring and modelling, perhaps even working through one of the three questions as a whole class and then using an even number of groups with each looking at one of the two remaining questions.

Higher ability students in a mixed ability class can be used to lead groups, with lower ability students being given a recording role to note the group's findings.

Assessment opportunities

- Reading: critical analysis
- **RAF 5**

Activity 2

Formal class debate on role models

Programme of Study link

Spoken English

- Participating in formal debates and structured discussions, summarising and/or building on what has been said

Description

Students hold a full formal debate on the topic of role models.

The motion could be: This house believes that schools should teach children how to choose effective role models.

Students should be divided into two large groups: those 'for' and those 'against'. It is best if this is done for them, rather than allowing them to choose based on their feelings. All students will need to research and prepare, and part of debating is finding the arguments and evidence to support your case whatever your personal feelings about the motion are.

There needs to be at least one main speaker for each team, but everyone will be expected to contribute to the debate.

The teacher can act as chair, or a student can be selected for this role.

Firstly, the two groups meet and have a brief discussion about possible research directions, dividing up the work between them all (ideally with some duplication).

Next comes the first research period (as homework or in school).

Then the two groups meet again and refine their arguments. They should pool all of the ideas that have come up as a result of their research, and divide them among the group so that each student (or pair of students, if the group is very large) has a different argument to finalise and present.

The next stage is more preparation and tightening up the arguments. Each team should have a leader who has a sense of what each person will be saying and can select participants based on the opposing team's last point or question.

Finally, the debate takes place. One person (or pair) speaks at a time, in formal style, and everyone else listens. Questions can be asked of each person/pair from members of the opposing team, and preparation time can be given before responses are expected (this may result in another person/pair coming forward if their point becomes relevant).

It can be helpful to introduce some formal procedures, such as everyone applauding when someone stands up to speak, and agreeing by calling 'hear, hear'. Negative comments should not be permitted, but criticisms can be phrased as questions at the proper time.

Learning outcomes

- Students will be able to research and contribute prepared statements to a debate.
- Students should be able to ask questions of the opposition.
- Students may be able to argue unprepared points.

Differentiation

Lower ability students should be enabled to present points that they have carefully prepared. They may find it easier to produce an effective formal statement for an argument that they do not agree with, as it is easier to slip into informal styles when debating a strongly held argument.

Higher ability students can be encouraged to respond to unexpected or unprepared points as they arise during the debate, and should be able to argue formally regardless of personal belief.

Assessment opportunities

- Spoken English: presentation and communication; discussion and knowledge about spoken language
- **SLAF 1, SLAF 2**

Unit assessment task

Description

Students write a report about how language is used to persuade. They will need to use subheadings to organise their ideas, and write using a formal and informative tone. Students should consider and include comment on:

- contexts in which persuasive language is found (including speech and writing)
- specific features of persuasive language (ideally including examples that they have found from a range of sources).

Learning outcomes

- Students will be able to show an understanding of the uses and features of persuasive language.
- Students should be able to explain a range of uses and features of persuasive language.
- Students may be able to differentiate between various persuasive usages and features.

Differentiation

Lower ability students can be allowed to collaborate and produce a report as a group, or subheadings can be provided to give them a frame to work within.

Higher ability students can be encouraged to include as wide a range of examples and ideas as possible.

Assessment opportunities

- Writing: style and vocabulary; form and structure
- **WAF 2, WAF 3, WAF 4**

UNIT 4 Real-world stories

Overview of unit

In this unit students will read a range of texts from the interesting genre of literary non-fiction. Literary non-fiction is non-fiction that reads like literature or poetry but is rooted in fact and real-life events.

Key words

Autobiography
Biography
Blog
Declarative voice
Diary
Figurative language
Hyperbole
Journal
Litotes
Pronouns
Review

Assessing learning prior to this unit

1. How familiar are students with the literary non-fiction genre?
2. Can they provide examples of texts from the genre?
3. What are students' current levels of reading, writing, speaking and listening?
4. What curricular targets do students have?

Key questions for this unit

1. What is literary non-fiction?
2. How do writers of literary non-fiction convey a sense of character, setting and atmosphere in their work?
3. How do writers of literary non-fiction create narratives to engage their readers?
4. How do writers of literary non-fiction use fact and opinion to affect the reader in their writing?
5. How does literary non-fiction differ from other non-fiction writing?

Example scheme of work

A six-week overview of how the texts and activities could be put together to form a teaching sequence.

Week 1	Week 2	Week 3
• Introduce students to the genre of literary non-fiction with Texts 1 and 2. • Through these texts students learn key reading skills including how to retrieve information and infer and deduce ideas from the text. • Students also learn about narrative structure, dialogue and how experience is portrayed for dramatic effect. Students will practise writing using evidence from the text. • Text 1 is aimed at Year 7 average to high ability students and Text 2 is aimed at Year 8 average to high ability students. A longer comparative writing task is included within the scheme at the end of Text 2 materials. The accompanying worksheets will help students to access this more difficult text and compare it with Text 1.	• Students build on their comprehension skills of retrieval and inference through the study of literary features, characterisation and description in Texts 3 and 4. • They also explore the use of intensifiers and exaggeration for the purpose of entertainment in Text 3 and the use of the third person and description in Text 4. • The final activity for Text 4 draws all study so far together in a synoptic comparative assessment of the features of all four subgenres of autobiography.	• Using Texts 5 and 6, the students study the subgenre of travel writing and analyse the ways in which the writer of Text 5 uses humour to engage the reader, whereas the writer of Text 6 uses a mixture of fact and opinion to put serious points across. • Students are also able to prepare and write their own travel piece for a specific purpose and audience. • Again, there is an opportunity for students to compare texts in Activity 3 of Text 6.

Week 4	Week 5	Week 6
• Using Texts 7 and 8, students are able to test their skills in comprehension of pre-1914 texts. They compare the different styles used by Scott and Pepys to record experience and to write for different purposes and audiences, and they record their own experience in a diary or journal.	• Students work through Text 9 and demonstrate their understanding of genre by writing their own elements of a contemporary blog. • They study the use of imagery and increase the level of sophistication of comparison by attempting a three-way comparison of the features of a blog and the other texts in this diary section.	• Text 10 is the final text and students use it to study the principles and features of a review and to analyse the language of AA Gill's restaurant review. • As a finale they are asked to consider the complex use of figurative language in this text and to appreciate his use of fact, opinion and irony. • Students are also given the opportunity to write their own review to put their knowledge of the genre into practice.

Assessing the learning outcomes of this unit

The activities in this unit provide for the full range of skills covering reading, writing and spoken English.
Reading tasks in this unit focus on audience and purpose, and a detailed understanding of content and meaning.
Writing tasks in this unit offer opportunities for writing comparative essays, diaries, descriptive pieces, interview scripts, magazine articles, and reviews.
Spoken English tasks include improvisation, advertising pitches, news reports and interviews, along with plenty of opportunity for discussion and debate.

Links between the texts

Texts 1–4 explore autobiography with a focus on an event from the author's own childhood or on an event that happened before the author's birth involving his or her ancestor/s.
Texts 5 and 6 are examples of travel writing by two authors using differing styles. The extract written by Bill Bryson is anecdotal underpinned with humour throughout, whilst Paul Theroux is more opinionated and critical of the subject matter.
Texts 7 and 8 are taken from famous journals, namely the diaries of Samuel Pepys and the last entry from the journal of Scott of the Antarctic. Both writers are recording their contemporary responses to what turn out to be important historical events. Text 9 is taken from the teenager Sophia Slater's blog – a modern-day diary format. She records her experiences of meeting the Dalai Lama.
The final text is of a completely different genre, that of review, or, more specifically, restaurant reviews. Although it focuses on food it also describes the setting, and its opinionated nature reveals the character of the writer as well as the meal under review.

Online resources

There are editable PowerPoint versions of all activities and Word versions of all worksheets available in Kerboodle.

In addition, there are exemplar student outcomes plus teacher notes and additional activities for the following activities from the Teacher's Book:

- Text 2: Activity 3
- Text 3: Activity 4 (video)
- Text 6: Activity 3

1: Boy: Tales of Childhood

Context

The text used here is from the famous children's author Roald Dahl's autobiography in which he writes about his early life, in particular the years he spent at a brutal boarding school in Wales. In the text, which reveals the 'the great and daring Mouse Plot', Roald and his friends are attempting to exact revenge on the miserable sweet-shop keeper, Mrs Pratchett, who is guilty not only of hating children in general but of being dirty. The text is coloured by the characterisation of Mrs Pratchett as a typical Dahl grotesque (an ugly caricature), similar to characters he would later create in his fiction such as Miss Trunchbull from *Matilda*. Characterisation and the telling of a story are the most important elements of the text.

This text is best suited for average to high ability Year 7 students.

Getting started

Generate a shared context for reading this text through these starter activities.

Starter 1

Students are asked whose life they would like to find out more about and why. What do they think would make a good autobiography? Everyone must write down two examples. Brief whole class feedback will probably cover famous people, celebrities, someone that the students admire or someone they consider has overcome a barrier in life. Elicit the style of writing, i.e. they would usually expect to see chronology, possibly diary entries, or some might include flashbacks. If there is time, touch on tone. Some students may mention humour or poignancy.

Starter 2

In pairs students are asked to think of an interesting story from their own life to tell each other. They should also explain why they chose this event. Is it because it is an interesting story? Does it say something important about their character? Or is it a mixture of both?

Further resources

Students may be directed to other negative characterisations from stories such as Scrooge from Charles Dickens' *A Christmas Carol* or Cruella de Vil in *101 Dalmations* (Dodie Smith). You may also wish students to carry out research into how schools have changed since the beginning of the 20th century, and look at other accounts of schools taken from classic novels such as *Jane Eyre* (Charlotte Bronte) and *Tom Brown's School Days* (Thomas Hughes). Other non-fiction accounts include Winston Churchill's account of the public school Harrow in *My Early Life: 1874–1904*, and stories from Gervase Phinn's books about his days as a school inspector.

Activity 1

Follow the clues to the character

Programme of Study link

Reading

- Making inferences and referring to evidence in the text

Description

Ask students to build up a profile of Mrs Pratchett and Roald Dahl himself as they read through the text (either individually or as a whole class). Ask them to look for evidence about the two characters in the text (Mrs Pratchett who is portrayed as a nasty character, and Roald Dahl who presents himself as a heroic character).

Working in pairs and using a table like the one below, students should take each character in turn and write words and phrases from the text that directly relate to the character in the first column and ideas they may deduce from the text in the second column.

Description of character from the text	What this suggests about the person

Feed back and discuss answers – if 'malignant pig-like eyes' is in the first column, discuss how it is not the description but the idea of 'malignant' and 'pig-like' that makes the reader think of a bad person. For Roald Dahl, expect to see 'They slapped me on the back. They cheered me and danced around the classroom' in the first column. The second column should contain details about how their actions present him as the hero of the moment. Emphasise the difference in terms of the contrast between direct information and indirect *clues* about someone.

Students could create their own heroic or unpleasant characters. They might draw the character and label the different features that suggest heroism, for example, soldier's uniform. They may also use dialogue in the form of speech bubbles and annotate the picture in the same way.

Learning outcomes

- Students will be able to identify words and phrases that describe the characters of Roald Dahl and Mrs Pratchett.
- Students should be able to explain what these words and phrases suggest about the character.
- Students may be able to create their own characters.

Differentiation

Lower ability students may be given the phrases already lifted from the text and asked to put them into the different columns.

Higher ability students can be asked to speculate on the qualities of Mrs Pratchett and Dahl by writing down three words that they would use to describe the characters to someone else.

Assessment opportunities

- Reading: comprehension; critical analysis
- **RAF 2, RAF 3**

Activity 2

Tell me a story

Programme of Study link

Reading

- Knowing how language, including text structure and organisational features, presents meaning

Writing

- Drawing on knowledge of literary and rhetorical devices from their reading to enhance the impact of their writing

Description

Give students a copy of the nursery rhyme Jack and Jill – included on Worksheet 4.2 Explain that they are going to break down the elements of a simple nursery rhyme to emphasise how structure is essential to any narrative.

Jack and Jill went up the hill → (Introduction)
To fetch a pail of water. → (Development)
Jack fell down and broke his crown, → (Climax)
And Jill came tumbling after. → [1]
Up Jack got and home did trot, → (Resolution)
As fast as he could caper;
And went to bed and bound his head → (Conclusion)
With vinegar and brown paper. → [2]

Provide the students with the separate parts of a narrative: introduction, development, climax, resolution and conclusion. Model the introduction then ask students to work in pairs and label the rest of the nursery rhyme. Less confident students could then work on another nursery rhyme or fairy story to embed these ideas, or they could be given the annotated nursery rhyme (see above) without having to work it out themselves.

Students can then be given the Dahl text separated into different sections of the narrative (without the conclusion). The students then have to put them in order and decide which bit of the narrative is missing. Less confident students may be told in advance that the conclusion is missing. This could be done as a paired activity (see differentiation suggestions).

Students should provide feedback and speculate on the conclusion based on the evidence of the text. They can then write their own conclusion in the form of two concluding paragraphs.

Finally ask students to think of an incident from their childhood (or make something up). If they have done Starter 2 they could use that idea. They should write down the main points of the narrative and then pass these notes to a partner. The partner then labels the narrative parts (as with Jack and Jill). If any parts are missing the students should write these below and return the narrative plans to their creators.

Students then read their narrative plans to each other or to the rest of the class.

Next they write up their narratives, making sure that they use all of the basic parts of the narrative.

Students peer assess their work for WAF3 with photocopy of levels for that specific descriptor.

Learning outcomes

- Students will be able to identify the parts of the narrative.
- Students should be able to plan out their own story using the parts of the narrative.

- Students may be able to write a well-structured narrative using the basic narrative arc.

Differentiation

Lower ability students can be further supported by working in pairs with a more able student to identify the longer sections from the Dahl text.

Higher ability students will need to reinforce their own learning by explaining and assisting in the paired part of this activity. As a challenge, higher ability students could also be asked to focus on the tone and style of their narrative, perhaps making it humorous, or to use a more formal style if they are secure in the structuring of their work.

Assessment opportunities

- Writing: form and structure
- **RAF 4, WAF 3**

Activity 3

Dialogue duo

Programme of Study link

Reading

- Knowing how language is used to present meaning

Spoken English

- Using intonation, tone, volume and action to add impact

Description

This activity focuses on the importance of dialogue in Dahl's account and how Dahl uses it to bring a real encounter to life, as the author of a fictional piece might.

Ensure that students are not looking at the text. Provide the excerpt (see Worksheet 4.1) with the verbs of speech missing. Working in threes or fours, students fill the gaps with what they think are appropriate choices, either what they remember to be the actual verbs or good synonyms.

Students then practise the excerpt as a piece of drama, taking on the roles of Thwaites, Mrs Pratchett and Dahl (to mime dropping the mouse into the gobstopper jar). They pay particular attention to delivering the lines appropriately according to the verbs they have chosen.

Watch a selection of performances. Discuss which worked best and why, noting down the most frequent verb choices. Compare briefly with the verbs in the text. How did the students (and Dahl) manage to bring the narrative and the characters to life? Were they believable?

Learning outcomes

- Students will be able to suggest alternative verbs other than those in the dialogue.
- Students should be able to comment on the use of verbs by Dahl and the choices he has made.
- Students may be able to comment on the effect that changing the verbs has on the text.

Differentiation

Lower ability students can be supported by creating balanced working groups so that they can draw on those with stronger reading/spoken English abilities. The colour coding on the excerpt helps to break down the text and emphasise who is speaking and when, so students can home in on the delivery of speech and its impact.

Higher ability students should be encouraged in the feedback elements of the activity to explain choices and evaluate the effectiveness of both their and Dahl's verbs of speech.

Assessment opportunities

- Spoken English: reading aloud and drama
- **RAF 5, SLAF 3**

SPAG focus

Rewrite the following sentences changing the italicised word to one of the vocabulary choices provided in brackets. Then explain how your choice adds to the sentence. Does it make it more informative, interesting or precise? How else might it change it?

- I went into the kitchen to make myself a nice cup of tea. (refreshing, hot, relaxing)
- The selection of sweets on the shelves all looked so tempting; I didn't know which to choose. (array, choice, display)
- I felt the warm sweet smell of hot chocolate wafting over me. (soothing, luxurious, comforting)
- When I popped the gobstopper into my mouth it broke. (shattered, splintered, cracked)
- She took the cake out of the oven and it smelt good. (sensational, delicious, mouth-watering)
- The cook poured the indefinable slop onto my plate. (splattered, ladled, dumped)

2: Angela's Ashes

Context

Angela's Ashes is presented in a very anecdotal style that builds up a picture of McCourt's poverty-stricken childhood in an Irish Catholic family. Some of these recorded memories are from before his birth, so they are stories passed down to him, and it becomes apparent that he comes from a line of strong mother figures who are struggling to bring up their families without much help from drunken fathers who do not face up to their responsibilities. Although the text is sad and poignant in places it retains a sense of humour and is never self-pitying. The conversational and dramatic style of writing, with frequent insertions of the present tense, reveal the often chaotic nature of his upbringing and of his forebears.

This text is best suited for average to high ability Year 8 students.

Getting started

Generate a shared context for reading this text through these starter activities.

Starter 1

'We had it hard, we did.'

Ask students to imagine or speculate how their parents' and grandparents' childhoods differed from their own. They should write or relate five differences between then and now, and give feedback to the rest of the class. As a class, discuss the differences (and any similarities) between the two.

Starter 2

Ask students to think of three interesting facts about a relative or friend that would sum up their life or character, e.g. 'Sarah was always quarrelling and falling out with the neighbours.' Or: 'Grandad carried a big stick and would wave it at anyone who annoyed him.'

Further resources

To gain a deeper understanding of the history and hardship that many of the Irish working class have faced over the centuries, able Year 8 children could read Jonathan Swift's essay on the Irish, *A Modest Proposal*. An introduction to satire and its purposes would be required.

Although it is set in South Africa under apartheid and focuses on racism, Beverley Naidoo's *Journey to Jo'burg: A South African Story* also focuses on the human struggle to overcome poverty and deprivation.

Both texts highlight the hardships that children suffer because of the society and situation they are born into.

Activity 1

Introduce a relative

Programme of Study link

Writing

- Writing clearly, accurately and coherently, adapting their language and style in and for a range of contexts, purposes and audiences

Description

McCourt introduces his relatives in a formal manner but soon changes to a conversational style. It quickly becomes obvious that the behaviour of his father, especially, does not match the formality of his introduction.

Students read paragraphs 1 and 5 where the reader is introduced to McCourt's father and mother. They need to look at the structure of each introduction and mimic the style when writing about a close relative. The aim is to write a few opening lines, but to create an impact. Is there one thing that stands out? Is there something quirky or funny about the person that they could include, or wild or mischievous? Clearly what they write can be an exaggeration of the truth. It could be completely imaginary, but it needs to sound authentic in order for the writing to be effective.

Suggested sentence starters include:

My mother/father (full name) was born/grew up (a few key details about his or her place of birth or early life.) Like/unlike his/her (stated relation) he/she (briefly describe an action that reveals a personality trait).

Partners should share their opening lines.

In the same pairs students should discuss using the following pointers:

- Which parts were interesting? Does this introduction make you want to read on?
- Does it retain a formal tone or switch quickly to an informal tone?
- Are there any snippets of information that you particularly liked?
- Are there any adjectives that you could use that sum up the opener?
- Does the writing style engage you (why/why not?) (Challenging)

Select a few outstanding examples to be read aloud to the whole class. Have a brief whole-class discussion about some of the bullet points above (as appropriate.)

Learning outcomes

- Students will be able to write a few lines describing a close relative.
- Students should be able to mimic the style of McCourt and add in an interesting detail.
- Students may be able to include a number of details and write the opening lines in a consistent style engaging the audience throughout.

Differentiation

Lower ability students can be given the suggested sentence starters and follow them closely. For the paired discussion, not all of the bullet points need to be covered, more emphasis could be placed on the content-based ones.

Higher ability students will be challenged by the question about writing style, which requires some language analysis. Select a few of the more able students to perform their opening lines. There may be an opportunity to step into the voice of that persona if they have included any spoken lines.

Assessment opportunities

- Reading: forms, conventions and language
- Writing: style and vocabulary; grammatical range and accuracy
- Spoken English: discussion and knowledge about spoken language
- **RAF 6, WAF 5, WAF 7, SLAF 2**

Activity 2

Understanding the impact of direct speech

Programme of Study link

Reading

- Knowing how language, text structure and organisational features present meaning

Description

Point out to students that although the text is full of recorded details of events before the author was born, he has manipulated the text to include a lot of direct speech. This helps to make the events seem more immediate and to take on greater significance. The use of episodes reported using direct speech also enables him to switch seamlessly between the past and present tenses.

Use Worksheet 4.3 to plot use of direct speech and its effects.

Learning outcomes

- Students will be able to retrieve relevant examples of direct speech and make a few comments about their effectiveness (content related).
- Students should be able to identify all of the relevant examples and make connections with how this aids the narrative.
- Students may be able to easily identify the examples, and comment on their effectiveness and how they add dramatic impact to the narrative.

Differentiation

Lower ability students can be supported by a partly completed chart to demonstrate the type of examples they are looking for and possible intended effects.

Higher ability students should be presented with a chart in which only one example is filled in, or a blank sheet with just the headings shown, as this will challenge them.

Assessment opportunities

- Reading: comprehension
- **RAF 2, RAF 3**

Activity 3

Compare and contrast the presentation of memories in *Boy: Tales of Childhood* and *Angela's Ashes*

Programme of Study link

Reading

- Making critical comparisons across texts

Writing

- Writing well-structured formal expository and narrative essays

Description

Students first need to use a detailed planning grid (Worksheet 4.5) to create a clear picture in their minds of the comparisons and contrasts between the two texts. This will help them to locate key quotations and examples from the two texts and to focus on language analysis. By completing the chart, students will then have a clear framework to work from when paragraphing their essay. (See online planning chart with examples.) Although the final essay will have to be done individually to provide a true and fair assessment, students can approach the planning stage working in pairs or small groups. Before writing, remind students about the importance of making a point clearly, supporting it with a quotation or example from the text, and then commenting on its effect.

Learning outcomes

- Students will be able to make comparisons and contrasts based on the content and characters in the two texts.
- Students should be able to explain the effect of the authors' choices of language, grammar or structure at points in their essay.
- Students may be able to maintain a comparison across the two pieces with comment on language and the writer's craft being embedded in their work.

Differentiation

Lower ability students will be supported by the examples already given in the chart. They do not necessarily have to fulfil every heading and could focus more on the characters and narrative content. Careful selection of pairs or small groups at the planning stage would also support them.

Higher ability students can be given a chart with just one comparative example. They can then provide evidence and comment for all of the headings. Emphasise that the language analysis columns are meant to be more challenging!

Assessment opportunities

- Reading: comprehension; critical analysis; forms, conventions and language
- Writing: style and vocabulary form and structure
- **RAF 2, RAF 4, RAF 5, RAF 6, WAF 2, WAF 3, WAF 4**

3: The curse of the spaghetti marrow

Context

This is an autobiographical piece by Jay Rayner, a well-known journalist and food critic. Jay's mother, the late Claire Rayner, was an agony aunt and TV personality in the 1970s and 1980s. This piece alludes to Jay's childhood and his mother's role as a TV cook. Nowadays, food and cookery programmes dominate the TV schedules, and it is unlikely that your students have not come across at least one of them. The prominence of this type of programme on television today will help to familiarise the students with the language of the text.

Getting started

Generate a shared context for reading this text through these starter activities.

Starter 1

Ask the students to write down two foods they like and two they dislike, and why. Is it taste, texture or association with different places or people that determines whether they like or dislike the foods?

Starter 2

Give students an item of food (the more exotic and controversial the better) which is not shared with the rest of the class. In pairs they give a verbal description of their food item as if their partner has never tasted it before. They need to use appropriate adjectives. Ask each student whether they would eat the food based on the description given by their partner.

Activity 1

Exaggerating the facts

Programme of Study link

Reading

- Knowing how language and vocabulary choice present meanings

Writing

- Considering how their writing reflects the audiences and purposes for which it was intended

Description

Read the text as a class. Split students into small groups (three or four per group would work well). Ask each group to identify examples in the text of where Rayner exaggerates the facts, for example, calling the marrow 'a cruel and unusual punishment'. Each group should aim to identify at least four examples.

Once students are happy with their examples, they should discuss what effect the exaggerated facts have – for example, often Rayner exaggerates for humorous effect or for emphasis. Each student should take one of the examples that their group identified and write an individual PEE (point, example, explanation) paragraph in which they explain how Rayner uses a certain word or phrase to exaggerate an idea to engage the reader.

It might be helpful to model an example for students. Using the phrase 'cruel and unusual punishment', students could write:

'Jay Rayner exaggerates his dislike for the spaghetti marrow by using the phrase "cruel and unusual punishment". This shows that he thinks having to eat the marrow is like being punished for no reason and is really unfair, and you could almost call it child abuse.'

Once each student has completed the PEE sentence, they should swap with another student in their group and give feedback about whether they have selected an example that is an exaggeration and what impact that has, i.e. is it for humour or to shock, even if it is in a self-deprecating, mock self-piteous way?

Students can answer the following question in a short essay format including a brief introduction and conclusion:

How does Rayner use humour or exaggeration to engage his reader?

They can put all of their PEE sentences together and add a suitable linking connective between each paragraph.

Finally they can write their own descriptive paragraph about their most/least favourite food, using exaggeration to engage the reader through humour or empathy. This piece can then be peer assessed against the writing criteria for WAF1and WAF2.

Learning outcomes

- Students will be able to identify some examples of exaggeration used in the passage.
- Students should be able to identify the effects of exaggeration and comment on its use in the passage.
- Students may be able to use exaggeration to the same effect in their own writing.

Differentiation

Lower ability students may benefit from a worksheet that provides most of the specific examples from the text so that all they need to add are the remaining examples and/or explanations.

Higher ability students could be further challenged of they are asked to include at least one metaphor to describe their chosen food, and to focus on appealing to the five senses in their writing.

Assessment opportunities

- Reading: comprehension; critical analysis; forms, conventions and language;
- Writing: style and vocabulary
- **RAF 3, RAF 5, RAF 6, WAF 1, WAF 2, SLAF 2**

Activity 2

Who is Jay Rayner?

Programme of Study link

Writing

- Drawing on knowledge of literary devices to enhance the impact of their writing

Description

This activity focuses on the purpose of autobiography – to tell the reader about the writer and his character, opinions and experiences.

Students look through the passage to identify any information that:

- tells them direct information about Jay Rayner (Jay's mother was a TV presenter in the 1970s who was also a TV cook; Jay was eight when he had to eat the spaghetti marrow; he liked curry, lamb ribs, McDonald's and Dayville ice cream and he didn't care about football. Football captains at his school never chose him for their teams)

- allows them to infer something about his character (Jay preferred rich, unhealthy foods rather than vegetables; Jay may not have been fit enough to play football because of the food he liked; he felt betrayed by his mother because she usually cooked food that he enjoyed and now she keeps giving him horrible food, which is like torture to him).

Now ask students to imagine that they are Jay Rayner and write a diary extract based on the information they have but expressed in their own sentences and using their own words where possible. For example they may write:

'I had to eat that disgusting boiled baby's head again today. I can't think why my mum is torturing me in this way – she usually cooks great stuff like curry.'

Alternatively, higher ability students could be challenged by writing their own diary extract in a similar style that reveals a different kind of personality entirely, such as a sporty individual who loves raw carrots and protein drinks!

Learning outcomes

- Students will be able to identify evidence in the text that tells them something about Jay Rayner's character.
- Students should be able to write a diary extract describing the events in the text.
- Students may be able to write in character using the persona of the young Jay Rayner to describe the events in the text or create their own believable persona if using the alternative activity.

Differentiation

Lower ability students will be able to follow the format of the original text.

Higher ability students will be challenged by having to maintain the same writing style and creating a consistent persona.

Assessment opportunities

- Writing: style and vocabulary
- **WAF 1, WAF 2, WAF 7**

Activity 3

Best meal/worst meal

Programme of Study link

Writing

- Drawing on knowledge of literary devices to enhance the impact of their writing

Description

This is a straightforward writing activity in which the students use the work they have done on exaggeration and description to write an account for an informal online blog in which they describe either the best or the worst meal they have eaten. They should concentrate on the food rather than the location or atmosphere, and use powerful adjectives, verbs, adverbs and similes for either a humorous or emotive effect on the reader.

They should be reminded about the correct register and features of an informal blog. You can then supply the bloggers' opening sentences: 'Hi, fellow foodies. I'm going to tell you about my favourite meal ever. Perhaps you could tell me about yours?'

Learning outcomes

- Students will be able to describe their best meal, using some descriptive techniques.
- Students should be able to describe their best meal successfully, using a variety of descriptive techniques.
- Students may be able to use contrasting vocabulary to describe their best and worst meal. Some students may also be able to explain and justify their language choices in a commentary on their work.

Differentiation

Lower ability students could first sketch and label their best/worst meal to help them to structure the piece.

Higher ability students could be directed to research more food blogs before writing to enhance their style.

Assessment opportunities

- Writing: form and structure; style and vocabulary
- **WAF 1, WAF 2, WAF 5, WAF 7**

Activity 4

The consequences of diet

Programme of Study link

Spoken English

- Participating in formal debates and structured discussion, summarising and/or building on what has been said

Description

In this activity students are introduced to a controversial statement concerning food, such as: 'Packed lunches should be banned'; 'Biscuits should be banned from sale'; 'School dinners are delicious'. They are then split into groups of four. Give them a specific argument that relates to the topic they will be debating. Two members of the groups have to produce written arguments for one side of the debate; the other two have to produce arguments against. One example could be as follows:

Topic: Biscuits should be banned

Ideas to debate could be:

- Health issues: biscuits are full of fat and sugar and this is harmful to people's health.
- Personal freedom – no one has the right to decide what we eat.
- Environmental impact – rubbish from biscuit packaging contributes to environmental pollution.
- Taste: Some biscuits are too horrible to contemplate (e.g. custard creams, Nice biscuits); none of them should be produced. Cookies may be exempted from the ban.

The two pairs then join together. The two sides have to deliver their own arguments verbally and debate the issue. To do this they should adopt a question/answer policy. Each member of the group asks two questions and gives two answers.

As an extension activity each member of the group should also make sure that he or she responds to at least one answer by making a further point either in support or against the answer, using counter argument. The whole class debate will be teacher assessed.

Learning outcomes

- Students will be able to write and verbally deliver arguments in favour and against their given topic.
- Students should be able to give reasoned arguments in writing and justify their opinions verbally.
- Students may be able to extend their arguments through the use of counter argument.

Differentiation

Lower ability students can be supported by careful group selection.

Higher ability students can be encouraged to further develop arguments with the use of counter argument.

Assessment opportunities

- Spoken English: presentation and communication; discussion and knowledge about spoken language
- **SLAF 1, SLAF 2**

4: Wild Swans: Three Daughters of China

Context

This text is an extract taken from Jung Chang's autobiography of her family's experience of living in China during a momentous period of history that spans the 20th century. The book focuses on the lives of three women: Chang's grandmother, her mother and herself. This means that although it is primarily an autobiography there are also many biographical elements within it. The text focuses on Chang's mother's first meeting with her mother-in-law shortly after her wedding to Chang's father. Clearly the event pre-dates Chang's birth so this detailed account was probably related to Chang years later when she was a young girl, and these facts make this text biographical rather than autobiographical.

This text is suitable for Year 8 higher ability students and Year 9 core ability students.

Getting started

Generate a shared context for reading this text through these starter activities.

Starter 1

Ask students to describe their favourite place, with the aim of being as factually accurate as possible. For example, somewhere they have been on holiday, their favourite restaurant or café, a relative's home. Make a few notes as prompts and then exchange descriptions with each other in small groups.

Starter 2

Kowtowing means to kneel and touch the ground with the forehead in worship or submission as part of Chinese custom or to act in an excessively subservient manner. Ask students in small groups to find three synonyms for the word 'kowtowing' using dictionaries, the internet or their own ideas.

Further resources

Chinese Cinderella by Adeline Yen Mah would be an appropriate parallel text for students to read at home. The autobiography is appropriate for young teenagers and is about Adeline's upbringing under the auspices of her father and stepmother in China during the Second World War. Culturally and historically this overlaps with *Wild Swans*.

Activity 1

Make it real

Programme of Study link

Writing

- Amending the vocabulary, grammar and structure of their writing to improve its coherence and overall effectiveness

Description

Ask the students to read the first paragraph of the text, close the book and then explain to a partner, from memory, what the house looks like. They can then check their account against the description in the book. How well did they do? Why is it easy to describe this house?

Next, one student draws a place that is described to them by another student. For example, it could be a room in their house or a relative's house. It should be somewhere they know well and can describe in detail. The person giving the description has to be as accurate as possible, and add a detail that reveals the character of the room's owner.

When finished they look at the finished drawing to check how well it has been described and reproduced. The students then look for the detail that reveals character.

Finally, students have to answer the question orally: What does the house in the text reveal about its owners?

Learning outcomes

- Students will be able to describe the house of Chang's grandmother-in-law.
- Students should be able to describe a setting accurately and add a detail that reveals something about their character.
- Students may be able to identify details from a setting that reveal character in a perceptive and insightful manner.

Differentiation

Lower ability students will need more prompting in this exercise, with the teacher supervising the reading and asking students to recall key descriptive details from the text whilst it is being read. For example:

- What is in front of the house?
- What is the furniture like?
- What does this suggest about the family?

You should also model the drawing exercise for less confident students.

Higher ability students can be challenged by using their five senses as far as possible when describing the room, i.e. not just relying on visual detail. Evoke the other senses too to conjure up a vivid picture of the location.

Assessment opportunities

- Reading: comprehension
- Spoken English: presentation and communication
- **WAF 2, WAF 5**

Activity 2

I was there

Programme of Study link

Reading

- Knowing the purpose, audience, form and context of the writing and drawing on this knowledge to support comprehension

Writing

- Amending the vocabulary, grammar and structure of their writing to improve its coherence and overall effectiveness

Description

Explain to the students that although Chang is describing the scene of the meeting between her mother and mother-in-law as if she is an eyewitness to the event, she is of course not present, and was not even born at that time. It is therefore a second-hand account, so perhaps it is not as reliable a piece of evidence as to the actual detailed events that day. This will need to be flagged up to students, but at the same time you can focus on how the inclusion of realistic detail compensates for this. Ask students to consider how she convinces the reader that this a real event. One of the ways is to see the scene through her mother's eyes by using her and her father's titles and possessive pronouns. Remind students that possessive pronouns indicate that something belongs to someone, e.g. his, her, mine, yours.

Now ask students to identify all sentences where Chang uses titles and the pronoun 'my'. Ask for ideas about why Chang does this and you should elicit the response that it makes the account personal and therefore credible (see the SPAG focus below).

Next ask students to use accurate description and possessive pronouns to write a short passage about an experience that has happened to a member of their family.

You could model your own story before asking students to come up with their own, and you could come up with suggestions for anecdotes, such as a family wedding, the reaction to a new baby in the family or a dad's return from active service as a soldier or a stint spent working abroad. Students may also like to think about family holidays and/or visits to relations as seen through the eyes of another family member.

This can be teacher assessed using the writing criteria focusing on the assessment focuses mentioned below.

Learning outcomes

- Students will be able to identify Chang's use of titles and possessive pronouns.
- Students should be able to explain why Chang uses these features and, in turn, use them in their own biographical writing.
- Students may be able to write in exceptional depth and detail about an experience, using the techniques of accurate description and third-person perspective with the use of first-person pronouns and titles.

Differentiation

Lower ability students will be supported by the highlighting activity to see where and why the possessive pronouns are used.

Higher ability students are expected to delve deeper into the use of the possessive pronouns and how they reflect the development of the narrative in the passage. Some of this is very challenging and will need careful guidance.

Assessment opportunities

- Reading: critical analysis
- Writing: style and vocabulary
- **RAF 2, RAF 3, RAF 4, RAF 5, WAF 1, WAF 2, WAF 3, WAF 7**

Activity 3

Kowtowing

Programme of Study link

Reading

- Learning new vocabulary, relating it explicitly to known vocabulary and understanding it with the help of context and dictionaries

Spoken English

- Improvising to focus on language use and meaning

Description

For this activity students should first look up the definition of kowtowing: to kneel and touch the ground with the forehead when worshipping or in submission as part of Chinese custom, or to act in an excessively subservient manner.

Divide the class into groups of three. The objective for each group is to either find another custom like kowtowing (look at the internet) or to make up a new one and then try to convince the class that it is a real custom.

Each member of the group prepares a short talk on a different aspect of the real or imaginary 'custom'.

In turn each group tells the class about their 'custom' and the rest of the class has to ask questions to determine whether it is real or not. The class votes on whether a custom is real and then the truth may be revealed. (This is a version of the panel game 'Call my bluff' which can be played at any time as a vocabulary building exercise, when students use random words and give real/false definitions to try to mislead their audience.)

Learning outcomes

- Students will be able to describe aspects of a real or imagined custom.
- Students should be able to use imaginative ways to describe in detail aspects of a real or imagined custom.
- Students may be able to use wit and originality when describing a real or imagined custom.

Differentiation

Lower ability students may benefit from using the worksheet which gives more detailed instructions.

Higher ability students could be given a specific country or culture and asked to carry out some research.

Assessment opportunities

- Spoken English: presentation and communication
- **RAF 7, SLAF 2, SLAF 3**

Activity 4

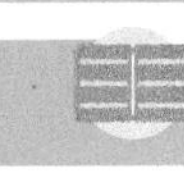

Comparison

Programme of Study link

Reading

- Making critical comparisons across texts

Description

This is a synoptic exercise designed to test students' understanding of the different features the four writers have used in Texts 1–4, respectively.

Students are asked to recall and write a list of the key features of autobiography that they have studied in this unit. They could subdivide them into language features, key focuses and the text in which they are found.

Students then answer the question:

Compare the way writers present their view of experience in two of the autobiographical texts in the student book.

Learning outcomes

- Students will be able to compare some features used by writers to convey experience in two autobiographical texts.
- Students should be able to compare four or more features used by writers to convey experience in two autobiographical texts.
- Students may be able to compare the features used by writers in depth and detail.

Differentiation

Lower ability students will require a writing frame that directs them to write PEE paragraphs, using comparative terminology such as: whereas, on the other hand, however, etc.

Higher ability students will be challenged by the analytical detail of the task and the rigour of making critical comparisons.

Assessment opportunities

- Reading: critical analysis
- **RAF 2, RAF 4, RAF 6, RAF 7**

SPAG focus

Reread the text and highlight every use of the possessive pronoun 'my' in one colour.

Now do the same for the possessive pronoun 'her' using a different colour.

Whereabouts in the text can you see most use of the possessive pronoun 'my?' Why do you think this is?

Overall in the passage why do you think Chang uses 'my' so often.

Elicit answers, including the following: Firstly she wants to create the impression that she was there and it complements the detailed description of the room, wanting to possess it although the house actually belonged to Chang's paternal grandmother. It makes the account more personal and creditable.

The frequent use of 'my' nearer the end of the passage also reflects the power struggle between the two, as in the final paragraph Chang describes this event as 'a little conquest' for her mother. In a small way it reflects the changes in the newly Chinese Communist society. Whereas traditionally the mother-in-law was more empowered, now the power is shifting towards the daughter-in-law in this passage.

Whereabouts in the passage can you see most use of the possessive pronoun 'her?' How does this reflect the power struggle between the two women?

Elicit answers that refer to the fact that in the first two paragraphs the emphasis is on the mother-in-law and what she possesses and how she was able to 'tyrannise' her daughter-in-law in the traditional society. There is also a lot of use of 'her' in the fourth paragraph, which reflects the point of the meeting and how she seems to be empowered by her throne-like chair. The possessive pronoun 'her' also adds emphasis to the detailed analysis of Chang's grandmother's physical description. After Chang's mother has kowtowed, the tension is released and she appears to have been accepted, so the emphasis moves away from the grandmother.

5: Down Under

Context

We now move on to a highly entertaining subgenre of literary non-fiction – travel writing. Although there has been an explosion of this kind of writing in recent times, writing about faraway places with both wit and wisdom has its roots in the grand tours of the 18th and 19th centuries. Although he has moved away from travel writing of late, the undisputed master of the genre for the last 30 years has been Bill Bryson. He uses a mix of witty anecdote, self-deprecating humour and surprisingly sharp and acute observations about the countries and places he visits. His writing is a master class in humorous writing and students will enjoy analysing his humour in the text from *Down Under* and attempting to replicate it when writing about their own favourite places.

This text is suitable for Year 8 core ability students.

Getting started

Students will benefit from looking at short extracts of early travel writing from the 19th century and being introduced to the genre via TV programmes such as *Coast*, any of the Michael Palin series, and *Great railway journeys* where Michael Portillo follows in the footsteps of his travel guide Bradshaw. Students may also become enthused by reading about their own area in travel magazines and Sunday supplements and considering what features they would choose to point out to prospective visitors.

Starter 1
Ask students for examples of good or bad holidays they have been on. What made the holiday a success or a disaster? Have they got any special memories of the holiday?

Starter 2
Make a list of five things that you think are essential for a good holiday. Students can volunteer ideas in whole class feedback. Come up with a class top five.

Further resources

Students can be directed towards *My Family and other Animals* by Gerald Durrell which is an account of his childhood experience of moving from the cold British climate to the warmth of Corfu and his life there.

Activity 1

Where's the humour?

Programme of Study link

Spoken English

- Improvising, rehearsing and performing their own story

Description
Inform students that Bryson uses three types of humour in this text: overstatement or exaggeration, understatement and self-deprecation. The three types are given on the accompanying Worksheet 4.4.

Read the text as a class and ask students to identify where the three types of humour may be found.

Next, ask students to recount to the class a serious (but not sad) story about themselves.

The class is to be divided into groups of four. The students decide on a suitable story from amongst the ones they had prepared to tell the class. Each group then tries to make the story funny by using one of the three types of humour. The group then prepare and perform the humorous version to the class.

Learning outcomes

- Students will be able to identify different examples of humour in the text.
- Students should be able to tell a story about themselves and make it humorous.
- Students may be able to make their stories humorous in several different ways.

Differentiation
Lower ability students could be asked to add just one of the examples of humour.

Higher ability students should be encouraged to add examples of all three types of humour.

Assessment opportunities

- Reading: critical analysis
- Spoken English: presentation and communication
- **SLAF 1, SLAF 2, SLAF 3**

Activity 2

Thoughts and feelings

Programme of Study link

Reading

- Checking their understanding to make sure that what they have read makes sense

Description
Students answer the question: 'What are Bill Bryson's thoughts and feelings about Australia and boogie boards in this text?' This is a simple question format question that some students find surprisingly difficult to cope with, possibly because there is a lot of emphasis on analysis of language, and yet this type of question asks students to reflect on what the text is really about and encourages them to look for hidden or implicit meanings.

Students read the text carefully and then make a list of Bryson's thoughts and feelings, and words or phrases that act as evidence for those thoughts or feelings. You could introduce this activity by modelling the first feeling – one of nervousness when he mentions 'awfully big waves'. When students have listed all the thoughts and feelings ask them to compare their lists with those of a partner before feeding back to the rest of the class.

Students then use this material to construct a piece of writing entitled: 'How the author conveys his thoughts and feelings in the text'.

Learning outcomes

- Students will be able to identify one or two of Bryson's thoughts and feelings about Australia or boogie boarding.
- Students should be able to identify a number of thoughts and feelings using evidence from the text.
- Students may be able to infer thoughts and feelings from the words and phrases they have identified.

Differentiation

Lower ability students may benefit from being given examples from the text to get them started: 'a remote-seeming strand', 'awfully big waves', 'vast and moody sea', 'explosive waves', 'my sagging trunks', 'the bay was surprisingly shallow'.

Higher ability students may like to write their own description of a scene that refers implicitly to their thoughts and feelings – such as the first day back at school after the summer holidays.

Assessment opportunities

- Reading: comprehension
- Writing: form and structure
- **WAF 3, RAF 2, RAF 3**

Activity 3

Advertising your dream holiday destination

Programme of Study link

Spoken English

- Giving short presentations

Description

Planning and presenting the dream holiday location

Students think of a place they know well and enjoy visiting. It might be a holiday destination or somewhere they visit frequently for day trips. They come up with five facts and opinions about the location. They can research websites to verify facts.

Remind them that a fact is indisputable, for example, you might describe a seafront as having many souvenir shops and cafés, whereas an opinion is how you think or feel. The same seafront might be described as gleaming in the summer sunshine, bustling with happy holidaymakers. Remind them that their description needs to be both succinct yet detailed to maintain the audience's attention. Use words economically. They should focus on their use of adjectives and include some emotive language. They might describe a venue as exciting or exhilarating or amazing for example.

Finally they need to come up with a strapline (an advertiser's slogan) for the destination. This will finish their presentation and should be catchy enough to be easily memorable.

They are going to present their work orally so their information needs to be clearly set out in bullet points on numbered cards so that they can maintain eye contact with their audience when presenting.

Learning outcomes

- Students will be able to find five facts and opinions and structure them into a short advertising pitch.
- Students should be able to incorporate effective use of adjectives and emotive language into their presentation.
- Students may keep the audience's attention throughout with good delivery and effective use of the language of advertising.

Differentiation

Lower ability students can be supported by following the structured steps of the task to enable them to feel confident with presenting in front of the class.

Higher ability students can be extended by the challenge of manipulating language for the purposes of advertising, and also by creating their own strapline, thus playing with language.

Assessment opportunities

- Spoken English: presentation and communication
- **SLAF 1**

Activity 4

Visit your home town

Programme of Study link

Writing

- Writing clearly, adapting language and style for purpose and audience

Description

In this activity, students demonstrate their understanding of Bryson's style by writing about their own home village, town or city in an article for the school newspaper or magazine. The article can describe the place itself or a particular event that has taken place recently or occurs frequently, such as an annual festival or carnival.

They will need to incorporate some of the humorous techniques Bryson uses in his own writing at the same time as painting a vivid picture of the location or specific event.

Students need to focus on the following:

- selecting some main features or characteristics and structuring the information into clear and logical paragraphs (first make a list of the attributes and downsides of their hometown/ staging of event)

- producing an accurate and detailed article
- deciding whether they are going to be positive or negative about the place/event. The latter might make self-deprecation an easier tool to use.
- maintaining a consistent tone throughout to aid the humour
- coming up with a headline that reflects the humorous style and tone of the article.

Whilst they are drafting, select students to read various paragraphs that clearly show they have grasped the use of humour. Thus the class will hear a range of styles and will be shown some snapshots, not the same information over again.

Learning outcomes

- Students will be able to write an article describing their hometown or an event it hosts, using detailed and well-structured paragraphs.
- Students should be able to include some humorous techniques with some success.
- Students may be able to write a humorous article with sophisticated use of a variety of techniques.

Differentiation

Lower ability students could be asked to write a detailed article that is either positive or negative in tone. Thus the activity is changed to suit their needs.

Higher ability students will be challenged by this extension activity, but they are supported by the clear planning steps and by hearing a selection of paragraphs from other students' work to aid inspiration.

Assessment opportunities

- Writing: form and structure; style and vocabulary
- **WAF 1, WAF 2, WAF 3, WAF 4, WAF 5, WAF 6, WAF 7, WAF 8**

6: The wild things at Mala Mala

Context

This text is taken from *The Dark Star Safari: Overland from Cairo to Cape Town* by Paul Theroux. Although written at the same time as *Bryson's Down Under* it has a more serious tone and offers a more political perspective. In this text Theroux sets the scene of his African safari by questioning the motivations of tourists who come to Africa only to be able to brag that they have seen the 'big five'. He suggests that tourists on safari have no interest in the African people, except as servants, and so perpetuate the colonial atmosphere of the 19th century. Theroux also refers to safaris as 'harassment' of wild animals.

The opinionated nature of this piece will enable students to debate and evaluate the arguments not only in this text but with regard to other travel issues, the main one being whether tourists actually spoil the areas they visit rather than helping the economies of emerging nations.

This text is suitable for high ability Year 9 students.

Getting started

A large number of tourists who visit Africa choose to go on safari as part of their trip. Paul Theroux looks at the ethics of this and considers who has most to gain. He looks at the attitudes of those tourists and at the effects it has on the host country.

Starter 1

Students read the text individually and then come up with three questions about the text for other students. One should be information based, but students should be encouraged to ask questions about Theroux's opinions. Questions might include: What tourist activity is Theroux criticising in this piece? How does he describe the animals' reaction to being spotted by humans? What tragic event does he make reference to in the piece? How does he describe tourists' attitudes to those who work at the safari sites?

Starter 2

In the second paragraph of this text Theroux uses adjectives to describe not only what the animals are doing, but to convey their characteristics, e.g. 'trudging elephants' and 'loping giraffes'. Ask students to make up their own adjectives for animals – each student can be allocated an animal or they can choose their own.

Activity 1

Establishing Theroux's opinion

Programme of Study link

Reading

- Making inferences and referring to evidence in the text

Description

Divide the class into six groups. Allocate each group one paragraph. Students have to find at least three examples that demonstrate Theroux's opinion about the safari experience. They then identify which parts of speech or linguistic devices he uses to put across his negative viewpoint.

Possible examples for paragraph 4: Verbs – negative connotations – an obsessive tick list idea reinforced in this paragraph:

'whisked to a game park', 'boast of having bagged photos', 'sounding like rambling over-privileged fatheads of a century earlier..'

Students give feedback and discuss the reasons Theroux gives for disliking safaris and safari-goers. Ask how his use of language exemplifies his opinion.

Learning outcomes

- Students will be able to identify three examples of his negative opinions in their given paragraph.
- Students should also be able to give feedback on this and at times identify the linguistic devices or parts of speech he manipulates to put across his opinion.
- Students may be able to consistently identify apt examples, and comment on the linguistic devices used and their effect in putting across Theroux's opinion.

Differentiation

Lower ability students should be allocated paragraph 1 or 2. They should be able to identify vocabulary and short phrases which reveal Theroux's negative opinion.

Higher ability students should be allocated paragraph 3 or 6. They should identify devices and explain how they reveal his mocking tone.

Assessment opportunities

- Reading: comprehension; critical analysis
- **RAF 2, RAF 3, RAF 5, RAF 6**

Activity 2

Advantages/disadvantages of modern-day tourism

Programme of Study link

Spoken English

- Using Standard English confidently in a range of formal and informal contexts

Description

Students work in small groups at first to discuss the advantages and disadvantages of modern-day tourism. Then collate students' ideas as a whole class by drawing a grid on the whiteboard and putting their ideas into columns, for example:

Advantages	Disadvantages
Example: Can bring much-needed money into a country and provide jobs for locals.	The local people may not see much of the new-found wealth and they may remain in poorly paid jobs.
If managed effectively, it can be a chance to educate outsiders about the local environment without a massive carbon footprint.	Often not much thought is put into the impact that tourism has on the environment, e.g. lots of high rise hotels and apartments are built.

Working in pairs, students script an interview on the subject of a prospective new seaside development that is being proposed to draw more tourists into the local area. The location is imaginary, but they will need to come up with a name and make the plans seem realistic. First they need to decide what type of facilities the development will provide, give a few details on the visual and environmental impact and on how it might boost the economy in an old-fashioned 'tired' seaside town. Mind-map all of these details. Quick drawings can be used to help establish a clear picture in their minds.

The script will be for a radio interview, so one student will take on the role of the show's presenter whilst the other, the interviewee, will choose one of the following roles:

- a representative from the local council
- a representative from a business forum
- a leader from an eco charity
- a youth worker.

Students script the interview around six key questions. Discuss and plan these questions first using the mind map and then decide on an appropriate order. When writing the script students need to focus on effective use of language, perhaps borrowing some of Theroux's techniques, and make the answers fit the chosen role of the interviewee. Remind them that some interviewees are likely to have a more positive attitude to the plan than others.

Students practise and perform their interviews.

Learning outcomes

- Students will be able to structure and perform an interview based on six questions.
- Students should be able to use language to portray either a positive or a negative attitude to the plans.
- Students may be able to consistently make interesting choices of language to back up the interviewee's opinion.

Differentiation

Lower ability students should be paired up with a more able student to help with preparation, scripting and performing. Consider each student's areas of strength.

Higher ability students will be able to reinforce their understanding by assisting their partner, and they will be challenged by trying to incorporate appropriately some of Theroux's techniques.

Assessment opportunities

- Spoken English: reading aloud and drama
- **SLAF 2, SLAF 3**

Activity 3

Compare and contrast the travel writing extracts of Bryson and Theroux (Texts 5 and 6)

Programme of Study link

Writing

- Writing for a wide range of purposes and audiences including well-structured formal expository and narrative essays

Reading

- Knowing the purpose, context and audience for the writing and drawing on this knowledge to support making critical comparisons across texts

Description

Students first need to plan the points for their essay on Worksheet 4.6. (Some examples have been completed on the worksheet as a starting point.)

Learning outcomes

- Students will be able to write about the differences between the two texts in relation to purpose and audience.
- Students should be able to write about the differences in style between the two texts.
- Students may be able to write about the differences between the two texts and give their informed opinion about which one is the most entertaining.

Differentiation

Lower ability students should be supported by breaking the task down into topic areas such as purpose and audience; style; and features of writing. It may also be appropriate for students to express a preference, although this works best with more able students who do not always go for the funniest text.

Higher ability students should be encouraged to express a preference for the writing style of one text and give reasons.

Assessment opportunities

- Reading: comprehension; critical analysis; forms, conventions and language
- Writing: form and structure; style and vocabulary
- **RAF 2, RAF 3, RAF 4, RAF 5, RAF 6, WAF 2 , WAF 3, WAF 4, WAF 5, WAF 6, WAF 7, WAF 8**

SPAG focus

Make several sets of cards with subordinate clauses, main clauses and conjunctions written on them. Distribute them to groups of students and ask them to spend two minutes matching up the elements to make complex sentences. When finished, ask them to look at the text and identify complex sentences.

7: Oates walks into oblivion

Context

The text is taken from the final diary entries of Scott of the Antarctic in March 1912. Captain Scott had set out with a team of men to reach the South Pole, only to reach it and discover that the Norwegian Amundsen had got there first. In the diary he recounts how their supplies have run low, but they are unable to reach a depot to restock due to a blizzard and are facing almost certain death.

Getting started

The diary is quite unusual in that it is not just a personal account of the expedition but also a scientific record and now a historical document. These final entries reflect Scott's sense of responsibility as the leader of the expedition for the unfolding tragedy, not just of his imminent death but that of others, and a sense of deep sorrow for the families who will be left behind. On reading these entries a number of different purposes and audiences become apparent, so it is essential to first establish the point of the diary.

Starter 1

Ask students if they have ever written a diary and why. Ask those who have if they are prepared to reveal their reasons. Establish that diaries are often personal and private and not necessarily meant for a wider audience. Also establish that diaries usually cover only a few years in a person's life or maybe a special event such as a holiday or an important family occasion – the written equivalent of photographs. Students will probably also volunteer the fact that most people start off with good intentions but then give up.

Starter 2

Ask students to read Text 7 quietly to themselves. What reasons can they give for why Scott wrote this diary? Expect the more obvious ones, such as a record of the trip with the intention of trying to keep the journal as objective as possible. Also establish that these are final entries where events have not gone in their favour, so the tone of the earlier entries would clearly have been different.

Further resources

The following texts cover the same subject matter of exploration. Joe Simpson's *Touching the Void* is a modern-day autobiographical account of a near-death experience when climbing, and of the moral dilemmas of that experience. Students might encounter this text again at GCSE.

Sir Ernest Shackleton's *South: Shackleton's Endurance Expedition* is a chronological retelling of one of his expeditions to the South Pole. This offers an interesting comparison with a gripping story to tell, but obviously he (and his men) survived to tell the tale.

Apsley Cherry-Garrard's *The Worst Journey in the World* is an autobiographical account from one of the survivors of Scott's fatal expedition.

Activity 1

Establishing the tone

Programme of Study link

Reading

- Knowing the purpose, audience for and context of the writing and drawing on their knowledge to support comprehension

Description

Ask students to consider the following questions in small groups. They might like to write their answers in bullet points or mind map them.

1. What strikes you about the diary? Is there anything that particularly stands out to you, bearing in mind the circumstances in which he was writing?
2. What conclusions can you draw about Scott from these final entries? (This requires an individual response.)
3. How would you describe the tone of Scott's writing?
4. What are the limitations of these diary entries in isolation?

Elicit responses. For question 1 students should cover the following points:

- the fact that he is still writing despite what is happening, a physical struggle to do so, a pervading sense of desperation, references to the continuing blizzard and not being able to reach the fuel depot, but he wants to continue to detail the facts of what is happening and record his opinion. He devotes a whole two paragraphs to testifying to Oates' selfless bravery. He clearly wants the diaries to be found and so is reaching out to a wider audience. Students might also spot Oates' famous final lines of understatement – 'I am just going outside and may be some time.'

For question 2 students will give more individual responses about whether they think Scott is brave or foolish. This links with question 4 as they should note that we cannot really judge from these final entries alone, as the reader does not know what decisions have been made beforehand which have led them to this situation. They may point out that he seems brave in the face of death. He appears to have accepted his fate.

For question 3 students' answers will cover a range such as:

- understated, controlled, but emotion clearly underlies the tone, elements of desperation. Also look for the fact that the tone changes – final plea

– trying to maintain 'a stiff upper lip' in the face of adversity. Remind students that the diary was written a hundred years ago and that Scott was part of a society that is very different from today's society. Expect students to disagree on questions 2 and 3 as the response is subjective.

Learning outcomes

- Students will be able to identify examples and to show their overall comprehension of the entries.
- Students should be able to pick up on the emotion that underlies the writing and cite examples.
- Students may be able to comment on the tone and the social historical context.

Differentiation

Lower ability students could be supported by bullet pointing their answers/using a mind map, as content is more important here than writing style.

Higher ability students should be asked to paragraph their response and to comment on social/historical context and how that may influence the text.

Assessment opportunities

- Reading: comprehension
- **RAF 2, RAF 3**

Activity 2

Purpose and audience

Programme of Study link

Reading

- Knowing the purpose, audience for and context of the writing, and drawing on this knowledge to support comprehension

Description

Remind students that this diary was written with a hoped for audience in mind, as he clearly wants the document to be found after his death –'Should this be found I want these facts recorded.'

With so little time left to write, he appears to be reaching out to several audiences.

Instruct students (individually or in small groups) to reread the entries and write down who they think the potential audiences are.

Answers should include:

- wider audience of the reading public back home – throughout Britain
- more personal audiences such as Titus Oates' mother (see paragraph 2)
- Oates' colleagues – his regiment
- his own family – his wife and son. The final line reads like a prayer or a plea – 'For God's sake look after our people.' 'People' could refer to the wider population, but it probably means the families who will be left behind following this tragic expedition.

Ask students to do the same again, but looking for purposes.

Answers should include:

- a factual account. References to weather conditions and their aim to reach the depot
- a personal letter. Emotion is most evident in the final sentences, a change to more emotive vocabulary
- a last will and testament. He wants to let their bravery be known, they are not going to shoot themselves, but let the death be 'natural'
- a plea/prayer. Final sentence – 'For God's sake look after our people.'

Learning outcomes

- Students will be able to establish the main purposes of the writing and some of the potential audiences for whom the diaries were written.
- Students should be able to spot all the purposes of the writing which are evident in the given extract, and be able to identify all the intended audiences.
- Students may be able to comment on the effect on the reader, bearing in mind the circumstances of the writing and the unusually broad number of audiences. They may be able to comment intelligently on the probable changing purposes of the diaries as a whole, not just this extract.

Differentiation

Lower ability students could be placed in carefully-selected small groups to support their reading of the extract. They could also be asked to come up with two of both the audiences and purposes to make successful completion of the task more attainable.

Higher ability students could be placed in carefully-selected groups giving them a chance to discuss the more subtle purposes and audiences of the piece.

Assessment opportunities

- Reading: comprehension; critical analysis; forms, conventions and language
- **RAF 2, RAF 3, RAF 4, RAF 5, RAF 6, RAF 7**

Activity 3

Writing your own diary

Programme of Study link

Writing

- Writing a range of other narrative and non-narrative texts, including arguments, and personal and formal letters, considering how their writing reflects the audiences and purposes for which it was intended

Description

Ask students to write their own series of diary entries about a challenge they have undertaken, successfully or otherwise. The entries should be in a consecutive order reflecting the chronology of events, but not necessarily daily. The diaries can reflect what actually happened or a different version of events with imaginary elements, but they need to sound authentic.

Learning outcomes

- Students will be able to write clearly about a challenging personal experience with some interesting detail.
- Students should be able to write a series of diary entries, of varying lengths, making their writing appear authentic, and retaining a chronological sequence.
- Students may be able to record changes in how they felt during the personal challenge which is reflected in the different entries. They may also be able to add extra details which may not actually have occurred, but still retain the ring of authenticity throughout their writing.

Differentiation

Lower ability students can be supported in the planning stages by answering the questions Who? What? Where? Why? How? to build up ideas and content. Next, ask them to focus in on a particular part of the challenge which affected them emotionally. Ask them to list quickly their feelings at this point. Emphasise quality not quantity. Remind them to think carefully about their choice of descriptive vocabulary in this piece of writing.

Higher ability students will need to sort out brief content and emotional impact notes for each of their entries, and sort out a logical series of events in the planning stages. Encourage them to use descriptive and specific vocabulary. Remind them about the features of the writing style based on their reading of diaries, and that they need to have a clear sense of purpose and audience before they start writing.

Assessment opportunities

- Writing: form and structure; style and vocabulary; grammatical range and accuracy
- **WAF 1, WAF 2, WAF 3, WAF 4, WAF 5, WAF 6, WAF 7, WAF 8**

SPAG focus

The use of short sentences in these final entries probably reflects a man struggling to survive but still managing to record events, rather than deliberate choices being made about writing style. Nevertheless the use of short sentences still has impact.

Describe the impact of the following:

'He was a brave soul. This was the end.'

Students should recognise that the brevity of the statements emphasises the finality of Oates' death and sums up his personality and humanity. We are told all we need to know without long passages of description.

Some of the sentences are longer but hyphenated, what is the effect of this?

'Blizzard bad as ever – Wilson and Bowers unable to start – to-morrow last chance – no fuel and only one or two of food left – must be near the end.'

Students should note that the hyphens have the effect of shortening and stilting the flow of the sentence, making this sound more like notes. It reflects that he is jumping quickly onto the next subject and emphasises that time is running out. The structure of the sentence perhaps reflects his state of mind.

8: Diary entry, September 2, 1666

Context

This text is from the diary of Samuel Pepys, a famous diarist from the 17th century. Pepys was born in 1633 and was a young man during the Civil War in England. He lived through two disasters – the plague and the Great Fire of London. The latter was actually a timely disaster in that it killed off the plague and resulted in sturdier and safer buildings being constructed. Also only a handful of people died in the Great Fire whereas the plague decimated the population of London. Pepys started his diary in 1660 and went on writing it until 1669, a few years before his death in 1703. He wrote about London, his home, his wife, his friends and himself, and about events such as the Great Fire.

This is a journey into the past. By now students should be familiar with the idea of a journal being an eyewitness to history. They may like to research the Great Fire of London, but it will be more productive to look for other examples of eyewitness accounts, and compare them to versions of the same event by two different people, or with an account from a history book. This will give them further insights into genre, purpose and audience. Students may research other accounts and different events – the Great Plague of London is a useful comparison to the account of the Great Fire, or you could ask them to research local events that have shaped their area's history.

This text is suitable for Year 8 higher ability students and Year 9 core ability students.

Getting started

The diary entry by Samuel Pepys is written in an upbeat tone even though it is describing a tragedy, but not a personal one. He aims to get across the astonishing impact of the spectacle of the Great Fire of London through the pace of the detailed description of what he witnesses.

Starter 1

Ask students to read through the text quietly to themselves. Elicit what it is about and check they understand that although a tragedy is being described Pepys comes across as being in awe of its power. Establish that this is an account of a spectacle and that he is an eyewitness to events. There is a sense of excitement in his writing. Emphasise that at the moment they just need to have a general idea.

Starter 2

Look up a definition of a spectacle and an eyewitness account in dictionaries so students are clear about what type of personal diary writing this is, i.e. it is personal in that he can give a first-hand account of events because he saw them with his own eyes, but he was not personally involved. Elicit that if someone had died in his family as a result of it, or if his house had been burnt down, the tone would probably be very different.

Further resources

Further reading of extracts from Pepys' diaries covering other aspects of his life and times.

History books (perhaps textbooks) covering the Tudor and Stuart periods.

Activity 1

Understanding the language and style

Programme of Study link

Reading

- Knowing how language, including vocabulary choice, grammar, text structure and organisational features, present meaning

Description

Students first need to be sure that they understand this 17th-century account. The cut and paste activity in Worksheet 4.7 asks them to put the sequence of events in the correct order and then match it to a modern-day version. During this part of the activity students are not allowed to look at the text. Once they have completed the ordering of Pepys' writing they can check it against the text. Students should feel more confident in their ability to understand the writing as a whole and not get bogged down by individual word choices.

Next students match the modern-day translations and insert them near the original text (Worksheet 4.8). To conclude, discuss what overall differences they notice in the language and style. Answers should include:

- different sentence structures with many clauses and not in the order they would usually expect
- far more use of the present continuous tense than in a 21st-century eyewitness account
- unusual grammatical structures
- some archaic use of vocabulary, such as 'hath'.

Learning outcomes

- Students will be able to order and match the text in Worksheets 4.7 and 4.8 and to verify their answers against the original.
- Students should notice a more florid writing style in Pepys' diary and different sentence structuring.
- Students may be able to comment in detail on the differences in the two versions and will make suggestions about the overall effect of Samuel Pepys' writing.

Differentiation

Lower ability students could work in pairs on the activity. Worksheet 4.7 is effectively split into 2 parts. They can be given this information so they are only putting in sequence 1–3 and 4–6. For Worksheet 4.8, give them clues to help with matching such as looking for numbers, times and people's names in both as those remain the same.

Higher ability students will probably take less time to complete the sorting and ordering so ask them to look for stylistic differences between the two and then ask them to feed back to the whole class as a conclusion to the activity.

Assessment opportunities

- Reading: comprehension
- **RAF 2, RAF 3**

Activity 2

Breaking news

Programme of Study link

Spoken English

- Improvising, rehearsing and performing in order to generate language and discuss language use and meaning

Description

Students should imagine that the Great Fire has occurred in modern times and it is breaking news. The news reporter is at the scene and is busy interviewing eyewitnesses.

- Students will be expected to script a modern-day interview with the eyewitness, e.g. Samuel Pepys or Jane. They will be assessed for speaking and listening and will ideally work in groups of three.
- They will need to refer back to details in the text and give them credible personas.
- Students will need to infer from the text details about Pepys, i.e. it is clear that he is not one of London's poor, and keep this in mind when scripting his responses. He could be given a modern-day profession. Perhaps he has filmed the fire on his mobile phone – will the interviewer make reference to this footage?

Next, students are told that the interview should use information from the original source material, but may infer ideas about Pepys' life and personality from the text. For example, the students may conclude that Pepys is an important man, as he knows the king, and that he expects to be treated with respect by the interviewer.

Discuss with students how news reports that are 'breaking news' often start. For example, it is clear that a feed is coming through to the presenter in the studio when they say something like: 'We're just receiving news of a fire that has broken out …'.

To provide further ideas you could use a clip from recent news to illustrate how the news broadcasters have to establish the facts of the situation. Allocate a scribe to make brief notes on how the news item is presented, e.g. recurring phrases.

Students practise their interview following a basic script outline but are also encouraged to improvise.

Learning outcomes

- Students will be able to contribute to the group script with relevant details based on the diary extract. All students are assessed on both the discussion and preparation elements and also on their performance, so those students with shorter speaking roles are not disadvantaged.
- Students should be able to script in the appropriate style of a breaking news item. (A clip will first need to be shown to reinforce this.) They will also be able to maintain the appropriate role when performing.
- Students may be able to improvise convincingly and remain in role whilst performing.

Differentiation

Lower ability students should be carefully grouped in threes so that they can draw on each other's strengths. Also support them by giving specific and defined roles within the group, such as looking for specific details in the text that hint at which social class Jane or Pepys belong to. And then build a persona from that, e.g. an appropriate job/profession.

Higher ability students are expected to build on the details from the text incorporating the correct language and style for an up-to-the-minute breaking news interview.

Assessment opportunities

- Spoken English: reading aloud and drama
- **SLAF 2, SLAF 3**

Activity 3

Comparing Scott and Pepys

Programme of Study link

Reading

- Making critical comparisons across texts

Writing

- Writing for a wide range of purposes including well-structured formal expository essays

Description

In this activity students compare the style and voice of the two diary/journal extracts, one written by Scott of the Antarctic and the other written by Pepys.

Students are asked to pick out words and phrases that illustrate that one text (Scott) is an impersonal account of a tragic event, whereas the other is a very personal account of a terrible fire.

Students then write a comparative essay entitled: 'How do the writers Pepys and Scott use language to convey their experience of important events in their lives?'

The essay may then be peer and/or teacher assessed for reading.

Learning outcomes

- Students will be able to write about the features of the two diaries/journals.
- Students should be able to compare some features of language, using appropriate connectives and evidence from the text.
- Students may be able to write in detail about the similarities and differences between the language used in the two texts.

Differentiation

Lower ability students should be given a writing frame in which they are provided with topic sentences for each paragraph and a list of comparative connectives to use (see Worksheets 4.7 and 4.8 from Activity 1).

Higher ability students may benefit from the teacher modelling the first point on the board and reminding the students of the comparative connectives they should use.

Assessment opportunities

- Reading: comprehension; critical analysis; forms, conventions and language
- **RAF 2, RAF 3, RAF 4, RAF 5**

Activity 4

'I was there'

Programme of Study link

Writing

- Writing for a wide range of purposes and audiences including stories, scripts, poetry and other imaginative writing

Description

Refer back to the Starters briefly and the fact that the text is an eyewitness account of a major event in Pepys' life. It is also a spectacle – something quite incredible to look at although it is a disaster. Emphasise that a spectacle could equally be a disaster or a memorably fantastic event. Both will remain in the memory because of their visual impact.

Students write their own diary entry of a major event in their life that can be easily described as a spectacle.

- In small groups they mind map ideas. Prompts include: recent major events that they may have been a part of, e.g. The Olympic Games – the games or the torch relay; the Royal Wedding; or the Queen's Diamond Jubilee. Students may not have been physically there, but they probably saw parts of the events on television. Some students might want to write about something more disastrous – a fire or flood – and writing from personal experience is likely to have more impact.
- Once students have decided on an idea, they need to do the following to complete the planning process before drafting:
    - briefly answer: What? When? Who? Where? Why? (And possibly How?)
    - sketch out a flow chart – the sequence of what happened must be clear
    - to keep the reader engaged they need to think about how they are going to describe events. They should appeal to all five senses, not just sight, and make interesting vocabulary choices. The reader needs to feel as if he or she is there too.
    - They can then write the opening paragraph, swap with a partner and give/receive constructive feedback.

Learning outcomes

- Students will be able to write a substantial diary entry about an event and describe it in detail.
- Students should be able to keep the reader engaged through their use of language and structure.
- Students may be able to combine the use of long and complex and short direct sentences in their writing to great effect and make more unusual and effective choices of language.

Differentiation

Lower ability students are supported by the mind mapping process to help them decide on an interesting idea. The other built-in planning stages can be used according to ability. When describing events students can be reminded to use interesting adjectives to improve the quality of their description.

Higher ability students should be reminded, when planning, about using a number of techniques to make their description effective and to keep the account flowing. Encourage them to go beyond their choice of adjectives (verbs are equally important to description) and to look at the whole structure of their piece and what they think has the greatest impact on the reader.

Assessment opportunities

- Writing: style and vocabulary; form and structure
- **WAF 1, WAF 2, WAF 3**

SPAG focus

As a means of extending students' vocabulary, ask them to look up the definitions of the following Latinate words from the text: infinite, endeavour, lamentable, clamber and perceive.

Make a list of synonyms either by consulting a thesaurus or as an extension activity where the most able students may attempt to come up with their own.

9: Coming Full Circle: My Meeting with the Dalai Lama

Context

This text is taken from an online blog that could be considered to be modern-day form of journal. Blogs are fascinating as they cover a vast number of subjects, from how to put on your make-up to serious political issues such as war and human rights discrimination. Blogs are everywhere on the internet, and related items can be found on social media websites such as YouTube, Twitter and Facebook. It is a good idea to establish how many members of the class are familiar with and have used this media. It is appropriate to discuss within the class the rise of social media and particularly the way in which it allows for self-promotion – or the promotion of a certain aspect of the self. It may be worth asking the question: Does social media hide as much as it reveals about individuals? This discussion could involve research into internet trolls, dating scams and the creation of false identities online.

One new feature that signals the need to capture the interest of a vast online audience is the blogger's profile. It has been included here as it provides us with some history about the blogger and is quite revealing about the kind of character and subject we can expect to see coming through the post itself. Another feature that also distinguishes blogs from conventional diaries and journals is the facility to comment on the blog post. Often the comments are as interesting as the original post and their diversity illustrates the different points that people pick up on when reading the same text.

This text is suitable for Year 9 core ability students.

Getting started

Generate a shared context for reading this text through these starter activities.

Starter 1

Students look up the definition of a blog. Then they suggest typical subject matter of a blog, e.g. sport stars, celebrities, food. Speculate on purpose and audience of each type.

Here is the Google definition of 'blog':

'noun: a personal website or web page on which an individual records opinions, links to other sites, etc. on a regular basis.

Verb: add new material to or regularly update a blog. E.g. "it's about a week since I blogged"'

(www.google.co.uk)

Starter 2

Students read the blog profile of Sophia Slater (without having access to the blog itself) and write down what they expect will be the subject of her blog. They feed back these ideas to the class. The class then reads the blog itself to see whether they were correct.

Activity 1  

Researching the Dalai Lama

Programme of Study link

Reading

- Understanding increasingly challenging texts through learning new vocabulary

Spoken English

- Giving short speeches and presentations, expressing their own ideas and keeping to the point

Description

In order for students to fully understand Sophia Slater's blog, they first need to research some of the references made in the text which are probably unfamiliar. Students need to make notes and write them up for a presentation.

Working in small groups students need to research the following:

- Who is the Dalai Lama? Establish the lineage too, as she refers to her great-great-grandfather meeting the thirteenth Dalai Lama, and she and her brother are lucky enough to meet the fourteenth Dalai Lama.

- Where exactly is Tibet? Where is Dharamsala? Briefly research the geopolitical situation surrounding Tibet and China's influence.
- What is a *chupa*? What are *khadas*? Google these two terms and find images. Discover the significance of these two things and establish their importance as a part of traditional Tibetan dress, and in its wider culture.

Note: Students need to support their written research for presentation with some carefully selected images.

Students collate and edit their research from the topic area they have been given. Present to the whole class.

Learning outcomes

- Students will be able to work as a team and research the information allocated using the URL links. They will also be able to present their research clearly supported by a few images.
- Students should be able to collate and edit their research so the feedback is succinct and totally relevant.
- Students may find further URL links and be able to add any additional relevant material into their presentation.

Differentiation

Lower ability students could be supported by working in mixed ability research groups so that they can draw on a range of strengths. The URL links give strong leads and focus the research so it is not endless. Alternatively, if groups are arranged by ability, allocation of the specific terms like khadas and chupa would be an appropriate choice for lower ability students.

Higher ability students can be allocated one of the more challenging topic areas that requires further research. They can also be asked to go beyond the suggested URL links already provided.

Assessment opportunities

- Reading: comprehension; form, conventions and language
- Spoken English: presentation and communication
- **RAF 2, RAF 7, SLAF 1, SLAF 2**

Activity 2

Meeting the Dalai Lama

Programme of Study link

Reading

- Making inferences and referring to evidence in the text

Description

In this activity the students prepare for and answer the question: 'How does Sophia give the reader the impression that meeting the Dalai Lama is important to her?' Students highlight words and phrases from the text that demonstrate how important this event is to Sophia. They should concentrate on two areas: the feelings and actions of Sophia herself, and her reports of what happens around her. What is the overall effect of this on the writing?

For example, students should come up with some of the following.

Feelings and actions:

- Refers to the whole event as 'the big day'. The title also refers back to her great-great-grandfather meeting the thirteenth Dalai Lama and she wants to show him the photograph
- 'My *chupa* had been ironed but I still smoothed away imaginary wrinkles in the deep red fabric. I folded and refolded my *khada*.'
- 'The moment had finally come!' Clear excitement that her turn had finally arrived.
- In the final paragraph she emphasises the symmetry of the occasion which obviously strikes her: 'One hundred years … we were holding hands … we'd fulfilled some sort of destiny.'

Activity around her:

- Second paragraph: build-up of detail reflects her anticipation and excitement.
- General feeling of excitement also mirrored in the other people's behaviour – 'Everyone was fidgety making polite conversation'.

Learning outcomes

- Students will be able to locate a few examples under both headings and put them into writing.
- Students should be able to find enough examples throughout the passage which support the impression that the meeting was important to the author.
- Students may be able to also comment on how the overall structure of the piece builds up to the actual meeting and thus emphasises its importance to the author.

Differentiation
Lower ability students can write their answers in bullet point or note format to help them focus on essential information.

Higher ability students should be asked to use the questions to help structure their response into a more formal and detailed short essay format.

Assessment opportunities
- Reading: comprehension
- **RAF 3, RAF 5, RAF 6**

Activity 3

Creating an identity

Programme of Study link
Writing
- Writing for a wide range of purposes and audiences

Description
Discuss with students beforehand what the purpose of a profile is – is it self-promotion or simply providing useful background information? Then the students should write a profile of themselves. They can look at Sophia Slater's profile for ideas and stylistic features.

Learning outcomes
- Students will be able to write a basic profile including personal details.
- Students should be able to write a bloggers' profile using the third person and include a range of salient facts about themselves.
- Students may be able to combine interesting anecdotes with factual details about themselves in a succinct manner.

Differentiation
Lower ability students could be supported by using a few of the key phrases from the source blog to help structure details about themselves.

Higher ability students can be challenged by being asked to make their blog more of a self-promotional piece rather than just detailing facts and anecdotes about themselves.

Assessment opportunities
- Writing: form and structure
- **WAF 2, WAF 3**

Activity 4

Write your own!

Programme of Study link
Writing
- Writing for a wide range of andiences and purposes, including a range of narrative or non-narrative texts

Description
In this activity students write their own blog. To make the exercise of writing their own blog more exciting students should use the link provided to read the rest of Sophia's blog, plus the associated comments (or you can print them off for students). They should then write their own blog about a memorable occasion or meeting in their own lives.

The students circulate their blogs to around five other students who comment on them by adding short posts (no more than two to three lines) on the subject and style of the blog. The students could be directed to complete the comments as a form of peer assessment, where students assess the blog against AF1 and AF2 of the writing criteria.

The following links might help students to get a better feel for a wider range of blogs:

- www.bbc.co.uk/blogs/tms/2011/07/jonathan_agnew_picks_his_five.shtml
- http://thoughtsfrombotswana.blogspot.co.uk
- www.southboundbride.com/category/real-weddings/real-weddings-by-location/free-state-weddings.

Learning outcomes
- Students will be able to write their own blog using a suitable style and describing events clearly.
- Students should be able to write an interesting blog and post relevant comments on other students' blogs.
- Students may be able to write in a convincing style with humour, emotion or persuasion according to the subject matter.

Differentiation
Lower ability students could be directed to use key phrases from one of the blogs listed above to help structure their paragraph.

Higher ability students could be encouraged to take on the overall writing style of one of the blogs they have viewed according to the subject matter they are using.

Assessment opportunities
- Writing: form and structure; style and vocabulary
- **WAF 1, WAF 2, WAF 3**

10: Table Talk: Oblix, The Shard

Context

This is an example of a restaurant review, a literary genre that has grown in popularity recently. These reviews are not only about the food, they are also about the restaurant, its setting and clientele as well as being a vehicle for the writers' opinions on a range of unrelated subjects. A.A. Gill's review of Oblix, the restaurant in The Shard (the newly constructed highest building in London) comes from *The Sunday Times* and is aimed at a middle-class audience who can afford to eat out at expensive restaurants, if not on a regular basis, at least on special occasions. The review is also entertaining even if readers have no intention of going to the reviewed restaurant, as the writing is sharp-witted and entertaining. Gill's opinions are provoking to the point of rudeness, but are engaging as they are humorous and intelligently expressed.

This text is suitable for Year 9 high ability students.

Getting started

Generate a shared context for reading this text through these starter activities.

Starter 1
Students consider what is reviewed in the press by coming up with a list of items that have been written about. Have they ever bought or experienced anything simply as a result of reading a review? Have they ever avoided anything for the same reason?

Starter 2
Ask students to read the review by A.A. Gill. Based on their reading, what star rating would they give the restaurant and why?

Activity 1

Match the review

Programme of Study link

Reading

- Reading critically through knowing how language, text structure and organisational features present meaning

Description

For this activity students should be given Worksheet 4.9 containing extracts from a number of reviews, but they will not be told which publication they are from. They are also given a list of publications and typical audiences. Their task is to match the review to its publication and target audience and to match this to its purpose. For example, there may be an extract from a restaurant review that appeals to fairly wealthy young professional clients. The purpose is not necessarily to just recommend (or not) the restaurant, but also to entertain. The worksheet will need to be cut up so that students can re-match the publication to the review and to the target audience. After a set amount of time (20 mins approx.) stop the activity and see how the students have got on. Were some more obvious than others?

Learning outcomes

- Students will be able to match some of the reviews to the publication and audience correctly.
- Students should be able to match all of the reviews to the publication and audience correctly. They will also be able to elaborate on the purpose by considering the content of the review.
- Students may also pick up on different writing styles according to the intended audience.

Differentiation

Lower ability students will be supported within the worksheet as some of the publications are more easily matched by clues in the titles that link with the content.

Higher ability students can be challenged to look at the style of the review and see if they can make more connections by inferring meaning from the text, i.e. reading between the lines.

Assessment opportunities

- Reading: critical analysis
- **RAF 3, RAF 6**

Activity 2

And that is a fact!

Programme of Study link

Reading

- Knowing how language, vocabulary choice and organisational features present meaning

Description

In this activity students learn how statements are not necessarily true – just examples of the declarative voice.

Begin by explaining to students what declarative voice is. The definition of 'declarative' is a word that can be used to describe any action or speech that makes a statement (e.g. I hate lemons. My brother is a woman.). Statements are not always accurate but they often sound like facts as they 'declare themselves' in an authoritative manner.

Ask students to read the rest of the text and identify all examples of fact and all examples of opinion. If students are young or not very confident, some examples or even the whole text may be given to them with fact and opinion already identified.

Give students a list of foods that have very different responses, e.g. marmite, olives, prawns. Put students into pairs – one who dislikes a food with one who loves it. Ask them to write a statement about the food like the ones A.A. Gill has used, the most basic being 'The marmite was like …' and the most elaborate 'The prawn … was not even on nodding terms …'.

(Extension) When finished ask the students to share their statements with their partner. Tell them that statements make use of the verb 'to be', but they are not necessarily fact as they are dependent on individual preference and opinion.

Learning outcomes

- Students will be able to recognise some uses of fact and opinion.
- Students should be able to recognise opinion stated as fact and create their own examples.
- Students may be able to use sophisticated examples of opinion expressed as fact.

Differentiation

Lower ability students can be given some of the examples of fact and opinion to get them started.

Higher ability students can be encouraged to come up with their own more elaborate examples of opinion dressed up as fact!

Assessment opportunities

- Reading: comprehension; critical analysis
- **RAF 2, RAF 3, RAF 5**

Activity 3

Write your own review

Programme of Study link

Writing

- Summarising and organising material, and supporting ideas and arguments with any necessary factual detail

Description

Inform students that they are going to write their own review. Students briefly discuss possible subject matter and share their ideas with the whole class. Write up the top 10 suggestions. Ideas might include: restaurants, films, fashion or leisure experiences, such as a bowling alley or ice rink. Students may want to reread some of the reviews they have looked at so far, so that a range of writing styles are fresh in their minds.

Before writing, the students need to decide on the following:

- what is being reviewed
- intended purpose and target audience
- important factual details as well as their own opinion. For example, a film review will need to include a plot summary without giving away too much
- whether the review will be positive or negative. Are they going to include a star rating?

Students then practise writing an opening paragraph and read it to a partner who can comment constructively. Emphasise that it is quality not quantity which is required here, as a review effectively offers a taster.

Learning outcomes

- Students will be able to follow the basic structure of a review.
- Students should be able to use language that is appropriate for the purpose and intended audience of the review.
- Students may be able to succeed in writing an entertaining review using humour, perhaps in the style of one of the reviewers they have read.

Differentiation

Lower ability students are supported by the stepped sequence of this activity.

Higher ability students can be challenged by asking them to mimick the style of one of the reviews they have read in preparation for this activity.

Assessment opportunities

- Writing: form and structure; style and vocabulary
- **WAF 2, WAF 4, WAF 5, WAF 6, WAF 7, WAF 8**

SPAG focus

For this activity students should revise the definition of metaphor and simile.

Give students a list of examples so that they can revise their knowledge and understanding of metaphors and similes.

UNIT 5 Horror

Overview of unit

This synoptic unit aims to support teachers and students in further developing the skills covered in the other four units of the book. To do this it uses a wide selection of texts – fiction, non-fiction, play scripts and poetry – all touching on the theme of horror.

Key words

Antonym
Character dynamics
Continuation
Déjà vu
Iambic pentameter
Linguistic feature
Memoir
Minor sentence
Narrative
Perspective
Subjunctive
Synonym

Assessing learning prior to this unit

1. What skills have students found the most difficult to acquire and apply so far?
2. What types of text and activity have given them the most enjoyment, and how can these be presented to them in new ways?
3. What weaknesses in English skills have the previous units revealed, and which of the texts and activities in this unit can best help students to meet their targets?

Key questions for this unit

1. Can I read for understanding?
2. Can I read with close attention to detail so that I understand the author's meaning and the effects that he or she is trying to create?
3. Can I write in a variety of forms and styles, paying attention to accuracy in sentence construction, punctuation and spelling?
4. Can I take part in discussions, clearly stating my point of view and listening to others so that I respond appropriately?

Example scheme of work

A six-week overview of how the texts and activities could be put together to form a teaching sequence.

Week 1	Week 2	Week 3
• Introduce students to the theme via two simpler modern texts: 'The Man with the Yellow Face' (Text 2) and *The Toymaker* (Text 3). • The texts provide opportunities for activities and assessment of inference and deduction, writing to build tension and discussion in groups. • The texts and activities are suitable for younger students and for those of lower to core ability	• The fiction of the past can be focused on by coupling 'The Tell-Tale Heart' (Text 1) and *Strange Case of Dr. Jekyll and Mr. Hyde* (Text 5). • The activities suggested in these texts will allow students to identify and comment on writers' purposes and the overall effect of the text on the reader, and will create opportunities for them to comment on writers' use of language, including grammatical and literary features at word and sentence level. • Students can start to appreciate horror writing of the past and thus relate texts to their social, cultural and historical traditions. • Whilst the reading in these texts is more demanding, a wide range of abilities can tackle the suggested activities with suitable support.	• A non-fiction focus will be useful at this point to remind students that the real world is unfortunately not short of horrors. • The two non-fiction texts in this unit, 'Hiroshima'(Text 7) and *Dispatches* (Text 8), provide insights for more-able students on recent history, and the range of activities suggested allows for reading, research, writing and oral presentation.

Week 4	Week 5	Week 6
• It would be wise to spend a reasonable length of time using the extract from *Macbeth* (Text 9). The suggested activities enable all abilities to come to the text with fresh eyes and to gain a great deal from it without regarding the language as a barrier. • Assessment using this text includes: o Identify and comment on the structure and organisation of texts, including grammatical and presentational features at text level. o Produce texts that are appropriate to task, reader and purpose. o Create and sustain different roles and scenarios, adapting techniques in a range of dramatic activities to explore texts, ideas and issues.	• Mystery and suspense is a keynote when 'The Monkey's Paw' (Text 10) and Flannan Isle (Text 6) are used. Both texts invite some background research, but both stand alone as excellent examples of how a mystery can be handled in fiction and poetry. • Core ability students will be able to appreciate Flannan Isle and show their ability to analyse rhyme and rhythm, together with the poet's treatment of the real-life mystery, whilst more-able students will be able to show their ability to emulate the written style of a Victorian tale of the macabre.	• The scheme of work might conclude with a look at the most up-to-date horror writing: *The Enemy* (Text 4), *Twilight* (Text 11) and *Dark Matter* (Text 12), each of which provide very different but equally intriguing angles on zombies, vampires and phobias, respectively. • The summative assessment task draws together many of the themes, skills and approaches suggested by the activities in the unit and can be used to provide a real incentive for students of all abilities to write on something that interests or excites them personally.

Assessing the learning outcomes of this unit

As this is a synoptic unit, the activities provide for the assessment of all assessment focuses covering reading and writing in the Secondary phase (RAFs 2–7 and WAFs 1–8). Thus reading for meaning and reading with regard to literary effect, purpose and viewpoint can be assessed, as well as the technical and compositional aspects of writing.

Speaking to others, with others and in role (SLAFs 1–3) is also covered in this unit.

The activities and suggestions will prepare students well for GCSE English assessment objectives in Reading and Writing (AO3 and AO4).

Links between the texts

All of the texts deal with some aspect of horror. There are extracts from Victorian fiction ('The Monkey's Paw', 'The Tell-Tale Heart' and *Jekyll and Hyde*) as well as very modern treatments of ghosts and ghastly events (*Dark Matter*, *Twilight* and *The Enemy*). Two non-fiction texts ('Hiroshima' and *Dispatches*) remind us that reality is often as brutal as fiction. Poetry finds a place in both Flannan Isle and, rather differently, in the extract from *Macbeth*.

Online resources

There are editable PowerPoint versions of all activities and Word versions of all worksheets available in Kerboodle.

In addition, there are exemplar student outcomes plus teacher notes and additional activities for the following activities from the Teacher's Book:

- Text 2: Activity 3
- Text 5: Activity 1
- Text 7: Activity 2 (video)

1: The Tell-Tale Heart

Context

Edgar Allan Poe is widely regarded as a master of the horror genre. He lived from 1809 to 1849 and earned his living from writing literary criticism, detective fiction and, of course, horror. The main themes in his stories focus on death, decomposition, premature burial and the reanimation of the dead. Students might be intrigued to know that he married his 13-year-old cousin in 1835 (on the marriage certificate her age is given as 21), spent most of his life drinking heavily, and died after being found wandering delirious on the streets of Baltimore.

Despite his rather odd personal life, his horror stories were very popular with the American public. 'The Tell-Tale Heart', from which this text is taken, shows the writer's skill in depicting a mad narrator and his despicable crime. In fact, the narrator's insanity results in him giving himself away to the police at the end of the story.

The language of this text makes it more suitable for Year 8 and Year 9 students.

Getting started

Why do we seem to gain a lot of pleasure from frightening ourselves? A preliminary discussion can explore the appeal of horror writing and films. Students may be able to give examples of stories or films that have terrified them, and now, at a distance, they can look more objectively at what it was that caused the fright.

Starter 1

Who are the great horror writers, film-makers and actors of today? Can the class compile a list of famous names? It is likely that Stephen King will come up, and it would be a good idea to make the point that Edgar Allan Poe was the Stephen King of his day.

Starter 2

Dictionary challenge: choose five less-familiar words from the source text and lead a race to look up each one and be able to give a definition in their own words (to show that they have understood the word, rather than simply reading out from the dictionary).

Further resources

Edgar Allan Poe: Complete Tales and Poems contains all the most famous works. However, Poe's works are also freely available on the internet via any search engine.

Two film versions of 'The Pit and the Pendulum' are also still in existence: a 1961 version starring Vincent Price (the final scene is available on YouTube: www.youtube.com/watch?v=uPG92YqKx5A) and a 1991 remake directed by Stuart Gordon.

Activity 1

A mad narrator?

Programme of Study link

Reading

- Making inferences and referring to evidence in the text
- Checking understanding to ensure that what they have read makes sense
- Knowing how language provides meaning

Description

Read the text with the class and establish their comprehension of the basic story line. Ask them to imagine that this is a statement made when the narrator has been arrested on suspicion of murder and that experts on mental health have been called in to advise on the sanity of the suspect. Working in pairs, ask the students to compile notes, using evidence from the text, to help come to an assessment of whether or not this man is mad. You may wish to point out to students lines such as 'I have told you that I am nervous: so I am.' and 'If still you think me mad, you will think so no longer when I describe the wise precautions I took for the concealment of the body.'

Take feedback to build up a case, always keeping the emphasis on exactly what is in the text rather than any unfounded assertions. It is likely that points arguing that the narrator is sane will have to be introduced by you to keep the necessary balance (note that he is fully aware of his actions; they are meticulously planned; he is able to describe events clearly and in detail). Come to a whole class conclusion and gather the most compelling evidence for that conclusion.

Learning outcomes

- Students will read the text closely, retrieving information and making inferences.
- Students should be able compile a body of evidence to support the assertion that the narrator is mad.
- Students may be able to demonstrate an understanding of how the writer constructs a character (the narrator who might be mad or perfectly sane, depending on how we read the text).

Differentiation

Lower ability students might need to be given two headings to help in their analysis of the text: What the narrator does/What the narrator says. This will help them to separate out actions that might be seen as those of a madman (cold-blooded murder) and ways of describing himself and his thinking in an effort to convince us that he is not mad.

Higher ability students need to be guided towards the understanding that the narrator is not a real person. Ask them to list phrases, rather than actions, suggesting an unbalanced mind (see the examples above) so that they begin to appreciate the concept of a character as a fictional construct.

Assessment opportunities

- Reading: comprehension; critical analysis
- **RAF 2, RAF 3**

Activity 2

A text from a different time

Programme of Study link

Grammar and vocabulary

- Using grammatical knowledge to analyse more-challenging texts
- Studying the effectiveness and impact of the grammatical features of the texts they read

Description

How do we know that this is not a modern text? Most students would be able to tell that this is 'old-fashioned writing', but tell them that they are about to become experts in linguistics (the study of language).

Divide the class into mixed ability groups of four. Provide a copy of Worksheet 5.1 (the source text on a blank sheet of A4) for each student. Alternatively, notes can be made in the usual English book.

Working as a group, students are to annotate the text to show why it is a text from a different time using four different aspects:

1. vocabulary – words rarely or never used nowadays
2. syntax – word order and/or sentence length and type not often seen in modern writing
3. punctuation – what is used and how it differs from a modern story
4. setting – evidence that we are not in a modern house.

Give each student in a group a number from 1 to 4. Allocate one of the aspects above to each number. Form new groups of four or five students, putting all 1s together, all 2s together and so on. Give these new groups 5–10 minutes to share what they have found out about their given aspect, and ensure that all students update their notes with any new ideas or information that they gain. Now ask students to return to their original groups and allow a further 5–10 minutes for each group member to inform the others of new ideas and evidence that they have brought back from their 'expert' group. At the end of this process, all students should have a richly annotated text containing detailed points on what makes the source a text from a different time.

If necessary, point out to students examples of 19th-century vocabulary, such as 'scantlings', syntax such as 'do you mark me well', punctuation such as the double hyphen and the excessive use of exclamation marks, and setting, as revealed by 'the flooring of the chamber' and the presence of 'a tub'.

Learning outcomes

- Students will understand why it is possible to say that this is a text written in a different time.
- Students should know that vocabulary and syntax indicate that the text is pre 20th-century writing.
- Students may acquire detailed knowledge and understanding of a range of linguistic features marking the text out as a pre-20th century text.

Differentiation

Lower ability students can be allocated the vocabulary or setting focuses. This will require them to find concrete examples of 'old-fashioned' words and aspects of houses.

Higher ability students should be asked to focus on syntax.

Assessment opportunities

- Reading: critical analysis
- **RAF 5, RAF 7**

Activity 3

Write like the master

Programme of Study link

Writing

- Writing stories, scripts, poetry and other imaginative text
- Using literary and rhetorical devices to improve the impact of their writing

Description

At the end of the text, the narrator seems to have everything in order and to have removed all evidence of a crime. This activity encourages students to continue – and finish – the story.

Briefly discuss with the class how the story might continue. (Draw attention to the title – it suggests a possible plot line.) At this stage, only broad ideas are needed – the more the better.

Through shared writing (taking contributions from students and discussing them before agreeing on a final version), arrive at a possible next sentence (after the end of the text). Focus the class on maintaining an appropriate style by reminding students of the features studied in Activity 2. You might come up with something like, 'Yet, as the dawn broke, there came a knocking at my door. The old man's single scream had been heard by my neighbour!'

As a guide for you, the next sentence in the actual text is: 'When I had made an end of these labors, it was four o'clock – still dark as midnight. As the bell sounded the hour, there came a knocking at the street door.'

Remind the class once again of the linguistic features they need to maintain (see Activity 2) and ask them to continue and, if possible, conclude the story.

Learning outcomes

- Students will use their knowledge of Poe's plot and style to write a continuation of the story.
- Students should be able to produce a finished story, showing elements of Poe's style.
- Students may produce a compelling continuation in a style that emulates Poe's.

Differentiation

Lower ability students may need help to come up with a simple list of the sequence of events leading to the end of the story. (You could suggest that the knock on the door was the police, and in talking to them the narrator somehow gives himself away.)

Higher ability students might like to compare their finished product with Poe's original (freely available on the internet). A side-by-side display would be both instructive and motivational.

Assessment opportunities

- Writing: style and vocabulary
- **WAF 1, WAF 2**

Activity 4

Author study

Programme of Study link

Reading

- Reading pre-1914 and contemporary English literature, including prose, poetry and drama
- Knowing how language provides meaning

Writing

- Writing well-structured formal expository and narrative essays
- Summarising and organising material, and supporting ideas and arguments with factual detail where necessary

Grammar and vocabulary

- Studying the effect and impact of the grammatical features of the texts they read
- Using linguistic and literary terminology accurately and confidently when discussing reading, writing and spoken language

Description

The most able can be stretched by asking them to produce an author study of the horror writing of Edgar Allan Poe. This would consist of reading the full version of 'The Tell-Tale Heart', at least two more short stories (e.g. 'The Pit and the Pendulum', 'The Fall of the House of Usher') and one of the longer poems (ideally 'The Raven'). It should then be possible to produce a longer piece of writing, perhaps consisting of a brief biography of Poe, a guide to the content and the themes of some of his works and an analysis of his writing style.

For the biography, encourage students to use more than one source and to blend information from both of them. This will ensure that information retrieval is suitably rigorous. For the content and themes, students should be encouraged to produce their own summaries, perhaps giving a word limit of 100 words for each story or poem. From this, they should be able to make inferences about Poe's themes and preoccupations. Activity 2 provides a good introduction to Poe's style, and students can be prompted to apply what they learned there to the other Poe texts that they have read, using a range of examples in order to arrive at a convincing analysis of the writing.

Learning outcomes

- Students will be able to demonstrate their understanding of the life and works of a major pre-20th century writer.
- Students should be able to bring a wide reading experience to bear on their author study.
- Students may be able to produce a detailed analysis of Poe's writing style and his themes, using their knowledge of his life to support that analysis.

Differentiation

Lower ability students can be given reduced reading demand and cover fewer areas in the written study.

Higher ability students should be challenged to complete the full task as given.

Assessment opportunities

- Reading: comprehension
- Writing: style and vocabulary
- **RAF 2, RAF 5, RAF 7, WAF 2, WAF 3**

SPAG focus

The task requires a detailed examination of syntax and punctuation. It can be further developed by looking specifically at the effect of the punctuation. Use Worksheet 5.2 (a version of the text in which dashes are replaced by commas and exclamation marks by full stops) to explore this. What difference does this make to the overall effect of the text on the reader? As an example, consider the final two words, each of which has an exclamation mark after it. This seems to heighten the sense of glee, verging on hysteria, that the narrator feels after concealing his crime.

2: The Man with the Yellow Face

Context

'The Man with the Yellow Face' is a short story by Anthony Horowitz, found in his collection *Night Bus*. The story uses the classic idea of a haunting premonition, but locates it in a strange photo emerging on a strip of four from a photo booth on York station. The photo appears just before the narrator boards an ill-fated train from York to London which crashes and leaves him severely injured, with a dreadfully burned, yellow face like the man in the photo.

The story is told in language that is suitable for low-to-middle ability Year 7 students, but the content may well appeal to a wide range of Year 7 and 8 classes.

Getting started

It would be a good idea to introduce this text with a few preliminary questions about premonitions. It is possible that some students, or people they know, may have had a premonition, or perhaps have experienced a feeling of déjà vu. Students can be encouraged to talk about this and speculate as to why they may occur – or even if they really exist.

Starter 1

Display the word 'ghost' and ask students to write down as quickly as possible five words or short phrases that come to mind. Collect a sample and add them around the central word on the display.

Starter 2

Ask students, in pairs, to come up with a definition of the word 'paragraph' and up to four guidelines for when we need a new one in writing. (The usual advice is to start a new paragraph when we have a new place, a new time, a new topic or a new speaker.) (This will be developed in one of the activities below.)

Further resources

The remaining stories in Anthony Horowitz's collection *Night Bus* are well worth reading, along with his other story collections in the *Black Apple* series: 'Burnt', 'Killer Camera' and 'The Phone Goes Dead'. There is also a collection of short stories by Maggie Pearson called *Short and Shocking*.

Activity 1

Setting the scene

Programme of Study link

Reading

- Studying the setting, plot and characterisation, and the effect that these have
- Referring to evidence in the text
- Knowing how language offers meaning

Description

Read through the text with the class, then focus on the paragraph beginning 'I went outside the photo booth' and the one that follows it (paragraphs 5 and 6). Conduct a quick question and answer session to establish students' understanding of the fact that we and the narrator are waiting for the photographs to come out of the machine, and that this will take about three minutes. Possible questions are: Why is the narrator waiting instead of going to board his train? Why does he need to wait? How long will he have to wait?

Ask students, working in pairs, to go through these two paragraphs and note down how the writer uses the senses to establish and develop the scene. What do we see, hear, smell? (The station environment, the clock, doors slamming, whistles, the smell of trains coming and going.) Some students might see that in the next paragraph we have touch, too.

Join pairs together to make small groups. Ask them to compare notes and come up with some ideas about how the writer uses the senses in order to establish the setting and build the tension. As a group, they are going to present a short verbal explanation of how the writer establishes setting and tension in the three-minute wait for the photographs. Allow 10 minutes for discussion and note taking, then ask groups to present their findings to the rest of the class.

Learning outcomes

- Students will be able to understand that the writer uses the senses to describe the setting of this part of the story.
- Students should be able to explain how the use of the senses contributes to the establishment of mood and the description of the setting.
- Students may understand and be able to explain how the writer creates tension, mood and atmosphere, as well as describing the setting, through the use of the senses.

Differentiation

Lower ability students can be put in pairs to make mixed ability groups for the main discussion. This will support them in coming up with ideas and wording their explanations.

Higher ability students need to be prompted to focus on the text at word level – looking at the effect of individual words or short phrases rather than expressing generalities – and encouraged to develop this word-level approach in their feedback to the class. For example, what is the effect of 'chugged' and 'shuddered' to describe the movement of trains?

Assessment opportunities

- Reading: comprehension; critical analysis
- **RAF 2, RAF 5**

Activity 2

A close look at paragraphing

Programme of Study link

Grammar and vocabulary

- Studying the effectiveness and impact of the grammatical features of the texts they read

Description

Ask students to compile a simple tally chart of the number of lines in each paragraph of the text. Take feedback to establish that the paragraphs have a range of lengths, but there is a high number of single-line paragraphs.

Through question and answer, remind the class of the basic 'rules' for starting a new paragraph: new time, new place, new topic, new speaker. It will be useful to have these written up on the board.

First, ask students to look at paragraphs 2 and 3 in the text and point out (or ask students to explain) that these are 'standard' in terms of following the rules for paragraphing. Then direct attention to the sequence of single-line paragraphs beginning with 'Four pictures' (page 81). Ask students, working individually, to note down for reference which 'rule' or 'rules' the writer has used in deciding on new paragraphs here. Take feedback. There may well be some confusion. (Is each new photograph a 'new topic'? Not really.) It should be possible gradually to elicit the idea that none of the rules really apply. Move the discussion on to consider why a professional and highly skilled writer 'does not know how to paragraph'.

Encourage rule breaking as follows: ask students to describe in writing skimming stones across a lake. They have four excellent, flat stones. Three of their throws do not work for different reasons, but the fourth is perfect. Each throw is to be described in a single-line paragraph. Select some students to read out their descriptions. Ask the class what the effect of this structure is (a cumulative building of tension, then a release or surprise). Help students to come to the conclusion that sometimes rules can be broken *for effect*.

Learning outcomes

- Students will produce a short written piece demonstrating paragraphing for effect.
- Students should be able to explain why they have broken the rules of paragraphing.
- Students may be able to explain how writers make conscious choices about grammar in crafting their writing.

Differentiation

Lower ability students may need a model of the single-line paragraph in the 'stone throwing' part of the activity. As an example, you could use 'First throw. Too high. The stone sank rapidly.'

Higher ability students should be able to suggest other ways writers have of building tension and may be able to write an example. You could suggest a long sentence, using multiple instances of 'and', to give a sense that an experience is never going to come to an end.

Assessment opportunities

- Reading: critical analysis
- Writing: form and structure
- **RAF 5, WAF 4**

Activity 3

Writing to build tension

Programme of Study link

Writing

- Summarising and organising material
- Applying growing knowledge of vocabulary, grammar and text structure to writing and selecting the appropriate form

Description

Remind students of the main outcomes of Activities 1 and 2: the appeal to the senses and the building of tension through the use of short paragraphs and minor sentences.

Set the title 'Waiting' and give the first line: 'Mum said she'd meet me here at the bus station 20 minutes ago, but there's no sign of her.'

Alternatively, through discussion, elicit a title and possible scenarios that will facilitate a piece of writing where a first-person narrator builds a sense of her or his surroundings as well as the tension of a period of waiting and an unexpected outcome.

Work with the class to build the success criteria for this piece of writing and have these on the board throughout the writing time.

Possible success criteria would be: use the senses of sight, sound, touch and smell; include at least two very short (one-line) paragraphs; use minor sentences occasionally for effect.

Allow 10–15 minutes for planning, then encourage the production of a piece of up to 400 words.

Learning outcomes

- Students will plan and write a piece of first-person narrative.
- Students should be able to include in their writing an appeal to the senses and a selection of short and longer paragraphs.
- Students may effectively build tension through the skilful use of techniques learned in Activities 1 and 2 in their writing.

Differentiation

Lower ability students should be supported at the planning stage to ensure that as many of the success criteria as possible are included in the plan. This can be achieved by reminding students of the criteria (displayed) and asking students to use them as a checklist, ticking off a feature when it is used.

Higher ability students should be challenged to produce a polished piece of writing that they can annotate to show the conscious choices made and techniques used to increase tension. In particular, encourage students to work on crafting sentences of different types and lengths, as noted in the SPAG focus.

Assessment opportunities

- Writing: form and structure; style and vocabulary
- **WAFs 1–8,** but in particular **WAF 1, WAF 2, WAF 4 and WAF 7**

SPAG focus

The one-line paragraphs in Activity 2 also provide an opportunity to revise sentence types. Most students will be able to recall the difference between simple and complex sentences, but may not have covered minor sentences.

As a reminder, you may need to point out that a simple sentence consists of a single clause and can be as little as subject followed by verb. ('He ran.') A complex sentence must have at least two clauses, one of which must be a main clause and one a subordinate clause. For example, 'The boys went out to play [main clause, has subject and verb and makes complete sense on its own] *although it was raining*.' [subordinate clause, introduced by subordinating connective and containing a finite verb, but does not make complete sense on its own].

Establish why each of the four paragraphs consists entirely of minor sentences (they have no verb). How would we make them into simple sentences? (And are they as effective?)

More able students might like to consider the case of 'looking' in the sentence 'Me looking stupid.' They may argue (correctly) that 'to look' is a verb, so this is not a minor sentence. This will provide an opportunity to refine the definition, pointing out that a simple sentence must contain a *finite* verb, and that 'looking' here is a *non-finite* verb (i.e. a verb that is not marked for person, tense or number).

3: The Toymaker

Context

The text is taken from *The Toymaker* by Jeremy de Quidt. The story follows Mathias, a young orphan in a travelling show who comes to possess a small piece of paper that hides a dark secret which people – including the evil Dr Leiter – are willing to kill for. Mathias tries to uncover the secret before he is caught by the sinister forces pursuing him. When the novel was published in 2009 it was shortlisted for several awards, but some reviewers felt that some of the scenes in the book were too violent for the younger age group it was aimed at. The novel certainly presents a fairly dark and disturbing view of human behaviour.

Year 7 students will perhaps gain the most from this text, but it will also appeal to lower and middle ability Year 8.

Getting started

The Toymaker features a toy that will never wind down because it has in it a still-beating sparrow's heart. Whilst this is obviously the stuff of fiction, it uses the perennial idea of the perfect toy – one that every child will want. Why are some toys thought to be better for children than simply giving them technology to amuse and entertain them?

Starter 1
What is the best toy that anyone in the class has had – or currently has? Why is it a favourite? Ask everyone to note down their answers to these questions, then take feedback.

Starter 2
If the class were at a design seminar for the next big smash hit toy, what would be its features? Generate a list of suggestions, then ask students to nominate and agree on their top five features, persuading others to share their view if necessary.

Further resources

The modern classic *Toy Story* films provide a wonderfully creative view of toys that have a life of their own.

Students might also like to see the wind-up doll sequence in *Chitty Chitty Bang Bang*, available at www.youtube.com/watch?v=PFMCrSYVN3A.

Dr Who fans might like to read *Toy Soldiers*, by Paul Leonard, a spin-off novel featuring missing children and toy bears.

Toys in the Attic by Daniel Ransom is a horror novel featuring possessed dolls – but it does contain some fairly graphic writing.

Activity 1

Character relationships

Programme of Study link

Reading

- Making inferences and referring to evidence in the text

Spoken English

- Rehearsing and performing play scripts and discussing language use and meaning, using intonation, tone, volume and action to add impact

Description
This is an activity that focuses on the relationship between the two characters in the text and how this is revealed. To experienced readers, the power dynamics between the characters in the text are fairly obvious, but this is not always the case for younger readers. Here, you may need to draw attention to the

words the characters use when they speak ('Tell her your real name, boy.') and to the descriptions of how the characters behave (Leiter looks with 'hard, dark eyes' whilst Mathias 'hesitates').

Divide the class into three groups. Within the groups, form pairs. Ask each pair to prepare and practise reading the text aloud, focusing primarily on the dialogue. Group 1 is to read the text, with Leiter being dominant and threatening, whilst Mathias is timid. Group 2 pairs will deliver a reading where both characters are of equal status. Group 3 pairs will give a reading where Mathias is clearly superior and Leiter is trying to wheedle information out of him (this will be difficult to achieve and might be reserved for the more able). Students in this group can be supported by giving them advice about how Leiter can be bending over and looking needy whilst using a whining voice, whereas Mathias can be standing upright and answering questions confidently with a firm, controlled voice.

Select two or three pairs from each group to give their prepared readings, then invite discussion on the difficulties involved and the clues in the text that indicate that group 1's reading is how the author intended the characters to come across.

Students may well notice that the text always has Leiter initiating topics and questions, that he 'speaks down' to Mathias and that he has a resource to use (the doll) that ensures he is in a superior position. Mathias, on the other hand, makes only two, single-word, responses and understands that he is in a terrible predicament because he will not be able to lie his way out of Leiter's clutches.

Learning outcomes

- Students will better understand how writers portray power relationships between characters.
- Students should be able to pinpoint some of the techniques writers use to indicate the power relationships between characters.
- Students may be able to use their knowledge of writer techniques to provide a convincing reading of the text that correctly indicates the power relationships between characters.

Differentiation

Lower ability students can be asked to read out just a few lines of dialogue, making it threatening or timid, as appropriate.

Higher ability students can be asked to take part in two different readings of the text from the three possibilities suggested above, and to explain to others what differences they had put into each reading.

Assessment opportunities

- Reading: critical analysis
- Spoken English: reading aloud and drama
- **RAF 3, SLAF 3**

Activity 2

What happens next?

Programme of Study link

Reading

- Making inferences and referring to evidence in the text

Spoken English

- Using Standard English confidently in a range of formal and informal contexts, as well as in classroom discussion
- Taking part in structured discussions, summarising and/or building on what has been said

Description

Establish with the class what we know about the characters and what exactly is happening in the text. (From Activity 1 it should be clear that Leiter is trying to force Mathias to reveal a secret, and is using the doll to separate truth from lies.) Working in small groups, ask students to come up with suggestions for (a) the immediate continuation of the scene and (b) the next phase of the story. Remind groups that their suggestions must be based on evidence in the text. For example, we know from the text that the doll can differentiate between truth and lies, so it is likely that Mathias's answer, 'No' is a lie and that the doll will indicate as much. What would happen then? Also, since Leiter is confident that he will find out the truth – and then extract Gustav's secret from Mathias – what would happen if the doll indicated that Mathias was in fact telling the truth?

Groups should try to come up with two possible continuations. Through discussion they should be in a position to present their findings to the class orally.

Ask each group to tell the class what they have come up with. Invite other groups to critique suggestions. In their original groups, ask students to agree on a version they are happy with, then, by contributing to a whole-class discussion, and by a process of negotiation, arrive at an agreed version of what will happen next.

Learning outcomes

- Students will be able to suggest a plausible continuation for the story and will take part in structured discussion.
- Students should be able to understand and be able to explain that their prediction is rooted in the text.
- Students may be able to offer different, but equally plausible, continuations and will discuss and negotiate an agreed version with skill.

Differentiation

Lower ability students should be encouraged to focus only on the immediate sequence of events. Ask them to come up with two different suggestions as to how this short action sequence will end.

Higher ability students should be challenged to think beyond their initial ideas by asking questions such as, 'So what would happen after that?' or 'That is a good suggestion, but can you think of a different one – one that is not obvious?'

Assessment opportunities

- Reading: comprehension
- Spoken English: discussion and knowledge about spoken language
- **RAF 3, SLAF 1, SLAF 2**

Activity 3

Showing who is the boss

Programme of Study link

Writing

- Writing stories, scripts, poetry and other imaginative writing

Description

Recall the outcomes of Activity 1. Or (if Activity 1 has not been attempted) through question and answer elicit information on the power dynamics between the two characters in the text. It should be clear that Leiter is trying to force Mathias to reveal a secret, and is using the doll to separate truth from lies. Leiter is threatening, overbearing and confident of his success, whilst Mathias is hesitant, nervous and afraid of what he will have to reveal.

Gather from the class a list of character pairs where one is clearly in a position of power or authority over the other (teacher–pupil; boss–worker; parent–child).

Ask students to choose one of these pairs and write a piece of dialogue that clearly shows the power relationship between the two. It is possible to keep the focus very much on the dialogue by asking for this as a play script, but it is probably better to allow some description between the speech, as in the text.

It may be necessary to revise the correct layout of play scripts or the correct punctuation of speech before beginning this activity.

Finally, pairs can read out some of the finished pieces, taking the two roles as appropriate.

Learning outcomes

- Students will be able to produce a written piece that shows the power relationship between two people.
- Students should be able to produce a correctly laid out or punctuated written piece that shows the power relationship between two people.
- Students may produce an accurately written piece that effectively shows a reader the power relationship between two people.

Differentiation

Lower ability students can have the opening of the dialogue modelled for them if necessary, pointing out both the correct layout or punctuation and some of the techniques that demonstrate the power dynamics between the characters.

Higher ability students can be asked to consider introducing a third character so that the dynamic shifts slightly.

Assessment opportunities

- Writing: style and vocabulary; grammatical range and accuracy
- **WAF 2, WAF 6**

SPAG focus

Remind students of the principal rules for punctuating dialogue correctly (see below), then use Worksheet 5.3 to provide practice in applying these rules.

Speech marks ('…') go around the words actually spoken.

The first word spoken has a capital letter.

A punctuation mark should appear before the closing speech marks. This can be a full stop, question mark or exclamation mark as appropriate. If the speech is followed by 'she said' or similar, and none of the punctuation marks already mentioned is appropriate, a comma is required.

When a new speaker begins, a new paragraph is required.

4: The Enemy

Context

Charlie Higson's *The Enemy* is the first in a series of four novels set in a post-apocalyptic world. A flavour of the novel's appeal can be gleaned from its blurb:

> When the sickness came, every parent, policeman, politician – every adult fell ill. The lucky ones died. The others are crazed, confused and hungry.
>
> Only children under fourteen remain, and they're fighting to survive.

Charlie Higson is also well known for his *Young Bond* series, which focuses on James Bond as a teenager. He is perhaps less well known as a writer and producer of radio comedy, including *The Fast Show*.

Readers are warned that the novel 'contains strong language and scenes of violence'. To some extent, of course, this is a marketing ploy since the series is squarely aimed at a younger audience, making this text ideal for Years 8 and 9.

Getting started

What would the world be like without adults to run it? An initial class discussion might draw up two lists: good points and bad points.

Starter 1

Try to imagine that when you woke up this morning there were no adults at all. They had all simply disappeared. Write down the first three things you would do.

Share initial lists with a partner, and then form small groups to compare notes.

Starter 2

Make up three different opening sentences to a story or novel that clearly indicate it is a horror story *and* hook the reader as well.

Further resources

The Enemy is the first in a series of five titles. The others are: *The Fallen, The Dead, The Fear* and *The Sacrifice*. There is also a website dedicated to the novels and various spin-off projects at www.the-enemy.co.uk/home.

Dystopian literature is of course a huge field. The classic novels are perhaps *Brave New World* (Aldous Huxley), *Lord of the Flies* (William Golding) and *1984* (George Orwell), but there is a whole genre, known as Steampunk, featuring novels set in alternative futures with different technologies. Students might well enjoy the *Mortal Engines* quartet by Philip Reeve, the *Chaos Walking* trilogy by Patrick Ness and *Blood Red Road* by Moira Young.

Activity 1

Debating violence

Programme of Study link

Spoken English

- Taking part in formal debates and structured discussions

Description

Point out to the class that some people have said this sort of writing (in the text) is unsuitable for the age range it is aimed at. Split the class into two halves and ask one half (individually or in twos or threes) to come up with as many reasons as possible to agree with this view. The other half of the class should work similarly on points against. For example, students in agreement might point out that young people should be shielded from too much violence in case it causes them to become less sensitive to it. There is also the argument that seeing and reading lots of violent material makes people violent. It is also often argued that childhood should be a time of optimism and innocence and that exposure to violence ruins this. Those against could say that there is no evidence linking violent acts to reading about violence, that children need to understand some of the realities of life, in moderation, and that most secondary age children are perfectly well aware that what they read or see on television is not real.

It should then be possible to run through the rules of formal debate and appoint speakers from the two halves of the class. A debate requires two speakers to propose the motion (to speak in favour of it) and two to oppose it (speak against). Each speaker has an uninterrupted turn to make their case (in the order for – against – for – against) and this is followed by contributions from the floor (the rest of the class). Students should be reminded that contributions from the floor are an essential part of a good debate, and everyone should have at least one idea that they would like to contribute if they are not a main speaker. Finally, one speaker from each side sums up their case.

You may want to run through some of the recognised conventions in this sort of speaking:

- a need for politeness and strict turn taking at all times
- a formal way of addressing the other side ('as our opponents have pointed out ...'; 'with respect, we feel it only right to contradict ...')
- the need for statements from the floor rather than questions.

It is also worth recapping on some persuasive techniques, amongst which are repetition, inviting agreement ('surely everyone will agree that ...') and pretending to concede a point whilst actually moving the argument back on to your side ('Whilst it may be true that ... it is much more likely that ...').

Conduct the debate and take a vote at the end. It is worth asking if anyone has changed their view as a result of listening to the arguments, and what particular points were the most persuasive.

Learning outcomes

- Students will be able to understand that there are two valid viewpoints about violence in texts written for young people.
- Students should be able to put forward verbally several points in support of one side of the argument.
- Students may be able to communicate a persuasive range of points in support of an argument.

Differentiation

Lower ability students would be best placed in the group coming up with arguments they personally support.

Higher ability students can take on roles as principal speakers.

Assessment opportunities

- Spoken English: presentation and communication; discussion and knowledge about spoken language
- **SLAF 1, SLAF 2**

Activity 2

Action, description and reflection

Programme of Study link

Reading

- Knowing how language provides meaning

Writing

- Using knowledge of literary and rhetorical devices from their reading to enhance the impact of their writing

Description

There are 11 paragraphs in the text. Ask students to jot down the numbers 1–11 and then to read through the text and note down either 'A' (for 'Action'), 'D' (for 'Description') or 'R' (for 'Reflection') against each number, depending on the content of the relevant paragraph. An 'Action' paragraph focuses on what happens; a 'Description' paragraph focuses on describing the scene or a character's emotions; a 'Reflection' paragraph is one in which the action momentarily stops and a character thinks about and analyses her or his thoughts and feelings. (Paragraph 8 might cause a problem in that it is technically 'Dialogue', but it can probably be accommodated under 'Action'.) Students will rapidly notice that there is only one 'R', but it would be worth pointing out that this is the longest paragraph of all of them.

Ask students in pairs to come up with suggestions about the proportions of paragraph types. Why would a writer do this? What is wrong with having unrelenting action?

Having established that variety is important so that readers do not become bored or desensitised – and also that the inner lives of characters are as interesting as what they do – ask students to produce a short piece of writing that uses all three elements under discussion. As a scenario, you might choose a boy/girl who is running away from some sort of danger.

Ask students to read out their work in progress – or use a visualiser if you have access to one – and to point out the balance of action, description and reflection that they have achieved.

Learning outcomes

- Students will know that a blend of action, description and reflection is desirable in narrative, and will attempt a piece of writing where this blend is applied.
- Students should be able to produce a more varied piece of narrative, showing an understanding of the need for a balance between paragraph types.
- Students may write a sophisticated piece of narrative in which action, description and reflection are skilfully blended.

Differentiation

Lower ability students can be asked for a specific output of two of the paragraph types, for example three action paragraphs followed by one reflection paragraph.

Higher ability students might be asked to weave in some dialogue in addition to the three paragraph types identified in the activity.

Assessment opportunities

- Reading: critical analysis
- Writing: form and structure
- **RAF 6, WAF 2**

Activity 3

Grammar detectives

Programme of Study link

Grammar and vocabulary

- Using grammatical knowledge to analyse more challenging texts
- Using linguistic and literary terminology accurately and confidently when discussing reading, writing and spoken language

Description

Students are going to build a profile of the writer by becoming detectives and carrying out a detailed examination of his grammar habits. There are three interesting grammatical features of this text that students can investigate: the use of adjectives; the sentence types chosen; and paragraph lengths.

Students can work individually on one or more of these features, or the class can be divided into small groups and each group given a feature to investigate and report back on. The basic approach is the same in either case: ask the question 'What do we know about Higson's use of …' and then support students in recalling the feature they are working on (e.g. What is an adjective? What is the difference between a simple, compound and complex sentence? How many lines are in each paragraph – and why?).

Students should spend some time collecting the evidence (identifying the relevant feature and counting occurrences) before moving on to the more important questions: Why does the writer do this? What is the effect on the reader?

When all of the evidence and views are put together, students can produce a final report on 'The style fingerprint of Charlie Higson: how to recognise the work of a master writer'.

Learning outcomes

- Students will be able to revise one or more grammatical features of writing.
- Students should be able to show their understanding of how one or more grammatical features contribute to a writer's style.
- Students may be able to produce a full analysis of the text, explaining features of the writer's style and its effect on the reader.

Differentiation

Lower ability students will find it easiest to observe and comment on paragraph length, followed by adjectives. You might like to model counting the lines in a paragraph, then underlining all of the adjectives in the same paragraph.

Higher ability students should be able to look at all three aspects: paragraph length, use of adjectives and sentence type.

Assessment opportunities

- Reading: critical analysis
- **RAF 5**

SPAG focus

This activity as a whole provides an excellent opportunity to revise and reinforce grammatical features, together with their overall effect. In particular, look at the writer's use of adjectives (usually defined as describing words that modify a noun).

Worksheet 5.4 provides an exercise in identifying and replacing adjectives so that their effect can be considered.

5: Strange Case of Dr Jekyll and Mr Hyde

Context

Strange Case of Dr Jekyll and Mr. Hyde first appeared in 1886, and appealed greatly to Victorian readers in its exploration of the nature of good and evil within the same person. 'Jekyll and Hyde' has since become something of a byword for 'split personality'. The idea has been developed in the 20th century through the emergence of superheroes, in particular The Hulk, a character students might well know.

The novel itself often appears on GCSE set text lists, so this text is ideal for Year 9 but would also appeal to more able Year 8 students.

Getting started

What happens when someone gets angry? What are the feelings associated with it? It might be possible to discuss with the class the rise of 'anger management' therapy. What do they think happens in these sessions?

Starter 1
Synonyms and antonyms. Call out a word followed by 'synonym' or 'antonym' – or both, one after the other. Students have to write down a suitable word each time. Useful starting words are: open, start, beautiful, allow and respect. Finish with the word 'angry'.

Starter 2
As a quick mental warm up, ask students to think of as many 'natural word pairs' as they can. An example would be 'fish and chips'. They should come up with any well-known pairings – which would then lead on to the introduction of Jekyll and Hyde.

Further resources

Stevenson's novella is a fairly difficult read for Key Stage 3 students, but the higher ability students might enjoy it. A guide to the plot, characters and themes may be helpful and is available at www.bbc.co.uk/schools/gcsebitesize/english_literature/prosejekyllhyde.

Exploring the dual personality brings in a whole range of superheroes. The starting point for any exploration of this genre should be www.dccomics.com. The idea of uncontrollable anger is picked up most closely in stories featuring The Hulk. There are a number of *Incredible Hulk* episodes on YouTube. The basic idea behind the character (and a good link to *Strange Case of Dr. Jekyll and Mr. Hyde*) is at www.youtube.com/watch?v=vZK9ZItBqoU from about 00:37 to 01:42.

Activity 1

The victim's viewpoint

Programme of Study link

Writing

- Using literary and rhetorical devices to improve the impact of their writing

Description
Imagine that the victim in the text survived, badly beaten and obviously shocked but nevertheless alive. How would he retell this event? It would be worth discussing with the class that the account in the text is written from the point of view of an observer who is recounting, a long time after the event, what she saw, so a good deal of the emotion is removed. How might the surprise, shock and pain be vividly recalled by the man assaulted?

You might like to use Worksheet 5.5 to model the opening sentence or two, pointing out the use of the first person. A start might be: 'As I walked along the lane I saw coming towards me a gentleman of about my age, walking with a heavy stick.' Students can continue with their account in the space provided on the worksheet.

Learning outcomes
- Students will be able to produce a draft of a first-person account of the assault.
- Students should be able to produce a finished first-person account that recounts the facts clearly.
- Students may be able to produce a polished first-person account that communicates the shock and the pain associated with the assault.

Differentiation
Lower ability students should be encouraged to concentrate on the events and on the victim's reaction.

Higher ability students should be challenged to maintain the style of the text even though the viewpoint has changed.

Assessment opportunities
- Writing: style and vocabulary
- **WAF 1**

Activity 2

Using direct speech

Programme of Study link

Writing

- Applying their knowledge of vocabulary, grammar and text structure to their writing

Description
Once students have worked with the text for a short time they will realise that it is a description given by an unknown person of a violent event that was recounted to him or her by the maid. This distancing effect is a deliberate choice on the part of the writer, but students could see the opposite effect by transforming the text into a dialogue between the maid and her close friend on the morning after the event.

It would be wise first of all to revise the correct layout and punctuation of direct speech, then to ask students in pairs to make notes on some of the actual words the maid and her friend might have used. Once these building blocks are in place students can be asked to work either individually or in pairs to transform the text (or part of it) into direct speech.

Learning outcomes

- Students will be able to produce a piece of written dialogue with the appropriate punctuation mostly correct.
- Students should be able to write a correctly punctuated conversation that reveals more of the maid's response to what she saw.
- Students may produce a dialogue, correctly punctuated, that gives insights into the maid's state of mind and provides a clear contrast to the source text.

Differentiation

Lower ability students will probably need to have the correct layout of speech modelled for them, and some suggestions of what might be said.

Higher ability students should aim to reproduce the tone of the original, whilst correctly punctuating a fairly long dialogue.

Assessment opportunities

- Writing: style and vocabulary; grammatical range and accuracy
- **WAF 2, WAF 6**

SPAG focus

This text is written in the past tense. However, in paragraph 2, the writer consciously uses two instances of the subjunctive: 'as if the subject … *were* of great importance' and 'as if he *were* only inquiring his way'. Draw attention to these verbs and ask if students know why the more conventional 'was' is not used. (The answer is that they occur in clauses expressing a condition that is not necessarily the case – as indicated by the words 'as if'.)

Students can practise this verb use further by inventing sentences using the expressions 'if', 'as if', 'wish' and 'suppose'.

6: Flannan Isle

Context

This text comprises the whole of W.W. Gibson's poem 'Flannan Isle', first published in 1912. It has remained a firm favourite, frequently anthologised, even though some of the stanzas may not be of the highest quality. The poem relates the mystery of the disappearance of the three lighthouse keepers from the Flannan Isles lighthouse in 1900. There are a number of mysterious incidents associated with this particular structure, and many folk myths have grown up about what a term of duty there might do to a person. A full account is at en.wikipedia.org/wiki/Flannan_Isles.

The poem is particularly suitable for Year 8 students, who will have developed the reading stamina to take in the whole text and consider its poetic features, but it can be enjoyed by all in Key Stage 3.

Getting started

A selection of famous, unexplained mysteries would be a useful introduction to the text. You might like to summarise some of the stories, or display a selection from list25.com/25-greatest-unsolved-mysteries-ever/

Starter 1

Thinking up rhymes. Give a starter word and allow one minute for students to write down as many rhyming words as they can. It is best to begin with an easy rhyme word such as 'tall', then work through more difficult initial words, for example 'stud', 'light', 'proof'.

Starter 2

What are the ingredients of a good mystery (preferably a real-life rather than a fictional one)? Ask students to list at least five and then put suggestions from the class together to form a master list.

Further resources

An excellent collection of narrative poems can be found at www.blackcatpoems.com/n/narrative_poems.html.

For those interested in the work of W.W. Gibson, most of his poems can be found at www.poemhunter.com/wilfred-wilson-gibson.

For examples of poems (some of them narrative) where the poet's skill was rather less than he imagined it to be, see the works of William McGonagall, and in particular his disaster poem (in more ways than one) 'The Tay Bridge Disaster'. They are collected at www.mcgonagall-online.org.uk/works.

Activity 1

What really happened?

Programme of Study link

Reading

- Checking their understanding to make sure that what they have read makes sense

Spoken English

- Giving short speeches and presentations, expressing their own ideas and keeping to the point

Description

Point out that this poem is based on a true incident. After a careful reading with the class, establish that they have understood the basic story through a brief question and answer session. Useful questions include those that establish the presence of the lighthouse, the fact that all three men were missing and there was no sign whatsoever of them, the fact that whatever happened was sudden (a meal was still on the table) and the fact that this was not the first strange incident in this location. Then ask students working in pairs or small groups to come up with key words that they would search on in order to find out more about the lighthouse in general and this incident in particular. (Good choices are 'Flannan Isles' + 'Lighthouse' + 'Mystery'.)

Ask students, working in the same groups, to research the mystery. Ask them to use the search terms established and to find at least three different sources of information. Each source should be summarised into no more than two paragraphs (this deters students from simply copying and pasting from the internet). They should bring their summary paragraphs to the next lesson. In that lesson, allow students time to work on, and eventually present, an account of the Flannan Isles mystery.

It would be useful to remind students of some basic presentation skills: they should not just read from a script or from PowerPoint slides. Visual aids should be clear, large and not over-detailed. Eye contact should be maintained with the audience. Voices should be varied to maintain audience interest.

As an extra challenge, ask students to weave some verses from the poem into their presentation, perhaps contrasting the poet's rather fanciful imaginings with the rather more prosaic accounts of what happened from the official investigations.

Learning outcomes

- Students will understand the story line of the poem and will take part in an oral presentation.
- Students should be able to show a detailed understanding of the events described in the poem and will be able to contrast these orally with different accounts.
- Students may demonstrate an understanding of the poem by placing verses from it in an oral presentation and contrasting these with alternative versions of events.

Differentiation

Lower ability students should be asked to focus on a simple contrast between the poem and the official investigation verdict. For example, the poet seems to suggest that the men may somehow have been transformed into ugly birds flying around the lighthouse, whereas the official investigation states that they were likely to have been swept away by a large, powerful wave.

Higher ability students can be asked to summarise and evaluate several different accounts of what might have happened, starting from the poem's version.

Assessment opportunities

- Reading: comprehension
- Spoken English: presentation and communication
- **RAF 2, RAF 3, SLAF 1**

Activity 2

Rhyme and rhythm

Programme of Study link

Reading

- Recognising a range of poetic conventions and understanding how they have been used

Description

Ask students to work in pairs to look at the first three stanzas and to come up with a description of (a) stanza length, (b) the rhyming pattern and (c) the rhythm.

Stanzas are generally four lines long. They use an ABBA rhyming pattern, but this is not consistently maintained. The rhythm is regular, with four stressed syllables per line (although again this is not consistently maintained).

Point out that this is a fairly conventional form for a narrative poem – a poem that tells a complete story. Having established the 'basic' form of four-line stanzas with a strict rhyming pattern, ask students to look at where the poet varies from this (see, for example, stanzas 5 and 6) and why they think he might do so. (Note that the rhythm hardly ever varies, but the rhyming patterns and stanza lengths do.) They should be prepared to give a verbal response if asked, on a particular stanza or a section of the poem, by commenting on the three aspects discussed and particularly emphasising the effect on the reader of any variations.

Learning outcomes

- Students will be able to describe the rhyming and rhythmic patterns in the poem.
- Students should be able to describe the pattern and show where the poet has moved away from it.
- Students may be able to demonstrate an understanding of the effects the poet is trying to achieve by establishing a basic pattern of rhyme and rhythm and then deliberately varying it.

Differentiation

Lower ability students may find it more difficult to work with the rhythm in the poem and can therefore be asked to become the resident experts on rhyme, which is simpler to grasp. Students should make a list of the rhyming syllables in each stanza and the pattern (usually ABBA). They should note down where the pattern is not followed. Having done this, they can make a significant contribution to class discussion of the poem's technical features.

Higher ability students can be asked to speculate on whether the variations are deliberate (for effect) or represent a lack of technique. There is no right or wrong answer here, merely an interesting discussion.

Assessment opportunities

- Reading: critical analysis
- **RAF 4, RAF 5**

Activity 3

A narrative poem

Programme of Study link

Writing

- Writing stories, scripts, poetry and other imaginative writing
- Using literary and rhetorical devices to improve the impact of their writing

Description

Well-known stories provide good subjects for students to attempt their own narrative poem. Remind them of the components required (these can be varied according to the ability of the class or individual students): rhyme, rhythm and (usually) stanza length. (See the notes for Activity 2.)

Some students may want to come up with their own stories, but this is more difficult. It might be best to offer a selection of traditional tales such as Cinderella, The Three Billy Goats Gruff or Jack and the Beanstalk so that students can concentrate on the poetic features rather than having to invent a story as well.

Learning outcomes

- Students will be able to write a version of a narrative poem with some success in using rhyming and rhythmical patterns.
- Students should be able to produce a narrative poem with more successful use of rhyme and rhythm.
- Students may be able to produce a polished narrative poem, showing skilful use of rhyme and rhythm.

Differentiation

Lower ability students may need your support in telling the story using a simple rhyming pattern in four-line verses.

Higher ability students will find the biggest challenge in handling the rhyme and rhythm, and they can be asked to use a more difficult story as the basis of the poem. As suggested in Activity 2, a rhyming or rhythmical pattern is often established and then deliberately varied by a writer to create a particular effect. Students can be prompted to use this idea in their own poems.

Assessment opportunities

- Writing: style and vocabulary; form and structure
- **WAF 2, WAF 3**

7: Hiroshima

Context

In 1946 John Hersey interviewed six survivors of the Hiroshima bomb and told their stories at length in order to give a human perspective to the event. A lot of Americans were unaware of the devastating effect of the atomic bomb, knowing only that it had brought about an almost immediate end to the war with Japan. Most came to understand what had been inflicted on the people of Hiroshima (and Nagasaki) only when they read the issue of *The New Yorker* magazine that was devoted entirely to Hersey's report, which was immediately regarded as a classic piece of journalism.

The text is probably most suitable for Year 9 middle and higher ability students, more because of the issues it raises than because of the language used.

Getting started

Generate a shared context for reading this text through these starter activities.

Starter 1

The key question raised by this text is the one of weapons of mass destruction. Students can be asked: If you had a weapon that you knew would inflict terrible suffering on people, but would also advance your cause, would you use it?

Using this question, ask students to divide a page into two columns headed 'Yes' and 'No' and then to put as many reasons as they can think of under each heading. Take feedback to establish the complexity of the issue. Yes points are likely to include the idea of winning for a just cause; of preventing further long-term suffering. No points are likely to include the means not justifying the ends; a threat being often more powerful than carrying it out.

Starter 2

Ask students to take one of the reasons they have come up with in Starter 1 and to develop it into a persuasive point to be made orally – perhaps lasting 30 seconds. Select some students to deliver these short speeches.

Further resources

There are numerous accounts of the development and use of the atomic bomb and also of the efforts over the last 70 years by many people to try to ensure that it is never used again. The two websites given in Activity 2 provide much of the background that students might need: www.cnduk.org and http://en.wikipedia.org/wiki/Nuclear_weapon.

The full text of John Hersey's article in *The New Yorker* is shown at http://archive.org/stream/hiroshima035082mbp/hiroshima035082mbp_djvu.txt.

Activity 1

The news and the people

Programme of Study link

Reading

- Knowing the purpose, audience for and context of the writing, and drawing on this knowledge to help understanding

Description

If possible, display the front pages of newspapers from August 1946.

The *New York Times* version is at www.nytimes.com/learning/general/onthisday/big/0806.html together with the text of the main articles.

A Google Image search using 'newspaper front pages nuclear bomb' will bring up several alternatives, although a careful selection will need to be made in advance.

Ask students to read the text and to note down the immediate differences they notice from the news reports (viewpoint, focus on the global/individual, statistics v. real people, triumph v. despair).

Explain to students that John Hersey's full report – about 30,000 words – formed the whole of one issue of *The New Yorker* – a magazine that in 1946 was normally devoted to 'lifestyle' features. Ask them to note down what they would say to someone who complained about this content in their favourite magazine.

Learning outcomes

- Students will be able to show their understanding of the difference between writing that focuses on an event and writing that focuses on individual people.
- Students should be able to develop their understanding of that difference by considering the issues raised as a result.
- Students may be able to develop their understanding of the difference in journalistic approaches and the issues raised as a result.

Differentiation

Lower ability students will be able to complete the 'differences' part, but not necessarily the part that refers to the *New Yorker* issue. For these students, take each of the suggested aspects above and support them in looking at the aspect under the two headings: 'Source text' and 'News reports'.

Higher ability students will be able to cope with both aspects of this activity.

Assessment opportunities

- Reading: comprehension
- **RAF 6**

Activity 2

The big issue

Programme of Study link

Spoken English

- Taking part in formal debates and structured discussions, summarising and/or building on what has been said

Description

Ever since the first nuclear bomb was dropped, a debate has raged over whether this is a weapon for good or evil. It is likely that students will not have considered this issue before, as they will have lived through a time when the nuclear argument (at least as far as weapons are concerned) has not been prominent.

Having read the text (and the newspaper front pages if Activity 1 has been completed) students should be in a position to carry out a structured discussion in groups. Ideally, each student in a group should have a particular role, and each role will require particular skills: the chair, who will invite contributions and summarise the arguments; a speaker who will argue that nuclear weapons are a necessity and that they have ensured peace for nearly 70 years; a speaker who will argue that they are a waste of time and resources since they can never be used; and a speaker who can provide a view on why some countries have the weapon but go to great lengths to prevent other countries from 'catching up'.

A more informed discussion will arise if there is time to allocate roles and then allow students to conduct research to support their viewpoint. Useful websites are www.cnduk.org and http://en.wikipedia.org/wiki/Nuclear_weapon.

Learning outcomes

- Students will be able to contribute informed points to a structured discussion.
- Students should be able to contribute points on a given aspect of the topic and will also participate in general discussion.
- Students may present a well-argued viewpoint in role and will also contribute thoughtfully to general discussion.

Differentiation

Lower ability students can be asked to chair the discussion and supported in having appropriate phrases to invite others to speak and to summarise what has been said. These students can be asked to open proceedings with a summary phrase beginning 'Today we are going to look at the difficult questions posed by nuclear weapons.' They should also be given short phrases to use when the discussion is underway, such as 'Thank you. Now I'd like to invite X to speak'; 'Would you like to answer that point, X?' and 'So, summing up what has been said ...'.

Higher ability students might want to take on the moral dilemma of arguing the case for countries who have the nuclear weapon but want to deny others the same facility.

Assessment opportunities

- Spoken English: presentation and communication; discussion and knowledge about spoken language
- **SLAF 1, SLAF 2**

SPAG focus

Skilled journalistic writing such as that in 'Hiroshima' requires the use of a variety of sentence types, and in particular well-developed sentences to carry a great deal of information. This activity encourages the development of well-formed sentences through adding different grammatical elements.

Start with the simple sentence, 'The boy ran'. Ask students to add particular elements as follows:

- an adjective before 'boy'
- an adverb after 'ran'
- a fronted adverbial phrase (e.g. 'With terror filling him ...')
- a relative clause after 'boy' (use 'who' as the relative pronoun)
- an adverbial phrase at the end of the sentence (e.g. 'towards the edge of the cliff').

This model establishes a well-developed sentence. Apply the idea by using two more starter sentences: 'The girl screamed' and 'Everyone froze'. Ask students to share their finished products and to compare them with the starting sentences in order to see the effect of adding these grammatical structures.

8: Dispatches

Context

The Vietnam war undoubtedly scarred Americans. The US government viewed American involvement in the war as a way to prevent a communist takeover of South Vietnam. This was part of their wider strategy of containment which aimed to stop the spread of communism. Ultimately, however, the immense loss of life, and defeat by an enemy perceived as no more than a 'peasant army', caused a violent upheaval in American domestic politics and a bitter divide in the country.

Few Americans not directly involved at the time had much sense of what fighting in Vietnam was really like. Michael Herr's *Dispatches* changed that, his memoir giving a disturbing picture of the chaotic, drug-fuelled American war effort in contrast with the propaganda messages coming from newspapers and newsreels (although television reporting later in the war became more transparent and contributed to a significant change in public opinion).

The themes and the writing in this text make it more suitable for higher ability students in Years 8 and 9.

Getting started

Most of the class will probably not know much about the Vietnam war. There are numerous YouTube documentaries covering this period of history, but a short overview is provided in www.youtube.com/watch?v=xOuyGpJpBhg.

Starter 1

Fact and fiction. Ask students to write a quick definition of these two terms and take feedback. Then ask for a definition of 'memoir'. Try to draw out the idea of a personal slant on events, and the fact that a memoir need not necessarily be of anything major, but could just be a recollection of small events in a person's life.

Starter 2

Ask students to write a list of the years they have been alive, from the age of five to the present (2008, 2009, 2010, etc.). Then against each year they should write one event (and only one) that they remember from that year. This can lead on to a class discussion of what types of thing we remember and consider significant in our lives.

Further resources

For those who are interested in the history of the Vietnam War, YouTube is the best place to start. There is a comprehensive series of documentaries covering all aspects of the conflict.

The war memoir is a popular genre. The best books can be found at www.amazon.com/The-Best-War-Memoirs/lm/RKXB7FG1JTKGM. In particular, students might like to work through *A Vietcong Memoir: An Inside Account of the Vietnam War and Its Aftermath* by Truong Nhu Tang, Jane Hamilton-Merritt and Doan Van Toai or *Palace Cobra: A Fighter Pilot in the Vietnam Air War* by Ed Rasimus, whilst in fiction the classic text is *All Quiet on the Western Front* by Erich Maria Remarque.

Activity 1

Shock and awe

Programme of Study link

Reading

- Knowing the purpose, audience for and context of the writing, and drawing on this knowledge to help understanding

Writing

- Writing a range of other non-narrative texts

Description

If students read the text merely for the information it contains, it seems like an account of a fairly minor skirmish. Ask students to establish the bare facts (an American base camp was overrun by the Vietcong, 10–15 Americans were killed; at the same time the American regional headquarters was heavily shelled).

How then does the writer introduce a sense of shock and awe at what occurred? It would be helpful briefly to secure understanding of these words in a military context: 'shock' refers usually to the enemy doing something totally unexpected, whilst 'awe' is used when instilling a sense of panic in the enemy because of the sheer power or skill with which you carry out an action or campaign.

Use Worksheet 5.6 to provide each student with a photocopy of the text and ask them to annotate it for the following:

- words or short phrases that give us the writer's viewpoint
- technical words to do with weapons of war
- words or phrases that surprise the reader (e.g. the survivors 'had become insane').

Having done this, ask students to write two or three paragraphs that sum up the overall effect of the passage. Support students in understanding that, for the sophisticated American military, this sort of operation by a 'peasant army' was impossible and threw into doubt everything they believed about how they should conduct the war. Encourage the production of 'Point, Evidence, Explore' paragraphs, keeping the focus on the actual words used by the writer to convey the horror of what happened.

Learning outcomes

- Students will be able to understand and describe the main events and the effect of the text.
- Students should be able to explain how the writer presents a sense of shock at the events described.
- Students may be able to write in detail about how the writer contrasts the events with their significance.

Differentiation

Lower ability students should be helped to concentrate on finding quotations in the text where the writer's viewpoint is noticed.

Higher ability students can be challenged to produce a detailed analysis of the text, drawing their evidence from different points in it.

Assessment opportunities

- Reading: comprehension
- **RAF 6**

Activity 2

Writing a memoir

Programme of Study link

Writing

- Using literary and rhetorical devices to improve the impact of their writing

Description

Look at the text to see how the writer has produced an account of an event, but has invested it with great significance, both for himself and the American military. (Activity 1 will make this clear.)

Ask students to plan and write about an event in their lives that, either at the time or later, they realised was important in some way. The aim is to produce a piece of writing in which the event itself is recalled in some detail, but its significance to the writer is also made clear. Point out that this can be a small, apparently unimportant incident. What matters is the significance attached to it.

As a fictional example, you might tell students of how a relative gave you a small locked box and said, 'You'll know when to open it.' This puzzled you at the time but soon after you learned that she had been diagnosed with cancer and had very little time left to live. Upon opening the box, you found a collection of photographs of you and her in very happy times.

Learning outcomes

- Students will be able to produce a piece of writing about a significant event in their lives.
- Students should be able to write in detail about an event in their lives and explain for readers the significance it had.
- Students may be able to produce a memoir in which a personal event and its significance is effectively recalled through carefully evoking the event and deliberately holding back the revelation of its significance in order to engage readers to the end of the piece.

Differentiation

Lower ability students will probably need to write separately about the event and its significance (perhaps one paragraph for each).

Higher ability students should be encouraged to blend the event's details and its significance so that the piece as a whole becomes a more subtle memoir.

Assessment opportunities

- Writing: style and vocabulary
- **WAF 1, WAF 2**

SPAG focus

Students will have learned about modal verbs in Key Stage 2, but it would be worth running a brief question and answer session to establish that they have been remembered (the verbs are: will, would, can, could, may, might, shall, should, must and ought).

Ask students to work in small groups and to put together a brief guide for their peers on what modal verbs are and why they are used. Encourage an understanding that these verbs indicate certainty, ability, tentativeness or obligation, depending on their use, and bring a finer degree of subtlety to writing.

More advanced students might be helped to remember that modal verbs exist only in a finite form (i.e. there is no infinitive form, such as 'to must' or 'to should') and they do not take inflections to indicate person, tense or number (e.g. it is correct to say 'he must' not 'he musts', as would be the case with non-modal verbs such as 'he jumps').

9: Macbeth

Context

Macbeth is one of Shakespeare's best-known plays. This text looks at part of one scene from the play and focuses on drama and characterisation rather than language (which should certainly not be a barrier in this text). At this early stage in the play Macbeth has been introduced as a hero, but has been shown to have serious reservations about killing the lawful king in order to further his own ambitions. Lady Macbeth, on the other hand, is immediately presented as a scheming, manipulative woman who seems to have no qualms about murder and its consequences.

The text and related activities are best suited to middle and higher ability Year 8 and Year 9 students.

Getting started

A quick class discussion on what is known about Shakespeare will pay dividends. Students are likely to have met the plays in one form or another from Year 4 onwards, and many will have completed a reasonably sophisticated study of some texts, and taken part in class performances, by the end of their primary phase.

Starter 1

Give students a blank piece of A3 or A4 paper and ask them to write the word 'Shakespeare' in the middle. Then allow five minutes for the development of individual mind maps that contain any words or phrases that come to mind or develop from the starting word. These can be shared and added to if desired.

Starter 2

Give students three minutes to write as long a list as possible of strong, dynamic, pushy characters in films, TV series and books they know. Share these lists, then ask how many of these characters are women.

Further resources

Charles and Mary Lamb's *Tales from Shakespeare* provides a good summary of the story of the play (and many others) and there are several film versions of the play, although these are usually rated 15+ and are not always suitable for students in Key Stage 3. Amongst the best known are Polanski's film version of the play, and the filmed version of the RSC production starring Ian McKellen and Judi Dench.

The full text of the play is freely available on the internet, making a study of key scenes relatively easy.

Students might be interested to read the scene in act 5 of the play where Lady Macbeth has been driven mad with guilt following the murder of King Duncan and has developed the obsessive habit of washing her hands.

Activity 1

Understanding the characters

Programme of Study link

Reading

- Reading Shakespeare
- Knowing how language provides meaning
- Understanding the ways that great dramatists make their works effective on stage

Spoken English

- Rehearsing and performing play scripts and poetry in order to discuss language use and meaning, adding impact by using intonation, tone, volume and action

Description

Students should read the text first, either as a class or in pairs or individually. Stress that the idea is to get the gist of what is being said and not to try to understand all of its complexities.

If desired, there are numerous film versions of this scene available, and students might appreciate seeing the characters come to life on stage or film.

Ask students to divide a page into two columns, headed 'Macbeth' and 'Lady Macbeth'. Under the respective columns they should write up to 10 lines that indicate that Macbeth is weak and afraid and up to 10 lines that indicate that Lady Macbeth seems strong and taking a lead in proceedings.

Examples for the Macbeth column include: 'This is a sorry sight' and 'I am afraid to think what I have done', whilst examples for the Lady Macbeth column are 'Infirm of purpose!' and 'These deeds must not be thought / After these ways'.

Pairs can then share their findings and come up with the best three lines from each column. As an extension activity, in pairs students can work on saying these lines, with suitable intonation and gestures, and then swapping roles. The aim here is to see how Shakespeare's words give clear guidance to the actors as to how the role should be played. As an example you can point out the line 'Give me the daggers' – clearly indicating an action – and 'Look on't again I dare not' – showing how Macbeth has become weak and terrified by what he has just done.

Learning outcomes

- Students will develop an understanding of the two characters in the text.
- Students should be able to explain how the play shows that Macbeth is the weaker character whilst his wife is stronger and more dynamic.
- Students may be able to show a well-developed understanding of the character dynamics by acting out key lines.

Differentiation

Lower ability students can practise saying one or two lines with a partner and need not feel exposed to the full glare of the class.

Higher ability students might work in pairs, taking three lines each and presenting an acted sequence to others. They should be encouraged to use voice (volume and intonation), gesture and movement to bring the text to life as much as possible.

Assessment opportunities

- Reading: comprehension
- Spoken English: reading aloud and drama
- **RAF 2, RAF 3, SLAF 3**

Activity 2

Generating tension

Programme of Study link

Reading

- Recognising a range of poetic conventions and understanding how these have been used

Description

Take students through a basic understanding of iambic pentameter. (A line of poetry with 10 syllables in five pairs that are stressed/unstressed, so that it sounds like: 'da DUM da DUM da DUM da DUM da DUM'). In the text, the line 'The death of each day's life, sore labour's bath' is a good example.

First look at some of the lines in the scene where a character has a longer speech and ask students to identify the rhythm – perhaps by copying out the lines with stress marks (/) over the stressed syllables.

Example: The death of each day's life, sore labour's bath

Point out that this is how noble characters spoke in Elizabethan plays.

Put students into groups of three or four and ask them to look at the whole text with a view to describing the way that Shakespeare manipulates the basic rhythm. Look particularly at where the lines are broken between characters whilst still preserving the iambic pentameter, and where the rhythm breaks down completely (if they think it does). Emphasise the importance of saying the lines out loud, with members of the group helping each other to hear the stressed and unstressed syllables.

Once groups have gathered plenty of evidence, ask them to consider what the effect of this rhythmic mayhem is – why does Shakespeare do it? Encourage them to the view that it helps to build the tension in the scene and underlines the sense of panic that the characters feel at this point. If the scene proceeded in regular lines, with each character having a speaking turn of four to five lines, the effect would be very static. Ask groups to feed back their findings and thoughts to the class.

At this point you may like to show a video version of the scene again, asking students to focus on how the rhythm never gets in the way of the performance, but actually enhances it.

Learning outcomes

- Students will develop an understanding of iambic pentameter and how it is used in this scene.
- Students should be able to understand and explain how the basic rhythm is manipulated by Shakespeare in the course of the scene.
- Students may demonstrate an understanding of the rhythmic effects in the scene and the overall effect of this on the reader/audience.

Differentiation

Lower ability students will need to spend some time in listening to and counting the syllables in selected lines. For this it is best to use full lines spoken by individual characters.

Higher ability students should be able to appreciate the rhythm in longer speeches and can support peers in hearing the stressed and unstressed syllables as well as developing their own explanation of where and why the rhythm is shared between speakers and/or disrupted.

Assessment opportunities

- Reading: critical analysis
- **RAF 4**

Activity 3

Writing the film script

Programme of Study link

Writing

- Writing stories, scripts, poetry and other imaginative writing

Description

The bare script contained in the text is, of course, a text for actors and directors to work with. One way to help students visualise the scene and bring it to life is to turn it into a film script that requires action statements.

Film scripts to use as models are freely available on the internet (for example, try www.imsdb.com/scripts/Amadeus.html – a good example of the blend of action and description that a script needs).

Worksheet 5.7 contains the beginning of a film script for this scene. It contains the basic elements of all film scripts, and it would be worth spending a little time looking at how it turns spoken lines into a much more visual medium through detailing what we are to see as well as what the actors say and do.

Students should continue from where the worksheet leaves off. Alternatively they can be given particular sections of the text to work on individually or in pairs.

Learning outcomes

- Students will be able to transform part of the original text into a film script.
- Students should be able to produce a film script of part or all of the text with actions included.
- Students may be able to produce a film script of the full text that includes a clearly visualised setting and actions for the actors.

Differentiation

Lower ability students can use a short section of the text (for example the opening 15 lines) and focus on adding actions to the script that make it clear what the actors will be doing. For example, they might come up with the idea that both characters are looking frantically around them, but not at each other, in lines 7–13.

Higher ability students should be challenged to produce a working film script, based on a model or models that they will have seen as part of this activity (see reference to source of film scripts). They should produce a film script that would look the same as those suggested and would give the actors and the director an equal amount of guidance to that in the professional scripts for shooting the film.

Assessment opportunities

- Writing: style and vocabulary
- **WAF 2**

SPAG focus

Explain that many words are formed by adding a prefix (e.g. 'bi-') or a suffix (e.g. '-ology') to a root word. Run a competition to see how many words students can come up with using the following:

- bi (two)
- aqua (water)
- aero (air)
- super (greater)
- micro (small)
- audi (hear)
- port (carry)
- trans (across)
- prim (first)
- phobia (fear)
- ology (study)
- tele (far off)
- graph (to write)
- re (again)
- pre (before)

10: The Monkey's Paw

Context

The text is the climax of a short story by W.W. Jacobs that was very popular in Victorian times, when there was something of a mania among the reading public for tales of the macabre. The story works on the well-known 'three wishes' structure and its appeal is in leaving the third wish to the reader's imagination, whilst providing a very clear indication of what might happen if it is not made.

This text is suitable for use with Year 8 and Year 9 mid- to higher-level ability students.

Getting started

Ask students if they know of any stories or films or TV programmes where wishes play an important part, and delve a little deeper to ascertain what the characters in the stories or films actually wish for and what happens as a result. There is a list of such films at www.allmovie.com/characteristic/theme/wishes-come-true-d1741.

Also draw attention to the saying 'Be careful what you wish for', and elicit an understanding of what it means.

Starter 1
Ask students to write down (in a numbered list) the answer to the question: 'If you had three wishes, what would they be?' Enable sharing of ideas in pairs and/or small groups and take feedback to establish the most popular wishes.

Starter 2
A 16th-century proverb goes: 'If wishes were horses, beggars would ride'. Write this up and ask (a) what it means and (b) how it could be updated for the modern age.

Further resources
Collections of short stories featuring ghosts and other macabre incidents are plentiful. The text comes from W.W. Jacobs' collection called *The Lady of the Barge*, and any of the collected stories of M.R. James would provide further material.

One of the most famous stories of this type is *Whistle, and I'll Come to You, My Lad* by M.R. James. It was adapted for TV by Jonathan Miller in 1968 and first shown on the BBC. It can be seen at www.youtube.com/watch?v=3j4MAzQiTxE.

The overture and introduction to Stephen Sondheim's musical *Into the Woods* is a fantastic piece of individual and ensemble singing based on different characters having different wishes, and it is well worth hearing.

Activity 1
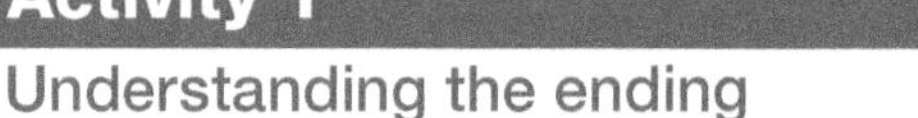
Understanding the ending

Programme of Study link
Reading
- Knowing the purpose, audience for and context of the writing, and drawing on this knowledge to help understanding
- Making inferences and referring to evidence in the text

Description
Read the text with the class. Ideally, it should be read by you, giving as dramatic a performance as possible.

Establish with the class that this story uses a traditional 'three wishes' structure. You may choose to trace through the text to establish what the first two wishes were. The writer deliberately refrains from telling us what the third wish is, and why it is made, but of course part of the enjoyment of the story is in the realisation of these 'facts'.

Ask students to work in pairs to come up with the words spoken by the father immediately following the line: 'he found the monkey's paw and frantically breathed his third and last wish'. They should try to create a line of dialogue that fits in to the original story. (Anything too modern should be rejected, with some discussion as to why it will not fit in with the way the story is written.)

Take feedback, and if desired work with the class to select the 'top three' versions of the line.

Learning outcomes
- Students will understand what the third wish in the story is.
- Students should be able to understand what the third wish is and will be able to suggest a form of words in which it might have been expressed.
- Students may show their understanding of the third wish by writing about it in a way that would make it seem part of the original text.

Differentiation
Lower ability students may need support in going back through the text to see the logical progression that makes the third wish inevitable. You may need to point out that the first wish (for money) comes true in an unexpected, gruesome way, and that leads on logically to the second wish – 'I wish my son alive again' – probably coming true in a horrible way.

Higher ability students can be challenged to add a paragraph to the story, containing the third wish, that fits the tone and style of the original.

Assessment opportunities
- Reading: comprehension
- **RAF 2, RAF 3**

Activity 2

An extra scene

Programme of Study link

Writing

- Applying their knowledge of vocabulary, grammar and text structure to their writing and selecting the appropriate form

Grammar and vocabulary

- Drawing on new vocabulary and grammatical constructions from their reading and listening, and using these in their writing and speech to achieve specific effects

Description

Following on from Activity 1, it would be a good idea to ask students, working individually, to add an extra scene to the end of the story in which the husband consoles his wife and explains how and why he used the monkey's paw to save her further grief. As far as possible, students should try to continue directly from the end of the story, writing in prose to match the original.

Peer assessment would be useful following this activity. Ask students to comment on two aspects of others' work: how well they have understood what the husband did and why; and how well the additional scene matches the style of the original.

Learning outcomes

- Students will be able to produce an extra scene to add to the end of the story.
- Students should be able to add an extra scene that shows an understanding of why the husband behaved as he did.
- Students may match the style of the original in an extra scene that fully explains the husband's actions.

Differentiation

Lower ability students can be asked to write a list of the points that the father would make when talking to the mother. By doing so, they can demonstrate their understanding of the story's three-wish structure and outcomes. Once this is done, they might be encouraged to summarise the story verbally for someone who has not read it.

Higher ability students should be challenged to write in an appropriate style. They will need to add both description and dialogue in their extra scene, and will need to look carefully at the features of the existing text in order to match it. They should note particularly that sentences tend to be considerably longer than in modern texts and that the husband speaks to his wife in a formal way.

Assessment opportunities

- Writing: style and vocabulary
- **WAF 2, WAF 7**

Activity 3

Researching Victorian horror

Programme of Study link

Reading

- Knowing the purpose, audience for and context of the writing and using this knowledge to support comprehension

Writing

- Writing notes and polished scripts for talks and presentations

Spoken English

- Using Standard English confidently in a range of formal and informal contexts, as well as in classroom discussion
- Giving short speeches and presentations, expressing their own ideas and keeping to the point

Description

Set students a research task: Victorian horror writing. Students can be randomly allocated a number from 1 to 4 and then given specific tasks as follows:

1. Who were the Victorian writers of horror and what did they write? (Include both British and American writers of the period.)
2. Why did Victorians enjoy horror writing to the extent they did?
3. Who was considered the best horror writer of the era? What would be a good example of his or her output?
4. Summarise three or four stories to give a sense of the type of plot and characters that the Victorians really enjoyed.

A useful starting point would be en.wikipedia.org/wiki/Gothic_fiction#Victorian_Gothic.

Groups can then be assembled containing students who have completed the different tasks. They can put their findings together to produce a presentation on 'Victorian Horror' that can be used as a formal oral assessment. It is important to ensure that everyone makes a contribution both in terms of the research findings they bring to the group and their part in the final presentation.

Learning outcomes

- Students will be able to undertake research on an aspect of Victorian horror writing.
- Students should be able to use their research as part of an oral presentation.
- Students may be able to use their own research and incorporate that of others to take a leading role in an oral presentation. They will cover more than one area of the topic, ranging across aspects researched by others.

Differentiation

Lower ability students can be allocated research tasks on the basis of how difficult each is. The easiest task is probably number 1 (2, 3 and 4 require more reading and note taking). Information required is mainly factual.

Higher ability students may undertake tasks 2, 3 or 4, which will require some summary and evaluation skills. For example, students will need to explain why certain writers were considered the best in this field and should be able to summarise the content of selected stories.

Assessment opportunities

- Reading: comprehension
- Writing: style and vocabulary; form and structure
- Spoken English: presentation and communication
- RAF 2, WAF 3, SLAF 1

SPAG focus

Victorian writing tended to use far more passive constructions than modern writing. Remind students of the difference between the two, using this example:

The boy broke the window

The window was broken by the boy

Note how the 'actor' (the boy) and the 'agent' (the window) swap places in the sentence, and the verb form changes.

Ask students to write a paragraph describing a minute or two of exciting action in a sports fixture. The paragraph should be written using entirely active sentences. Paragraphs can then be swapped, and students can be asked to rewrite someone else's paragraph using as many passive constructions as possible.

As a further activity, students can be asked to comment on the differences between the two versions. Why does the sports report not work very well in the passive?

11: Twilight

Context

Stephanie Meyer's *Twilight* saga was a phenomenal publishing success in the first decade of this century. The writer's skill lay in introducing vampirism to characters and settings from American high-school stories and films with which readers would be very familiar. There was also the trick of making the 'lead vampire' compellingly handsome, attractive and mysterious (if rather pale skinned!). The novels, and the film adaptations, are written with a focus on action rather than subtle character development.

This text is most suitable for higher ability Year 8 students, and all students in Year 9.

Getting started

In most classes there will be students who can name the novels in the *Twilight* saga (*Twilight, New Moon, Eclipse, Breaking Dawn*) and who have probably seen all of the films. It would be helpful to ask them to tell others some of the basic ideas and plot lines in the stories.

Starter 1

Give students three minutes to write down everything they know about vampires. Take feedback to establish a comprehensive knowledge base for the class. Most students will know, for example, that vampires can be forced to flee by making the sign of the cross at them, that they can be killed by driving a wooden stake through their hearts, that they bite the necks of virgins, that they drink blood and hate garlic, etc.

Starter 2

Run a quick challenge/competition in which students, in pairs, have to write down as many action verbs as possible (run, thump, jump, throw, etc.) in two minutes. Establish a winner, checking that the words written down are actually verbs. As an extension activity, run the challenge again, but this time only for stative verbs (be, have, feel, etc. – verbs that indicate a state of being).

Further resources

For those who like their series novels, the *Twilight* saga encompasses four novels and gave rise to five films. The novels also heralded a huge resurgence in vampire fiction aimed at teenagers. en.wikipedia.org/wiki/Category:Vampire_novels has 80 pages devoted to vampire novels.

The original vampire novel is probably *Dracula* by Bram Stoker, although there are accounts of beings who feast on human blood stretching back to Vlad the Impaler in the 15th century.

Activity 1

Action!

Programme of Study link

Reading

- Checking their understanding to make sure that what they have read makes sense
- Making inferences and referring to evidence in the text

Description

Because the text is part of a long, climactic sequence in the novel it is possible that readers move very rapidly through it and miss some of the detail that the writer has been careful to include. This *activity forces* a close reading of the text.

Ask students to read through the text quickly. They should then pair up, and each member of the pair has 30 seconds to tell the other what has happened in what they have just read *without looking at the text again*. Following this, it would be worth exploring with the class what features were remembered by nearly all readers and what were less frequently recalled.

Ask pairs to look through the text again, and this time to write down a numbered list of the sequence of actions in the order in which they occur. For example, start with:

1 James either kicks or punches Bella in the chest.

2 Bella staggers backwards into the mirrors on the wall.

Join the pairs to make groups of four and compare lists to arrive at a 'master version'. To reinforce what has been learned here, ask students to explain why there might be so many discrete actions in a very short piece of text (lead them to an understanding of the nature of a climax in a thriller).

Learning outcomes

- Students will be able to recall the main actions taking place in the text following a close reading of it.
- Students should be able to put a detailed set of actions into the order in which they occurred.
- Students may be able to build on their close reading of the text to develop a greater understanding of a climactic sequence in a popular novel, for example by describing how the actions build in violence and intensity as the text progresses.

Differentiation

Lower ability students should be encouraged to compile a complete list of actions in the text.

Higher ability students will need to explain how and why the author creates a rapid sequence of many actions. (The answer is that it takes readers on a journey towards the climax of the action.)

Assessment opportunities

- Reading: comprehension
- **RAF 2**

Activity 2

Vampires: fact or fiction?

Programme of Study link

Reading

- Knowing how language provides meaning

Writing

- Summarising and organising material, and supporting ideas and arguments with any necessary factual detail

Description

Explain to the class that an online encyclopaedia for younger readers (up to the age of 11) requires an update for its article on vampires. Use Worksheet 5.8 to show the class the headings in the Wikipedia entry on vampires (en.wikipedia.org/wiki/Vampire) and draw attention to the contents list. Discuss with the class which of these headings would be more suitable for younger readers (for example 'Folk beliefs' and 'Film and television') and if there are any areas or aspects that might need to be covered differently bearing in mind the age and reading ability of the target audience. (Examples might include 'Porpyria' and 'Psychodynamic understanding'.) The idea is to come up with a set of headings that can be used as the skeleton for a piece of informative writing.

Students might need to be reminded that informative writing for a younger age group generally uses short, clear sentences, technical vocabulary (and a glossary is provided), diagrams, charts or tables as appropriate. It is usually written in the present tense.

Once the headings are agreed, students can be set to research some or all of them and to write the respective sections. It is important to maintain a focus on the audience, and to use the students' work as it progresses to discuss with the class whether or not it is suitable for under-12s – and why.

As a 'real-world test' it might be possible to send one or more final versions of the article to a partner primary school and obtain feedback from Year 5 and Year 6 pupils.

Learning outcomes

- Students will be able to produce some informative text for younger readers.
- Students should be able to adapt information successfully for younger readers, using the features noted above.
- Students may be able to produce a well-written and interesting information text that meets the needs of younger readers.

Differentiation

Lower ability students need to avoid information overload, so it would be a good idea to give them a specific aspect to focus on, for example 'Modern films and novels featuring vampires' together with a range of information texts for 10- and 11-year-old readers. (The school library should have plenty of these.)

Higher ability students can be encouraged to write their own sections. They can support others in making their writing suitable for younger readers as well as writing their own texts. They should be able to check that the features outlined above are present and that the text as a whole is appropriate for the target audience, in that it matches in many ways the texts from the library that are used as models.

Assessment opportunities

- Reading: comprehension
- Writing: style and vocabulary
- **RAF 2, WAF 2, WAF 7**

SPAG focus

Remind students of the importance of using a range of punctuation, including, in Key Stage 3, ellipses, hyphens, colons and semicolons. (These might have to be modelled if students are unclear about their use.)

Ask students to come up with five sentences that use two or more of the punctuation marks above, but to write them down without any punctuation at all. Working in pairs, the sentences can be swapped and partners can supply the missing punctuation and explain why it is used.

12: Dark Matter

Context

Dark Matter, the novel from which this text is taken, marks something of a departure for Michelle Paver. Her *Wolf Brother* series, aimed at young adult readers, has been phenomenally successful, but she has moved away from this type of writing to produce a highly acclaimed ghost story. One reviewer said that 'The novel virtually defines a new genre: literary creepy.'

This text is most suitable for middle and higher ability Year 9 students.

Getting started

Is it possible to be afraid of something merely by thinking about it? Can people be driven to do things out of a sense of fear or panic even though part of them knows that there is really nothing there? This would be a fruitful area to discuss before reading the text.

Starter 1
Why are we afraid of the dark? Ask students to come up with at least four reasons individually and then take feedback to build up a full picture.

Starter 2
What are the ingredients for an excellent opening to a story or novel? Ask pairs to make a list (together with any good examples they know of) then share the results to arrive at a rich mixture.

Further resources

A good starting point is Michelle Paver's website: www.michellepaver.com.

Modern ghost-story writers tend to rely more on the idea of suggestion than apparition. The *Independent* considers the 'Best 10 ghost stories' here: www.independent.co.uk/arts-entertainment/books/features/the-10-best-ghost-stories-8231292.html – *Dark Matter* is one of them.

A famous film using the theme of real or imagined haunting is *Don't Look Now* (although you are advised to view it first before deciding whether to show all or part of it to your students). The film, if shown or recommended, would not be suitable for students below Year 9.

Activity 1

Narrative hooks

Programme of Study link

Reading

- Making inferences and referring to evidence in the text
- Studying setting, plot and characterisation, and the effects of these

Description

The text is the opening of the novel. Ask students to read the text and come up with a written list of the techniques the writer has used to tempt readers to continue. If prompts, are needed you might like to use: sense of mystery; violent events; unreasonable fears (phobias); desolate settings; the need not to bring back painful memories.

Ask students to speculate on why we should start a novel with a letter that appears to contribute nothing at all to the story. Why is this a clever device by the writer? Students may be able to see and suggest that the letter in fact sets the outline of the story very well. It acts as a 'teaser' in that we know something terrible happened but not what or how.

Ask the class to come up with possibilities for the next sequence in the novel. Will it be from Dr Murchison's point of view? From Jack Miller's? From someone else who was on the expedition? From the author, acting as an omniscient narrator (not likely, given the way the novel starts, but possible).

For those who are desperate to know, the novel continues with Jack Miller's account of how he first met those who were to go on the expedition with him.

Learning outcomes

- Students will be able to list some of the techniques the author uses to engage readers.
- Students should be able to produce a list of 'narrative hooks' and make a guess as to what might follow the opening.
- Students may be able to produce a comprehensive list of 'narrative hook' devices and suggest a plausible way of continuing to engage the reader with the next sequence in the novel.

Differentiation

Lower ability students should be set a target for the devices they can find (for example 'four different ways the author gets you interested'). See the first part of the activity for possible examples to help students.

Higher ability students can be asked to come up with three continuations, then to choose one and explain why they feel it is the most likely.

Assessment opportunities

- Reading: critical analysis
- **RAF 3, RAF 5, RAF 6**

Activity 2

Being the author

Programme of Study link

Writing

- Using knowledge of literary and rhetorical devices from their reading and listening to enhance the impact of their writing

Description

Following on from Activity 1, students can be invited to select a point of view that appeals to them for the next sequence in the novel and to think up a likely scenario. They should then plan and write the sequence, or part of it, bearing in mind that at this stage the aim is still to intrigue the reader and draw him or her further into the story. Point out that it is usual to introduce at least one of the main characters at this stage, and to have something happen that sets the story going.

Ask for volunteers to read out their work once they have completed two or three paragraphs and collect the views of other members of the class as to whether it is meeting the core requirements. It will be useful at this point to check the text to make sure that anything written does not contradict the information given there.

Learning outcomes

- Students will be able to write part of the next possible scene or sequence in the novel.
- Students should be able to write part or all of the next sequence, using some of the ideas contained in the opening.
- Students may be able to write the next scene or sequence in the novel, building on the opening and maintaining the reader's engagement.

Differentiation

Lower ability students might be given a viewpoint for writing the next scene: the opening mentions Jack and at least two companions. One of these can tell the next part of the story.

Higher ability students should keep the emphasis on intrigue. They should be able to show how they have used at least one of the elements in the opening to build on the reader's curiosity in their scene.

Assessment opportunities

- Writing: style and vocabulary
- **WAF 1, WAF 2**

Activity 3

Questions to a writer

Programme of Study link

Writing

- Personal and formal letters

Grammar and vocabulary

- Knowing and understanding the differences between spoken and written language, including differences associated with formal and informal registers, and between Standard English and other types of English

Description

Point out that the novel from which the text is taken marks an unusual departure for the author, Michelle Paver. She has had great success with her *Wolf Brother* series (see www.michellepaver.com/*wolf*-brother for details of the worldwide success of these novels). To write *Dark Matter* must have required a lot of research and planning, and where did the idea come from in the first place?

Ask students, possibly working in pairs, to come up with five questions that they would need to ask the author in order to collect material for a profile of her and a promotional piece about her new book. Revise the correct layout of a formal letter (perhaps using Worksheet 5.9) and then ask students individually to draft a letter to Michelle Paver asking her about the inspiration for and writing of *Dark Matter*.

As an additional incentive, you may like to indicate that the best letter will be sent to the author on behalf of the class.

Learning outcomes

- Students will be able to formulate questions to ask an author.
- Students should be able to formulate questions and to put these into the form of a letter to the author.
- Students may be able to use the questions they have formulated as the basis of a formal letter to the author that is both polite and interested in possible answers.

Differentiation

Lower ability students should be supported in coming up with well thought out questions to the author. (For example: 'What made you want to write a ghost story?')

Higher ability students should be encouraged to adopt the correct degree of formality when writing to someone they do not know personally. (See Worksheet 5.10, referred to in the SPAG focus below.)

Assessment opportunities

- Writing: style and vocabulary
- **WAF 2, WAF 7**

SPAG focus

This activity provides an opportunity to revise the differences between formal and informal language. In particular, you might like to focus on higher-level vocabulary (more Latinate words), impersonal constructions: 'It seems to us …' and modal verbs (could, should, would, might). Worksheet 5.10 helps to investigate this.

Unit assessment task

Description

A new magazine, *The Dark Side*, for young adult readers is being launched. It will feature stories and non-fiction (informative) articles dealing with the macabre – ghosts, poltergeists, strange manifestations, vampires, the living dead, psychopaths – and is asking for submissions from 11- to 14-year-olds.

The editor needs pieces between 400 and 2,000 words and is interested in 'stories, poems, play scripts and articles that make readers think, and possibly shiver. Nothing too obvious, graphic or violent, just well-written material that will grab a reader's attention'.

Invite students to write pieces for the magazine. They should make individual choices about whether they will write fiction or non-fiction. Following this, they should outline the topic or story they will produce, and then write it.

It would be possible to run this activity as a genuine competition, with prizes for the best entries and publication on the school website or VLE for the winners.

Learning outcomes

- Students will be able to write a piece using some of the techniques learned in this unit.
- Students should be able to write an effective piece using some of the learned techniques.
- Students may be able to use what they have learned in this unit to write a compelling piece suitable for sharing with a wider audience.

Differentiation

Lower ability students may be variously supported to write at length by giving them topics to use, starting sentences or paragraphs, and/or outlines of a story or non-fiction piece to work from. First establish the kind of piece they would like to contribute. (Fiction or non-fiction? Topic?) Then provide similar texts and/or writing frames as appropriate. There is an opportunity to work with lower ability students as a guided group, helping them with the planning and writing of similar topics.

Higher ability students should be challenged to adopt a professional approach to the task of writing at length, looking carefully for and at similar material that already exists, then writing and rewriting their material until they are satisfied that it meets the criteria and shows off their skills as writers.

Assessment opportunities

- Reading: comprehension; critical analysis; forms, conventions and language
- Writing: style and vocabulary; form and structure; grammatical range and accuracy
- **RAF 2, RAF 3, RAF 4, RAF 5, RAF 6, RAF 7, WAF 1, WAF 2, WAF 3, WAF 4, WAF 5, WAF 6, WAF 7, WAF 8**

Name .... Class .... Date ....

Newspaper headlines

Write 1–2 sentences per headline stating whether you believe the headline is real or made up, and your reasons for thinking that.

When deciding, think about what the story accompanying each headline could be about, unusual headlines and stories you may have experienced, and what type of publication such a headline might appear in if it is real.

NUNS IN FIGHT AGAINST STRIPPERS

____

I'll fight council over sausage roll

____

Church window nearly smashed

____

YAWNING ALMOST KILLED MAN

____

Factory creates four jobs

____

LIFEBOAT CALLED OUT TO HELP WITCH

____

POSITION FOR PANTO PONY POO PERSON

____

Name .... Class .... Date ....

Diamond nine theme ranker

1a. Rank the following statements about zoos. Cut out the boxes and organise them into a diamond formation of your own with the statement you agree with most strongly at the top moving down to the one you agree with least or not at all at the bottom.

Zoos are a form of family entertainment

It is now harder to touch and see animals

Zoos protect rare species from extinction

Zoos educate the public about animal behaviour

Zoos make money out of animals

Creatures in zoos are caged and cannot grow properly

Zoos provide a safe home and regular food for animals

Zoos run breeding programmes for endangered species

Animals have the same rights as humans

1b. When you have finished, compare your diamond nine ranking with those of other students. Explain to them why you have ordered the statements in the way that you have. Change your rank order if you want to as a result of your discussions.

2. Now write a further nine statements about zoos and rank them in the diamond formation.

When you have finished, compare your diamond nine ranking with those of other students. Explain to them why you have ordered the statements in the way that you have. Change your rank order if you want to in the light of your discussions.

Name .... Class .... Date ....

Arguments against

Use the table below to list your arguments against children working for pocket money. The first row has been done for you.

Use the final column to rank your arguments in order of importance.

Writer's points	**Evidence**	**Your argument**	**Your evidence**	**Order of importance**
Teenagers should not be given money just because they ask for it.	Working gives children responsibility and confidence.	Teenage years are soon gone and should not be spent working.	The teen years last for seven years. If you work from 18 to 65, that is more than enough working years.	

Name .... Class .... Date ....

Child employment: what is allowed by law?

In employment law, work is taken to mean paid hours in employment, and a child refers to a person who is under 13 years old. There are many laws protecting children from exploitation.

1. What do you think 'exploitation' means? Use a dictionary if you are not sure.

____

____

2. Use the internet to help you sort the following statements into true or false. Use a dictionary to help you understand any difficult words.

A Children may not work before 7.00am

B Children can work up to 8.00pm at night

C Children cannot work in a betting shop

D Children are allowed to work in a pub with the landlord's permission

E Children can work in a factory as long as it is not harmful to their health or education

F Children may work a maximum of 15 hours a week during term time

G Children may work a maximum of two hours on a Saturday and Sunday

H During school holidays children may work as many hours as they wish if it is the weekend

I Schools have to arrange a work permit for students to participate in work experience

J Children participating in paid performances (TV/theatre etc.) have to have a chaperone

K Once a child reaches 17, they can work full time and on Sunday

Name .... Class .... Date ....

Emotive language and factual report

Emotive language is the use of words and phrases that create an emotional response and appeal to the reader's feelings. Emotive language is designed to make the reader feel a certain way, such as feeling sorry for someone, or feeling sadness, shock or relief.

1a. Put these words that feature in the article in order from the most emotive to the least emotive.

kids tearaways louts yobs people offenders criminals citizens victims pensioners

b. Explain your choices. An example has been completed below for you.

Tearaway – this is a very emotive word. It suggests a young person who is out of control and who is reckless. In the article, the 'tearaway' is presented as on the path to destruction before an ASBO helps to put the life of that person back on track.

2a. Tone refers to the writer's attitude towards what is being written and towards the reader. A writer can change the tone of writing through choice of language. This means that particular words can be added to show a writer is angry, disappointed, happy or worried, for example. The word 'tearaway' above is used to show the writer feels angry and negative towards teenagers with ASBOs.

Pick out three more examples of emotive language from the article. Replace these three words with alternatives that make sense in the sentence but completely change the tone and meaning of the text. For example, the word 'dodgy' in the phrase 'dodgy ASBOs' could be swapped for 'effective' or 'successful', which suggests ASBOs work, whereas 'dodgy' suggests ASBOs are not successful.

b. Using one of your alternative words, explain in detail how this change occurs and what its effect is on the reader.

Name .... Class .... Date ....

Emotive language and factual report

Emotive language is the use of words and phrases that create an emotional response and appeal to the reader's feelings. Emotive language is designed to make the reader feel a certain way, such as feeling sorry for someone, or feeling sadness, shock or relief.

1a. Put these words that feature in the article in order from the most emotive to the least emotive. This means you should put the words in order from the word that you think will have the greatest effect on the reader's feelings down to the word that you think will have the least effect on the reader's feelings. Some words can suggest much more to readers than other words and you should consider this in your response.

tearaways yobs offenders victims pensioners

b. Explain your choices. An example has been completed below.

Tearaway – this is a very emotive word. It suggests a young person rather than an adult or 'pensioner'. Readers might think it describes someone who is out of control and who does not think of the consequences of their actions. In the article, the word 'tearaway' is used to suggest the person is going to get into serious trouble if nothing is done, but an ASBO could help to sort out their life.

2a. Tone is the feeling the writer has towards the reader and the feelings he has about what he is writing about. A writer can change the tone of writing through the language used. This means that words can be added to show a writer is angry, happy or worried, for example. The word 'tearaways' above is used to show that the writer feels angry and negative towards teenagers with ASBOs because the word exaggerates and suggests those with ASBOs are out of control.

Pick out three more examples of emotive language from the article. Replace each of these three words with a different word that makes sense in the sentence but completely changes the tone and meaning of the text.

For example, the word 'law-abiding' in the phrase 'law-abiding citizens' could be swapped for 'awkward' or 'moaning', which would suggest the citizens (people) are complaining for no reason. In contrast, 'law-abiding' suggests the citizens are innocent people who follow the law.

b. Using one of your new words, explain in detail the effect it could have on the reader.

Name .... Class .... Date ....

Witness statement

You are going to write a witness statement. Choose whose you are going to write:

attacker victim bystander witness

Use the sentence starters below to begin your paragraphs.

Bystander or Witness

I was attending the Notting Hill Carnival with some friends. We were standing near …

I saw a man … who was …

I heard … and I saw …

The man with the knife was wearing ...

He looked ...

Victim

I was enjoying the sights at the carnival but it was very crowded. I was standing near … when I heard ...

I suddenly felt ... because …

I saw …

I noticed a man who ...

When I looked down, I saw ... and I felt …

Attacker

I was at the carnival and it was very busy. I was standing near … when I heard …

I thought that I was in danger because … so I …

People were …

I felt …

I started to run because …

Then …

I did not mean to …

Name .... Class .... Date ....

'gh' words

Some words have a silent 'gh', like 'sight', but in others the 'gh' sounds like 'f', as in 'enough'. Sometimes the 'h' is silent and 'gh' just sounds like 'g', as in 'ghost'.

1. Read the 'gh' words below and put them into the correct column of the chart according to whether the 'gh' has an 'f' sound, a 'g' sound or is silent.

tough brought taught

rough ghetto laugh

cough though thought

'gh' sounds like 'f'	'gh' sounds like 'g'	'gh' is silent
enough	ghost	sight

2. Use each of these words in a sentence of your own.

Name .... Class .... Date ....

Writing a newspaper obituary

Newspaper obituaries are typically written by a professional writer and provide important and accurate information to the public. Use the guidelines below (and in Text 7) to write your own obituary of a famous person who is no longer alive. For example, you could choose a person from history like Elizabeth I or a celebrity like Michael Jackson.

Basic guidelines for writing newspaper obituaries

1. Deceased's first name, middle initial and last name, separated by commas, followed by age

   Do *not* use the word 'aged' before the numerical age.

2. County and town where they lived

   Do not use a specific street address for the deceased.

3. Cause of death (optional)

4. Place of death (optional)

   Though this is optional, it is usual to mention where the deceased died, for example at home, in hospital or in a nursing home.

5. Date of death

6. Occupation

   Give their job title if relevant. More than one occupation can be listed. In the case of a famous person, this is where you would explain their achievements and what they are famous for. Try to write in chronological (date) order and select the most important or biggest achievements.

7. Marriage

   Give name of wife/husband and the date of the marriage. There may be further comments to make on the marriage if the wife/husband was well known too.

8. Left behind/survivors

   Give the name of the wife/husband if they are still alive and of any children in the order that they were born.

Name .... Class .... Date ....

Comparing captions

Use this writing frame to help you compare the effects that two different captions to the same photograph may have on readers.

Both newspapers refer to the petrol cans as 'jerry cans'. This word links to …
and suggests … Readers may think …

The Times, a broadsheet newspaper, describes the man as a shop owner, which suggests he is … However, the *Daily Mirror*, a red top newspaper, leaves this information out. This might be because … It suggests … Readers may think …

The *Daily Mirror* uses the word 'hoard', which suggests the man is …
whereas *The Times* … The effect of this on readers is …

The Times describes motorists as 'panicked', which suggests … and makes readers think the man in the photograph is … The *Daily Mirror* does not tell us that the man is going to sell the petrol to motorists, which might make readers think …

Overall, the caption from … is more effective because … whereas the other caption from … is …

Name .... Class .... Date ....

Commenting on vocabulary used in the texts

Follow the instructions below to help you analyse the way the judges use language to describe the contestants' macaroons.

Step 1: Select words and phrases used to describe the macaroons

In the space below, list words and phrases which the judges use to describe and comment on the macaroons.

Step 2: Explain why those words and phrases were chosen

Think carefully about what the judge may have wanted to achieve with each word or phrase. For example, they may have wanted to:

- have an effect on the contestants' thoughts and feelings (e.g. reassure or encourage them)
- describe the macaroons in a clear and striking way
- explain how macaroons can or should be made.

Add a brief note to each word or phrase above to explain what you think the judge intended.

Step 3: Write analytically about three words or phrases

Choose three words or phrases from your selection which you feel have been used for different reasons. Now write out your ideas into a full analytical paragraph.

You could use this frame to help you:
[name of judge] describes Jason's macaroon by saying '[insert your chosen word or phrase]'. He/she uses this word/phrase because/in order to ...

You could develop this further by adding a comment on the effect of the word or phrase. For example, you may feel that the phrase 'makes you smile' is effective because it suggests an effect that the macaroon has when you eat it. This would be reassuring to Jason because it tells him that the judge is really pleased with his macaroon.

Name .... Class .... Date ....

Comparatives and superlatives

Below you will find the outline of a newspaper review of an episode of a television talent show. Your task is to complete it by filling in the gaps. Some but not all of the words you need should be comparatives or superlatives. Decide what sort of word should be where, and decide how to describe the various acts mentioned in the review. Once you are happy with the overall text, go back and write an interesting title.

Reminder: Comparatives are formed by adding *-er* to the end (e.g. brighter) or by using 'more' in front of an adjective (e.g. more brilliant). Superlatives are formed by adding *-est* to the end (e.g. brightest) or by using 'most' in front of an adjective (e.g. most brilliant).

Talent TV: ____________________

Last night's instalment of Talent TV was ____________ than ever. There were some ____________ acts, while others were just ____________.

A highlight of the show was Juggling Jim: his act was ____________ that I have ever seen. We were glued to the TV during his performance. However, his manners were ____________; I don't think I've seen anyone talk to the judges like that before!

But we all watch these programmes for the weird and wonderful, don't we? And last night's episode did not disappoint. Who could forget the ____________ Humeira with her voice that was ____________ than ____________? Never mind the perfectly ____________ Al with his acrobatics – that had to be the ____________ act of the series, surely?

Name .... Class .... Date ....

Writing creatively in the first person

Follow the steps outlined below to complete this creative writing task using ideas from Text 3: Emma Hearts LA.

The task

Write a first person account of a character's feelings about a change in family circumstances. Their feelings should be strong ones, but can be positive or negative. The character may be based on yourself, or completely invented. The change could be one of the following or an idea of your own:

- family moving overseas
- changing schools
- a new baby in the family
- no more pocket money due to family budget tightening
- a grandparent moving in because they need care.

Getting help from the text

Have another look at the text Emma Hearts LA to help you see how a piece like this can be written. Think about how we know that Emma is not happy about the move. (She does not exactly say so straight out.)

You could write your piece like this, as a conversation between your character and someone else (perhaps arguing with a parent, complaining to a friend or excitedly discussing the changes with a sister or brother). Alternatively you could write a diary-type piece where your character explains how they are feeling and why.

Planning what to write

What change are you going to write about?

How does your character feel about this change?

What is your character like? (For example, are they basically you, or are you going to pretend to be someone else for this task?)

However your character feels about the change, what reasons do they have for feeling this way?

What questions might they want to ask about it?

How might your character's family respond to their feelings?

Name .... Class .... Date ....

Direct speech

Your task is to produce a set of rules for writing direct speech. Looking at the text in your book will help you. You should think about:

Punctuation:	What must (or can) be used, and where does it go?
Capital letters:	Where are these required?
Speech tags (words like 'said'):	Where can these go?
Layout:	How do you paragraph a conversation?

Some challenges:

- What if you do not use a speech tag? How else can you show who is speaking?
- What if you want to put a speech tag in the middle of a line of dialogue?
- What different kinds of punctuation can you use at the end of a line of dialogue?

Rules for writing direct speech

Name .... Class .... Date ....

Features of text messages

Text messages are considered **multimodal** texts because they are a mixture of written language (the written mode of communication) and spoken language (the spoken mode of communication). Your task is to organise examples from text messages along a continuum to show how different aspects of the texts are more like speech while others are more like writing.

Using a continuum line rather than just making a 'spoken' list and a 'written' list means that you can be a bit more subtle.

Spoken Written

'Hey'
Informal greeting

For example, you might decide that 'hey', as an informal greeting, is more like speech than writing, although it is not true that it could never be written. This means that it should go nearer the 'spoken' end than the 'written' end, but not completely at the end of the line.

The list of features below may help you to label the aspects that you notice in the texts.

Features found in text messages

Number homophones (both on their own and as part of words), e.g. *4, l8r*

Letter homophones, e.g. *u, b*

Clipped letters from the end of words, e.g. *seein*

Phonetic spelling, e.g. *evryone*

Deleted letters (especially vowels), e.g. *tmrw, hlp*

Slang and colloquial words, e.g. *gonna*

Initialisms (where the letter names are said), e.g. *idk, h/w* and acronyms (where it can be said as a word), e.g. *lol*

Informal greetings, e.g. *hey, hey hun*

Exaggerated phonetic spelling/elongated words, e.g. *pleeease*

Non-standard use of punctuation for effect, e.g. *?!?!?*

Compressed grammar (missing out non-essential words), e.g. *Hey u ready? U ok?*

Symbols and emoticons, e.g. *xxx :-)*

Name .... Class .... Date ....

Writing a formal letter

Imagine your school wanted to ban slang in the same way as the school in Text 5. This worksheet will help you to prepare a formal letter to express your views about this. Your letter may be addressed to your head teacher or school governors, or to the local newspaper. You will need to show some understanding of why this ban has been suggested, and express your own views about the importance and relevance of Standard English, and about how it can be taught or encouraged in school.

Gathering your ideas

Make a few notes here about how you feel.

Jot down the reasons that the school wants to have this ban here.

Can you link any of your feelings to the school's reasons? Or if not, what counter-arguments can you make to the school's likely arguments for a ban?

Structuring your letter

Formal letters need a clear and coherent structure. Can you organise these key elements into the best order?

polite and formal opening

polite and formal closing

overview of your reaction to the idea (i.e. do you agree)

main points of your argument, with reasons for your claims

brief statement of who you are (i.e. why this is relevant to you)

Vocabulary bank

I support this view because ...

I feel this would be unhelpful because ...

Although I accept that ..., I believe that ...

It is my view that ...

It is important to consider...

I am unable to support this idea because ...

Name .... Class .... Date ....

Presentation on your own use of language

You will be giving a short presentation about your use of language. This worksheet will help you prepare what to say, whether you are working on your own or as part of a group.

What could be interesting about how I use language?

Here are some examples from two students, to show you some areas you could consider:

Humeira:

I speak Gujrati at home with my parents and sometimes with some friends.

When I speak to Gujrati speakers at school, sometimes we use both Gujrati and English in the same conversation.

I've been speaking English since I started school.

I play the flute, so I know some special words relating to music.

I use some catchphrases from my favourite TV shows with my friends.

I never swear but I do use slang with my friends.

Joe:

My parents moved here from a different region, so sometimes I pronounce words differently from other people in my class.

My mates and I often have silly words for things that other people don't understand.

I play computer games a lot and have picked up some words from these that I use in conversation now.

I love new slang expressions and use them a lot with my friends, but adults often don't understand them.

When I was little, I couldn't say hard 'c' sounds so I called our cat a bat and my family still call her 'bat'.

What about examples?

When you prepare your notes for your presentation, it would be best if you had some examples or particular words and phrases for each influence on your language. For example, if you have a different accent from the one spoken in the region you live, what are some of the best words to show this?

Name .... Class .... Date ....

Analysing the poem, carousel style

Point for discussion at this station:	The voice in this poem is that of a newsreader using a 'BBC accent', and yet the poem is not written in Standard English. Which do you think are the most interesting examples of this non-standard language? Why do you think Leonard has done this? How would the impact of the poem be different if it was written in Standard English?

Point for discussion at this station:	This poem is said to express Leonard's anger at the way people with accents are treated or thought of. What evidence of anger can you find in the poem?

Point for discussion at this station:	Think about features that you expect to find in poetry (e.g. rhyme, rhythm, similes, etc.). Which of those features do you find in this poem? What about it makes it a poem?

Point for discussion at this station:	The poem talks to us directly, seeming to assume that we speak with an accent. Find at least one example for this and discuss what the effect of this could be. How do you feel, reading this poem?

Name .... Class .... Date ....

Analysing the structure of the text

Analysing the structure of successful texts can help you to collect ideas to use in your own writing. In this case, an effective speech may help you to see what is needed to help a listening (rather than a reading) audience follow your text.

What to focus on

Firstly, how does the language used in the text help to lead the audience through it?

Here are some ideas of things you could look for and note below:

- words and phrases that act as signposts through the text (e.g. 'so', 'and'), getting our attention and pointing out to the audience that a new idea or something connected to the last point is coming next
- examples of topic sentences
- examples of repetition (of ideas, of phrases and of patterns).

Extension: looking more closely

Bearing in mind that this text was written to be spoken aloud, how do you think its sentence structures help it to be successful?

Which types of sentence can you find in this text? For each type, note an example and try to explain how it would help the audience to easily understand Malorie Blackman's point.

Name .... Class .... Date ....

Statements about language

Below you will find a set of statements, representing a range of attitudes about language.

Statements

Everybody should speak Standard English without a local accent. Then we would all understand one another better.

I like hearing different accents. I think it is all part of our mixed culture and we should be proud of it.

Telling someone else to change the way they speak is like saying they are not good enough as they are.

Speaking in slang is wrong and shows that you are not clever enough to have a good vocabulary.

Some accents are just better than others. Some are cool, some make you sound stupid or like a criminal, and some are just boring.

When someone speaks in a posh way, you just know they think they are better than everyone else.

If there were not any different accents, that would be boring.

Some people are ashamed of their accent and feel like they should change it. They should not have to feel like that.

I have a favourite accent that I like to hear.

There are accents that I dislike.

Although it does seem a bit unfair, sometimes people need to change their accent for their job to help people understand them better.

I do not think I have an accent.

Name .... Class .... Date ....

Advertising and audience appeal

Look at the comments below about audiences and how they might be attracted by the advertising slogans in Text 1. Which of the slogans do you think each comment is about? Use your existing knowledge of the products and their advertisements as well as the words in front of you.

1. The commanding tone of this slogan suggests that it is targeting people who want to participate in sport but may have other demands on their time.

2. The playful rhyme of this slogan implies that the product is for children and families.

3. This slogan appeals to animal lovers by reminding them that people can treat animals like objects, as though they are the latest toy and can be forgotten quickly.

4. The chatty style of language helps this slogan to appeal to people looking for something fun and not serious.

5. This slogan targets busy families by suggesting that the shop does small things which make a difference in people's lives.

6. This company promotes its products as being luxurious and its advertising is aimed at women who they suggest deserve something extra special.

Once you have decided which slogan goes with each sentence, turn the sentence into a full point by adding in the slogan (or part of it) as a quotation. For example:

The commanding tone of 'Just do it' suggests that Nike targets people who want to participate in sport but may have other demands on their time. The slogan seems to encourage them and also to give them permission. It also suggests that Nike products will help you to just get on with it, perhaps freeing you from unnecessarily complicated preparation.

Extension
Produce similar points for other slogans that you are familiar with.

Name .... Class .... Date ....

Analysing tone/address to audience

Use these prompts to help you explore how this leaflet addresses its audience of 'normal' adults (as opposed to those who consider themselves heavy drinkers).

Aspects to explore

Find examples of these aspects of the text. They help it to be persuasive by playing down the issue and making it seem like something everyone should think about.

Ways that alcohol itself is presented as being to blame

Ways that drinking too much is presented as an easy mistake to make

How cutting down on drinking is shown to be simple

How they try to present serious information (such as warnings about health risks) in a way that is not too frightening

How the health benefits of drinking less are emphasised more than the dangers of drinking too much

How the audience is addressed

Write down anything else you feel helps the writer of the leaflet to achieve their persuasive purpose.

Name .... Class .... Date ....

Glossary of persuasive language features

Use this glossary to help you identify features of persuasive language in Text 3. Note that sometimes one quotation could be an example of more than one technique (the 'mocking' example below is also a rhetorical question).

Alliteration	Using repeated consonant sounds, e.g. 'crazy credit crunch prices'.
Anecdote	A personal example or a story about an individual to illustrate a point: 'a friend of mine had this experience …'.
Direct address	Talking directly to the reader, e.g. by using 'you'.
Emotive language	Language intended to affect the readers emotionally, e.g. by making them feel guilt, anger or sympathy.
Fact	Something that can be proved to be correct, e.g. 'children are dying of starvation.'
Metaphor	Comparing two things without using 'like' or 'as', e.g. 'Education is the light that can guide children out of poverty.'
Mocking	Making an opposing idea seem ridiculous, e.g. 'Can you believe some people are suggesting …?'
Opinion	Something believed or thought, not a hard fact, e.g. 'children do not deserve to die.'
Patterning in sentences	Repeated sentence patterns or structures, e.g. 'Ask not what your country can do for you; ask what you can do for your country.'
Repetition	Using the same word, phrase or sentence more than once.
Rhetorical question	A question used to provoke the readers, or to get them thinking; a question that does not require an answer.
Statistics	Facts in the form of figures such as absolute numbers, e.g. '3,000 accidents were associated with the use of mobile phones last year' or percentages, e.g. '35 per cent of accidents last year were caused by mobile phones'.
Triplet/power of three	A pattern of three things, e.g. a word or phrase repeated three times, or a set of three words or phrases which go together, e.g. 'children who could grow up to be doctors, teachers or lawyers'.

Name .... Class .... Date ....

Understanding the speech

This sheet will help you to understand Henry's speech, both in terms of what it says and in terms of how Shakespeare makes his points.

Summary

In this speech, King Henry V is trying to encourage his soldiers to fight even though they are outnumbered. He does this by getting them to picture the future, when they will be able to look back on this day with pride and other men will wish they had been there. He makes being outnumbered seem like a good thing, as they can be even prouder of their success, and he makes it seem like a privilege to be one of those fighting. He reminds them all that the next day is St Crispin's Day, as this will make it easier for them to remember in future what they were doing on this day.

Evidence search

Find as many examples as possible of Henry talking about and making reference to the idea of pride.

Which phrases show us how other men will feel?

Where does he talk about being outnumbered and make it sound positive?

List the different times he refers to St Crispin's Day or 'this day'.

Extension

Use some of the evidence you have gathered to write up one or more analytical points about how the speech works as a piece of persuasion.

Name .... Class .... Date ....

What kind of a king is Henry V?

Work through this sheet to help you answer the question above.

How could you describe Henry V, based on this speech?

Note down as many ideas as you can about what Henry V is like. The prompts below may help you.

Using adjectives and descriptive phrases

Referring to your ideas above, make a list of adjectives or descriptive phrases to describe Henry V. Each idea above should give you at least one adjective or descriptive phrase, but do not worry if some of your ideas seem to lead to the same word or phrase.

For example, if you thought that pride was important to Henry V, you could describe him as proud or a proud man.

Organising your ideas

Now that you have a list of ideas, decide which you think are the most important or most obvious in the speech. You could rank them from most to least important, or use the pyramid below, which allows you to have some at the same level as each other. If you have more ideas than there is space for, just include the most important ones.

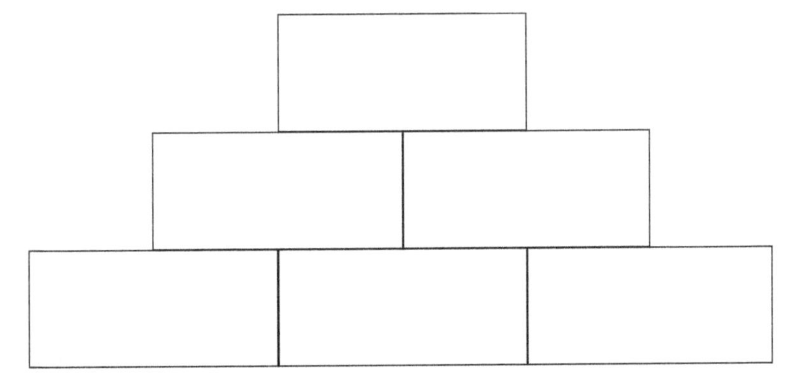

Name .... Class .... Date ....

Analysing the Clairol advertisement

Complete this analysis of the text by filling in the gaps.

This advertisement for hair dye features a prominent picture of a couple who appear to be

____

This implies that using the product can help you to have

____

Most of the picture is taken up with ____, which helps the audience to focus on the product.

This brand of hair dye seems to be targeted at women who ______________________________

This is shown through

____

Continue your analysis by answering the following questions:

- Does this dye seem to suggest a drastic change in colour or something more natural?
- Which words and phrases tell you this?

Name .... Class .... Date ....

Inventing a book and writing its blurb

First, use the prompts below to help you plan the main story line of your imaginary book:

- Who will be your main character? To write the blurb, you will need a name and you will need to know a bit about them. What does he or she like? What kind of person is he or she?
- In most (if not all) stories, the main character has some kind of problem to solve. What is the problem for your main character? Has he or she lost someone or something? Does he or she need someone or something? Is something bad about to happen to them?
- Is there a villain in your story? If so, what is the villain like?

Next, write the blurb of your book. Remember to:

- use your main character's name
- introduce the main problem he or she faces
- show the reader how difficult it will be for him or her to succeed
- make the audience want to know what is going to happen (but do *not* give away the ending!)
- check the blurbs in Unit 4, Text 6 for more ideas on how to write this.

Name .... Class .... Date ....

Analysing the open letter – ideas to help you get started

You are working towards analytical sentences which follow this structure:

Amnesty International uses … [feature], e.g. '…' [quotation] in order to … [explanation].

Features worth looking for

Try to find examples of the following to help you analyse this text:

emotive language (words and phrases which are there to make the reader feel)

pronouns (I, you, he, she, we, they)

formal language (particularly in this case relating to politics or the law)

patterns of three (clusters of three related ideas or lists with three items – it does not have to be the same word or phrase used three times)

flattery or empathy (paying compliments to or showing understanding, in this case towards the Russian authorities rather than the wider audience)

Remember to think carefully about the **reason** each feature is used. What **effect** is it likely to have? This will give you something to say in the 'explanation' part of your analytical sentence.

Name .... Class .... Date ....

Sentence construction in the open letter

Many of the sentences in this text are complex, using different kinds of subordinate clause. The table below labels some of the parts that make up the first two sentences.

Clause	Type	Comment
As the one-year anniversary of your trial approaches,	Adverbial clause	
around the world,	Adverbial	
Although you were the most visible of the protesters,	Adverbial clause	
through your imprisonment,	Adverbial	
we are writing to assure you that,	Comment clause	
we know that	Comment clause	
who have suffered in the protests	Relative clause	
about whom we are also very concerned	Relative clause	

Look at how these parts of the sentences contribute to the text.

Can you come up with an explanation of what adverbials, comment clauses and relative clauses can be used for? Write your explanations in the 'Comment' column of the table.

Can you find other examples elsewhere in the text? Write them in the space below.

Name .... Class .... Date ....

Exploring formal speech

Follow the steps below to explore the concept of formal speech.

Organising speech by formality

Put these six kinds of talk in order, from the most formal to the least formal:

- television soap (e.g. *Eastenders* or *Coronation Street*)
- conversation with a friend about a personal problem
- the Queen's speech at Christmas
- medical appointment
- debate competition
- reality television programme (e.g. *Made in Chelsea* or *Big Brother*)

What do you think affects the formality of each of these? For example, you may consider factors such as the relationship between the speakers or between the speaker and the audience; expected rules of different kinds of speech; privacy; location.

Looking at the debate transcript

Answer the following questions:

- Which features of spoken language (e.g. fillers, pauses or other hesitations) can you find in this transcript?
- Which features of persuasive language can you find in this transcript?
- Where do each of these kinds of feature occur in the transcript?
- Can you explain your answers (i.e. why the features are focused where they are in the transcript)?

Extension: formality in written language

Can you come up with four more kinds of written language with different degrees of formality to complete the spectrum below?

Least formal	Note on the fridge (e.g. 'Don't forget milk!')
	______________________________
↓	______________________________
	______________________________
	______________________________
Most formal	Medical textbook full of technical vocabulary

Name .... Class .... Date ....

Excerpt with the verbs of speech missing

Without looking at the original extract, add your own choice of verbs of speech in the gaps.

Think about what seems appropriate for each character and then compare this with Dahl's text.

How close were you?

Key

Red: Mrs Pratchett Light blue: Dahl's friends Green: Dahl

'One Sherbet Sucker, please,'

Thwaites ...., holding out his penny.

[Short paragraph describing the moment when Dahl puts the mouse in the Gobstopper jar.]

'And one Bootlace, please,'

.... Thwaites .... When I turned round, I saw Mrs Pratchett, holding out the Bootlace in her filthy fingers.

'I don't want all the lot of you troopin' in 'ere if only one of you is buyin','

she .... at us. 'Now beat it! Go on, get out!'

As soon as we were outside, we broke into a run. 'Did you do it?'

they ....

'Of course I did!' I ....

'Well done you!' they .... 'What a super show!'

I felt like a hero. I was a hero. It was marvellous to be popular.

Name .... Class .... Date ....

Jack and Jill

Jack and Jill went up the hill

To fetch a pail of water.

Jack fell down and broke his crown,

And Jill came tumbling after.

Up Jack got and home did trot,

As fast as he could caper;

And went to bed and bound his head

With vinegar and brown paper.

Name .... Class .... Date ....

Use of direct and indirect speech in *Angela's Ashes*

Indirect speech (one example only)	Direct speech examples (select 5 from the 7 examples in the extract)	Speaker	Intended effect
1	'as a wee lad your poor father was dropped on his head … can be a bit peculiar.'	His paternal grandmother	It almost sounds like she is excusing his father's wayward behaviour. Caricatured – cartoon image but also poignant.
2			
3			
4	'Get out of it. Out. If you stay here a minute longer … Get out.'	His maternal grandmother	Adds dramatic impact. Her outburst seems very much in the here and now. Repetition adds to this.
5			

Name .... Class .... Date ....

Types of humour

Identify the types and effects of humour in the extract. Fill in the gaps.

Bryson is very adept at using words economically. Sometimes he manages to combine two of these at the same time with even greater effect. Look out for this too!

Work through the extract chronologically.

Type of humour	Example	Effect
		They were actually just splashing around and having a good time. The total overreaction makes it humorous.
Understatement and overstatement		
	'she gave the kind of big, languorous wave … only an Australian … an appropriate response to a death-at-sea situation'	
	'Glen, never having seen anything quite this grotesque on an Australian beach'	
		A really serious incident just seems so ridiculous and cartoon like, almost as if the arm could be stuck back on again.
Overstatement		
	'I was tentatively eager … jumped aboard and sank like an anvil.'	

Name .... Class .... Date ....

Compare and contrast the writing styles of Dahl and McCourt

Remember: Point Quote Comment

	Narrative content (incident described)	Description of characters/ impressions given	Use of tenses	Use of speech	Style/tone	Structure
Roald Dahl *Boy*	Focuses on one incident from his childhood – lets the reader in on a secret – the boys' hiding place where they find the mouse, builds up to revenge on Mrs Pratchett.				Builds up the detail to a climax. Aware of the author controlling the narrative – talks about importance of 'striving to be truthful.' More serious and dramatic.	
Frank McCourt *Angela's Ashes*	A series of anecdotal incidents that date from before the author's birth which involve accidents. The writer is made privy to the secret, as is the reader.				More informal and flows seemlessly from one event to the next. Elements of humour to suggest childlike qualities of the child not quite understanding – 'wonder why anyone would give money for a head like that.'	

Name .... Class .... Date ....

Bryson and Theroux comparison

	Content	Purpose of audience	Style and tone	Linguistic and poetic devices
Bill Bryson		To entertain; to inform (historical references).		
Paul Theroux	Personal experiences too – own 'home-made' safari, move on commenting about the white concept of 'going on safari'.			

Name .... Class .... Date ....

Samuel Pepys' diary entry of the Great Fire of London

Understanding the flow of events

Key sections about what happened, without the extra descriptive details, have been jumbled up. Cut them up and sort them into the correct order. Once you are sure of the order, check them against the original extract, before sticking them in your exercise book.

So I rose … and went to her window … I thought it far enough off, and so went to bed again, and to sleep.

she hears that above 300 houses have been burned down tonight … is now burning down all Fish Street, by London Bridge. So I made myself ready … and walked to the Tower; and there got up on one of the high places, … and there I did see the houses at the end of the bridge all on fire, and an infinite great fire on this and the other side … of the bridge.

Jane called up about three in the morning, to tell us of a great fire they saw in the City.

Everybody endeavouring to remove their goods … poor people staying in their houses as long as till the very fire touched them … And among, other things, the poor pigeons, I perceive, … burned their wings and fell down.

So down [I went], … to the Lieutenant of the Tower, who tells me that it began this morning in the King's baker's house in Pudding Lane, and that it hath burned St Magnus's Church and most part of Fish Street already.

So I rode down to the waterside, … and there saw a lamentable fire …

Name .... Class .... Date ....

Samuel Pepys' diary of the Great Fire of London

Understanding the flow of events – modern-day version

The statements below describe Pepys' account of The Great Fire, but they use more up-to-date vocabulary and structure. Sort out the correct order and then match the statements with the sections from Pepys' diary in Worksheet 4.7. Slot the modern version in the right places so they become a handy translation that you can refer back to. Or place them on an opposite page of your exercise book alongside the ordered sections from the Pepys extract. Remember to be sure of the order before you stick any down.

So I got up and went to the window, thinking it was far enough away I got back into bed and went back to sleep.

Jane got me up at about 3am to tell me about a huge fire that had broken out in the city.

I spoke to the tower security guard who told me it had started in Pudding Lane at the King's baker's this morning and it had already burnt down St Magnus's Church and most of Fish Street.

She told me that over 300 houses had burnt down last night and now the fire has spread along Fish Street by London Bridge. I got up and dressed and went straight to the Tower.
I climbed up to get a better viewpoint and saw that the fire had taken hold for miles around.

Everybody tried to remove what they could from their houses … the poor stayed in their houses as long as they possibly could, getting out in the nick of time …

So I rode down to the waterside and saw a huge and terrifying fire …

Name .... Class .... Date ....

Review extracts

Article source/writer	*Guardian*, 20 October 2013, Jay Rayner
Review extract	What they make of the fusty 'second home in Tuscany' options I can't imagine, but that food is very good. There is a starter of sweet-salty clams amid a stew of borlotti beans and chorizo that has us sucking at the shells. There is a whole roast partridge on a mess of creamy polenta studded with butter-seared ceps, with a little sticky jus to keep everything moving. At the end there is a cast-iron pan of black and purple grilled figs tumbling apart, with dollops of cream, walnuts and dribbles of sticky honey. So far, so bargain-basement River Café.
URL link	www.theguardian.com/lifeandstyle/2013/oct/20/the-tavern-restaurant-review
Audience	Middle-class audience with enough disposable income to dine in such a pub. Appeals to both males and females, who are young(ish) professionals.
Purpose	To entertain as well as to inform (whether to recommend the establishment or not).

Article source/writer	The *Telegraph*, 27 June 2013, Tim Robey
Review extract	Despicable Me, the animated supervillain comedy from 2010, was an average flick with a neat enough premise. In Despicable Me 2, it's gone. You see, Steve Carell's bald, beaky hero, Gru, is now a reformed soul, occupied with round-the-clock childcare rather than dastardly plots to steal the moon and whatnot. The withdrawal of his evil motives is so complete that the movie's very title feels like a misnomer – what we get this time is Grumpy Old Me at best, or Secretly Lovable Me, or Doting Me. And none of these 'Me's are very much fun.
URL link	www.telegraph.co.uk/culture/film/filmreviews/10145597/Despicable-Me-2-review.html
Audience	Although the author is reviewing a children's film, the article is aimed more at adults with young children as they are far more likely to be reading broadsheet newspapers. The vocabulary used in the review is aimed at an older audience than the film itself.
Purpose	To inform and entertain. The review warns against seeing the film as it apparently does not live up to *Despicable Me*, although it gives the impression that children would still enjoy it but their parents would not.

Article source/writer	*Cycling Weekly*, product reviews
Review extract	Verdict: As a whole package, it's a very capable bike and a great platform for a budget road racer. Yes, the finishing kit and brake calipers are down at the budget end of things but a compromise needs to be struck somewhere and it wasn't in the frameset. If you are going to struggle to squeeze a pricier ride past the financial controller then this is a solid bike to upgrade.

Name .... Class .... Date ....

URL link	www.cyclingweekly.co.uk/tech/bikes/129642/1/merida-scultura-comp-904.
Audience	Clearly aimed at adults who enjoy cycling and take it seriously. The practical detail included suggests the target audience have enough disposable income to spend on such an item and probably fall into the 25–45 age bracket.
Purpose	Purely to inform and review the bike as the reviewer gives his or her opinion on whether the bike represents value for money.

Article source/writer	*Bella* magazine, women's clothes section
Review extract	Take a walk on the wild side in this seriously sexy animal print jumpsuit. With frilled cap sleeves and a v-neckline, this is perfect for making an impact this season. Make it even fiercer by teaming with high heels and accessorising! Patent belt included. Pearly button fastening at back. Approx length 137cm/54" (based on a UK size 8 sample). 90% Polyester 10% Elastane. Natasha wears a UK size 8 and her height is 5'6" UK size 8 = EU 36/US 4/AUS 8.
URL link	http://shop.bellamagazine.co.uk/browse/womens-clothes
Audience	Aimed at a predominantly female audience who are probably in their twenties.
Purpose	To inform and give a positive review. The write-up includes not only detail about the impact the garment will have, but also lots of practical details such as available sizes, materials used and dimensions.

Article source/writer	*Daily Mail*, movie review of *This is Us*, One Direction film, 30 August 2013, Paul Tookey
Review extract	Reviewers will be queuing up to badmouth the new One Direction movie. A chap in front of me actually booed the opening image, which was the logo of Syco, Simon Cowell's company. Fortunately for its commercial prospects, this pretty much defines the kind of movie that is critic-proof. Fans of the biggest boyband in the world will need no encouragement to watch a rockumentary that brings them up close and more-or-less personal with their youthful heroes. The big surprise here is that even non-fans should find themselves warming to the five lads in the group.
URL link	www.dailymail.co.uk/tvshowbiz/reviews/article-2406227/One-Direction-film-This-Is-Us-review-Chris-Tookey.html#ixzz2IshxxeFZ
Audience	The film is aimed at a different viewing audience from the reading audience of this newspaper. The majority of their readers are likely to be in their thirties or forties and old enough to have primary school-aged children or teenagers. The review is to help the parents decide whether they want to accompany their children to see the film.
Purpose	To inform and comment, and to cautiously recommend.

Name .... Class .... Date ....

A text from a different time

The old man's terror must have been extreme! It grew louder, I say, louder every moment! --do you mark me well I have told you that I am nervous: so I am. And now at the dead hour of the night, amid the dreadful silence of that old house, so strange a noise as this excited me to uncontrollable terror. Yet, for some minutes longer I refrained and stood still. But the beating grew louder, louder! I thought the heart must burst. And now a new anxiety seized me --the sound would be heard by a neighbour! The old man's hour had come! With a loud yell, I threw open the lantern and leaped into the room. He shrieked once --once only. In an instant I dragged him to the floor, and pulled the heavy bed over him. I then smiled gaily, to find the deed so far done. But, for many minutes, the heart beat on with a muffled sound. This, however, did not vex me; it would not be heard through the wall. At length it ceased. The old man was dead. I removed the bed and examined the corpse. Yes, he was stone, stone dead. I placed my hand upon the heart and held it there many minutes. There was no pulsation. He was stone dead. His eye would trouble me no more.

If still you think me mad, you will think so no longer when I describe the wise precautions I took for the concealment of the body. The night waned, and I worked hastily, but in silence. First of all I dismembered the corpse. I cut off the head and the arms and the legs.

I then took up three planks from the flooring of the chamber, and deposited all between the scantlings. I then replaced the boards so cleverly, so cunningly, that no human eye --not even his --could have detected any thing wrong. There was nothing to wash out --no stain of any kind --no blood-spot whatever. I had been too wary for that. A tub had caught all --ha! ha!

Name .... Class .... Date ....

'The Tell-Tale Heart': punctuation matters

In this version of Text 1, dashes have mostly been replaced by commas, and exclamation marks by full stops.

What difference do you think this makes to the effect of the text on the reader?

> The old man's terror must have been extreme. It grew louder, I say, louder every moment. Do you mark me well I have told you that I am nervous: so I am. And now at the dead hour of the night, amid the dreadful silence of that old house, so strange a noise as this excited me to uncontrollable terror. Yet, for some minutes longer I refrained and stood still. But the beating grew louder, louder. I thought the heart must burst. And now a new anxiety seized me, the sound would be heard by a neighbour. The old man's hour had come. With a loud yell, I threw open the lantern and leaped into the room. He shrieked once, once only. In an instant I dragged him to the floor, and pulled the heavy bed over him. I then smiled gaily, to find the deed so far done. But, for many minutes, the heart beat on with a muffled sound. This, however, did not vex me; it would not be heard through the wall. At length it ceased. The old man was dead. I removed the bed and examined the corpse. Yes, he was stone, stone dead. I placed my hand upon the heart and held it there many minutes. There was no pulsation. He was stone dead. His eye would trouble me no more.
>
> If still you think me mad, you will think so no longer when I describe the wise precautions I took for the concealment of the body. The night waned, and I worked hastily, but in silence. First of all I dismembered the corpse. I cut off the head and the arms and the legs.
>
> I then took up three planks from the flooring of the chamber, and deposited all between the scantlings. I then replaced the boards so cleverly, so cunningly, that no human eye, not even his, could have detected any thing wrong. There was nothing to wash out, no stain of any kind, no blood-spot whatever. I had been too wary for that. A tub had caught all, ha. Ha.

Name .... Class .... Date ....

Practise your punctuation

The following paragraphs have either no punctuation, or very little. Put in all the punctuation required.

1. I think he said that its going to be a fine day for the match I don't she protested there are black clouds already it looks like rain to me
2. Where are we going then he asked I thought you said the beach she replied didn't you I might have said the beach he went on but now I've changed my mind I think we'll go up on the hills instead that way the dogs will still have a good run but they won't get all covered in sand it's not you that ever washes them down she said grumpily I quite fancied the beach today.
3. No she screamed I'm not going that way why ever not he said a look of amusement coming over his face it's never bothered you before has it you know very well I could never go through that damp dark passage not after what happened to tina tina had it coming to her he said with a sniff she never took any safety precautions so it's no wonder she got in a bit of bother is it a bit of bother she said her voice rising to screaming pitch again tina's dead that's hardly a bit of bother
4. pull down the blinds he said sadly it's getting dark and I really don't want to see any longer what's going on out there there there she said moving closer to him I'm sure they won't find anything under that great white tent it's just a precaution he looked at her for a long moment before he spoke they suspect me of murder don't they
5. all's well that ends well Rhiannon said brightly that's a play by Shakespeare isn't it I'm really glad you could make it we've had a really lovely weekend yes haven't we Briony said we must do it again and soon we'll put a date in our diaries right now Rhiannon said her enthusiasm almost getting the better of her oh yes it's going to be super

Name .... Class .... Date ....

The art of the adjective

In this section of *The Enemy* by Charlie Higson, the adjectives that have been underlined replace those used by the writer. Below the text is a list of the original adjectives.

Can you work out which adjective goes where?

Do you think the originals are more effective than the replacements? Can you explain why?

> Arran was filled with a wild rage. With a loud roar he lashed out to right and left, smashing his club into the grown-ups, shattering bones, breaking noses, loosening teeth, closing eyes. He was hardly aware of what was going on around him.
>
> When a mother came at Arran, blonde hair flying, he gripped her by the throat and squeezed. Her head thrashed from side to side, her dirty hands flapped at him. Her hair whipped out of her face so that for a moment he saw her clearly.
>
> Her nose was wrinkled by disease. There were boils and sores covering every inch of skin. Her lips were pulled back from yellow teeth showing rotting, raw gums.
>
> Everything about her was smelly, ugly, rough – apart from her eyes. Her eyes were blue.

Original adjectives

inhuman	blind	half rotted away
black	long	disgusting
degraded	scabby	beautiful
broken	great	shrunken

Name .... Class .... Date ....

A horrific attack

As I walked along the lane I saw coming towards me a gentleman of about my age, walking with a heavy stick.

Name .... Class .... Date ....

Shock and awe

During the early morning of 7th February something so horrible happened in the Khe Sanh sector that even those of us who were in Hue when we heard news of it had to relinquish our own fear and despair for a moment to acknowledge and pay tribute to it …

Five kilometres south-west of the Khe Sanh Combat Base, sitting above the river which forms the border with Laos, there was a Special Forces A Camp. It was called Langvei … The camp was larger than most Special Forces camps, and much better built. Its bunkers were deep, solid, with three feet of reinforced concrete overhead, seemingly impregnable. And sometime after midnight, the North Vietnamese came and took it. They took it in a style that had been seen only once before, in the Ia Drang, attacking with weapons and tactics which no-one imagined they had. Nine light tanks, Soviet T-34s and 76s, were deployed east and west, closing in on the camp so suddenly that the first sound of them was mistaken by the Americans for a malfunction of the camp generator. Satchel charges, Bangalore torpedoes, teargas and – ineffable horror – napalm were all hurled into the machine gun slits and air vents of the bunkers. It took very little time. An American colonel who had come on an inspection visit to Langvei was seen charging the tanks with nothing but hand grenades before he was cut down. (He survived. The word 'miracle' doesn't even apply.) Somewhere between ten and fifteen Americans were killed and as many as 300 of the indigenous troops. The survivors travelled all night, most of them on foot, arriving at Khe Sanh after dawn, and it was said that some of them had become insane. At the same time that Langvei was being overrun, Khe Sanh received the most brutal artillery barrage of the war: 1,500 rounds that night, six rounds a minute for more minutes than anyone could bear to count.

Name .... Class .... Date ....

Macbeth: the movie

INT. NIGHT. MACBETH'S CASTLE

LADY MACBETH IS PACING IN AND OUT OF THE SMALL POOLS OF LIGHT THROWN BY THE RUSHLIGHTS ON THE WALLS. SHE IS CLEARLY AGITATED BUT AT THE SAME TIME EXCITED.

MACBETH: [Voice-over] Who's there? What, ho!

LADY MACBETH RUNS TOWARDS THE SOUND THEN STOPS.

LADY MACBETH: Alack! I am afraid they have awak'd and 'tis not done.

Name .... Class .... Date ....

Organising information: Wikipedia on vampires

Headings used:

1 Etymology

2 Folk beliefs

2.1 Description and common attributes

2.1.1 Creating vampires

2.1.2 Identifying vampires

2.1.3 Protection

2.1.3.1 Apotropaics

2.1.3.2 Methods of destruction

2.2 Ancient beliefs

2.3 Medieval and later European folklore

2.4 Non-European beliefs

2.4.1 Africa

2.4.2 The Americas

2.4.3 Asia

2.5 Modern beliefs

2.5.1 Collective noun

3 Origins of vampire beliefs

3.1 Slavic spiritualism

3.2 Pathology

3.2.1 Decomposition

3.2.2 Premature burial

3.2.3 Contagion

3.2.4 Porphyria

3.2.5 Rabies

3.3 Psychodynamic understanding

3.4 Political interpretation

3.5 Psychopathology

3.6 Modern vampire subcultures

3.7 Vampire bats

4 In modern fiction

4.1 Literature

4.2 Film and television

4.3 Games

5 Notes

6 References

7 External links

Name .... Class .... Date ....

Formal letter layout

Your address road
Your address town
Your address postcode

Receiver's address road
Receiver's address town
Receiver's address postcode

Date

Dear [Name or sometimes 'Sir or Madam']
Subject of letter [often in bold and centred]

Text of letter begins here

[paragraphs should not be indented, but there should be one blank line between paragraphs]

Text of letter ends

Yours faithfully [if you used 'Sir' or 'Madam' after 'Dear'. If you use a name after 'Dear' at the beginning, you should use 'Yours sincerely' instead]

Signature

Your name printed under your signature

Name .... Class .... Date ....

Getting the tone right

Here are two versions of the opening paragraph of a letter to an author. Can you explain the differences between them?

Version 1

Me and the rest of my mates in our class were wondering what got you into writing a ghost story. It's not as if you'd done one before, was it? We reckon you could have carried on writing those adventure stories and made loads of money. I bet someone's gonna make one of them into a film soon, yeah?

Version 2

On behalf of my class at school, I would be very interested to know what it was that provided the inspiration for your new ghost story. It seemed to us that you had great success with your series of adventure stories, and there have been rumours of a possible film deal shortly, so we came to the conclusion that this completely new direction must have been sparked by a moment of inspiration. I would be most grateful if you could let us know whether or not this idea is correct.

Task

Now here is a further paragraph following on from version 1. Can you rewrite it so that it is more in the style of version 2?

Another thing that we wanted to ask was how you found out all that stuff about the Antarctic. We're dead certain that you haven't been there, but the writing about it's pretty good so it seems like you have. How do you do that? It's not that we're asking you to give away any author's secrets, but it'd be interesting to know how you go about it. Thanks!

Optional marking scales

Reading

Band	Comprehension	Critical analysis	Forms, conventions and language
9.3	• Perceptive understanding of texts is demonstrated, with ideas synthesised and evaluated from more than one source, and sophisticated use of reference incorporated to support argument. • Impact of vocabulary is explained and discussed across a range of texts, drawing on the most appropriate strategy to interpret unfamiliar words. • Coherent interpretation of texts is developed, based on astute and detailed reading, demonstrating insight.	• Analysis of how specific linguistic, structural and grammatical features are used deliberately to create impact and elicit a particular response in a range of texts. • Full and perceptive comparison between texts, drawing out similarities and differences in an analytical and critical discussion. • Detailed exploration of how texts are shaped by readers' responses, and well-argued critical and cogent responses to texts.	• Analysis of how different forms, conventions and other features can be adapted in a range of texts to position the reader and create particular effects. • Some detailed analysis of how the English language has changed over time, with an appreciation of some of the different influences and the impact they have had. • Confident and integrated use of literary, linguistic and grammatical terminology supporting perceptive and thoughtful critical comments on features in texts.
9.2	• Detailed understanding of texts is demonstrated, with ideas synthesised from more than one source, and precisely selected evidence is used to support and develop arguments. • Some consideration of the impact of the choice of vocabulary across different texts is demonstrated, drawing on a wide range of strategies to interpret unfamiliar words. • Interpretations of texts are detailed and based on close and careful reading, developing ideas and drawing out connections.	• Some analysis of how linguistic, structural and grammatical features are used in a range of texts to create specific effects. • Detailed critical comparison between texts, with some analytical explanations. • Exploration of how texts are shaped by readers' responses, and critical opinions are developed, supported by well-argued reasons.	• Some analysis of how different forms, conventions and other features can be adapted in a range of texts to fulfil purpose and create a particular impact. • Some analysis of how the English language has changed over time, with a detailed evaluation of some of the different influences and the impact they have had. • Confident use of a range of literary, linguistic and grammatical terminology, supporting critical and analytical commentary on texts.

Reading continued

Band	Comprehension	Critical analysis	Forms, conventions and language
8.3/9.1	• Clear understanding of the difference between main and subsidiary ideas is demonstrated, with some ability to summarise and synthesise information, supported by well-selected evidence. • Clear and precise explanation of an increasingly wide vocabulary, using a range of strategies, including dictionaries, to interpret unfamiliar words. • Inferences develop an interpretation of texts, exploring ideas and beginning to make connections.	• Detailed exploration of how a variety of linguistic, structural and grammatical features are used in a range of texts. • Critical comparisons between texts, including some ability to contrast ideas, with explanations of comments. • Discussion of how texts are shaped by readers' responses and critical, personal opinions are developed, supported by sound reasons.	• Detailed exploration of how form, conventions and other features of texts can be adapted to fulfil a particular purpose and create effects. • Exploration of the ways the English language has changed over time, evaluating some of the different influences and the impact they have had. • Mostly confident use of literary, linguistic and grammatical terminology, helping to support detailed and critical commentary on texts.
8.2	• Main ideas and subsidiary ideas are understood and summarised in a range of texts, with well-selected evidence used to support arguments. • Clear explanation of vocabulary, including some unfamiliar words, supported by use of dictionary and other strategies. • Inferences across a text or texts, beginning to explore layers of meaning.	• Some exploration of how different linguistic, structural and grammatical features are used in a range of texts. • Critical comparisons are made between texts, with some explanation of comments. • Some exploration of the effect of texts on different readers, with developed personal and critical opinions offered.	• Some exploration of how form, conventions and other features of texts can be adapted to create particular effects. • Some exploration of the ways the English language has changed over time, considering some of the different influences and the impact they have had. • Use of appropriate literary, linguistic and grammatical terminology helps support effective commentary on texts.
7.3/8.1	• Understanding of the difference between main and subsidiary points in a range of texts is shown, with appropriate evidence used to expand ideas. • A range of strategies, including dictionaries, is used to interpret and explain unfamiliar vocabulary. • Inferences across a text, or texts, begin to show some evidence of development and exploration.	• Some discussion of how linguistic, structural and grammatical features are used in different texts. • Some critical comparisons made between texts, with some development of comments. • Some consideration of the effects of texts on readers, and personal, critical opinions show evidence of some development.	• Secure understanding of the main forms, conventions and features of different texts, with some awareness of how these can be adapted for impact. • Some discussion of the ways the English language has changed over time, recognising some of the different influences and the effect they have had. • Secure knowledge of terminology to support explanation of literary, linguistic and grammatical features in texts.

Band	Comprehension	Critical analysis	Forms, conventions and language
7.2	• Clear understanding of explicit meaning is shown, with main points of some texts summarised, and relevant evidence used to support ideas. • A range of strategies, including dictionaries, are used to interpret unfamiliar vocabulary. • Inferences based on evidence across a text, with some development.	• Some explanation of aspects of language and structure, including grammatical features. • Comparisons are made between texts, with some expansion of comments. • Understanding of the effect of texts on the reader is shown, and personal opinions are justified with straightforward reasons.	• Knowledge of the main forms, conventions and features of different texts is shown. • Understanding of some of the changes that have occurred to, or influences on, the English language over time. • Developing knowledge of some of the relevant terminology to discuss literary, linguistic and grammatical features in texts is shown.
7.1/6.3	• Straightforward understanding of explicit meaning, main ideas are identified and some evidence is used to support ideas. • Some range of strategies, including dictionaries, used to interpret unfamiliar vocabulary. • Inferences based on evidence from different points in a text, with some explanation.	• Some straightforward aspects of language and structure are identified, including grammatical features. • Straightforward comparison is made between texts, with limited development of comments. • Understanding of effect of the text on reader is shown and straightforward personal opinions given.	• Recognition of some of the forms and conventions of texts. • Awareness of some of the changes that have occurred in, or influences on, the English language over time. • Familiarity with some appropriate terminology to discuss literary, grammatical and linguistic features in texts.

Writing

Band	Form and structure	Style and vocabulary	Grammatical range and accuracy
9.3	• Imaginative and skilful adaptation of form used to address a range of purposes and create impact on the reader, across a range of texts. • Structure and organisational devices are deployed flexibly and adroitly to fulfil the purpose of the writing and position the reader.	• Style draws on a range of techniques and is nuanced to be appropriate to purpose and audience, and to meet the requirements of a task. • Use of vocabulary is ambitious, judicious and sometimes deliberately surprising.	• Varied syntax is used in a range of writing to convey ideas and create impact for the reader. • A range of punctuation is used with precision and accuracy to create effects; errors are rare or untypical. • Spelling is correct, with errors untypical or evident only in very unusual words.

Writing continued

Band	Form and structure	Style and vocabulary	Grammatical range and accuracy
9.2	• Across a range of texts, form is adapted to meet the purpose of the writing, drawing on a range of conventions. • Information and ideas are skilfully controlled and organised, with a range of devices used to position the reader.	• A range of stylistic features within a deliberately chosen style are used to create particular impact for purpose and audience. • A wide, ambitious and imaginative vocabulary is used across a range of texts with precision.	• Syntax is varied and apposite, showing an ability to adapt features for particular forms of writing. • A range of punctuation is used with precision and accuracy to create effects: there may be one-off errors in more complex sentences • Spelling is correct with only occasional errors in irregular or unusual words.
8.3/9.1	• The form is adapted to suit the purpose of the writing, showing familiarity with a range of conventions. • The structure is controlled, with paragraphs used to position the reader.	• Consistent use of a range of styles, including formal and informal, appropriate to purpose and audience. • Vocabulary chosen is varied and ambitious, and selected to fulfil the purpose of a task.	• Syntax is used with some skill to create particular effects. • A range of punctuation is used with precision and accuracy to create effects; there may be some errors in more complex sentences. • Spelling is almost always correct, though there may be errors in some less common, irregular or commonly misspelled words.
8.2	• There is some adaptation of form, appropriate to purpose and audience, in some texts. • A clear structure and a variety of paragraphs are used to support the purpose of the writing.	• The chosen style is mostly sustained throughout the writing, appropriate to purpose, audience and level of formality. • A wide vocabulary, including some ambitious words, is used appropriate to the purpose of a task.	• Sentence structures are chosen and adapted to meet the requirements of the task. • A range of punctuation is used for clarity and impact, with only occasional omissions or errors. • Spelling is mostly correct, though there may be occasional errors in less common, irregular words.
7.3/8.1	• Use of form shows secure understanding of purpose and audience across a range of texts. • The structure of the writing is clear, with connectives used to signal the sequence of ideas in the text and secure use of paragraphing.	• A range of stylistic features, including those appropriate for formal writing, used to support the purpose of the writing. • A range of vocabulary is used, including technical, literary and subject specific language, to match purpose and style, and sometimes for particular effect.	• A range of sentence structures is used, almost always securely, with some adaptation to the purpose of the task. • A range of punctuation is used, mostly securely, to clarify meaning and sometimes for effect. • Most spelling is correct including less common, irregular words.

Band	Form and structure	Style and vocabulary	Grammatical range and accuracy
7.2	• The main features of a form are used, mostly securely, showing understanding of purpose and audience. • The overall structure of the writing is clear, supported by appropriate use of paragraphs.	• Some range of stylistic features is used, mostly appropriately, to support the purpose of the writing. • Vocabulary is selected to match the purpose and style of writing, mostly appropriately, including some technical and literary language.	• A range of sentence structures, simple, coordinated and complex, are used, mostly securely, though there may be occasional errors. • Some range of punctuation is used, mostly securely, to achieve clarity in texts. • Most spelling is correct, including common irregular words and some less common words.
7.1/6.3	• The main features of a form are used, showing understanding of purpose and some awareness of audience, though not always sustained throughout. • Writing has straightforward overall structure, with mostly secure use of sections or paragraphs.	• Some stylistic features are used, mostly appropriately, to match the purpose of the writing. • Some range of vocabulary is used, mostly appropriately, for purpose and audience.	• Some range of sentence structures is used, mostly accurately, though there may be a lack of variety or some lack of control when more ambitious structures are attempted. • Punctuation of sentences is mostly accurate, with some use of other punctuation, e.g. commas and apostrophes for omission. • Spelling of most regularly constructed words and common irregular words is accurate.

Spoken English

Band	Presentation and communication	Discussion and knowledge about spoken language	Reading aloud and drama
9.3	• Complex and contradictory ideas are cogently conveyed and examined, with structure adapted to create particular impact and position a range of audiences. • Language, including vocabulary, grammatical constructions and rhetorical features, are deliberately deployed to enhance the points made and create particular impact on the audience.	• Well-judged and pertinent contributions help to develop discussions, synthesise important ideas and draw others in, sometimes offering a new perspective or solution, to complete a task effectively. • An appreciation of the significance of Standard English is demonstrated; it is used confidently and articulately, when relevant, in a range of contexts. A variety of appropriate terminology is used to explore conventions and features of oral communication in some detail.	• Reading aloud is exceptionally skilful and assured, demonstrating an ability to adapt voice and delivery appropriately to material, purpose and audience. • Complex ideas and relationships are explored across a range of play and other drama activities, demonstrating sophisticated use of voice and action, and an ability to reflect perceptively on performance.

Band	Presentation and communication	Discussion and knowledge about spoken language	Reading aloud and drama
9.2	• A range of information on complex topics is coherently explored, with some adaptation of structure to create impact, for a range of audiences. • A varied and precise vocabulary, range of grammatical constructions, and rhetorical techniques are used skilfully to achieve impact on the audience.	• Sustained and considered contributions to discussions demonstrate an ability to develop key ideas, identify and summarise important ideas and draw others in to complete the task effectively. • There is clear understanding of the importance of Standard English; it is used consistently, when relevant, and conventions or features of oral communication are explored using appropriate terminology.	• Reading aloud demonstrates skill and assurance across a range of texts, with voice adapted to suit purpose and audience. • Skilful exploration of relationships and themes, demonstrated across a range of plays and other drama activities through the use of well-chosen and adapted voices, actions and commentary.
8.3/9.1	• Information and ideas on topics of some complexity and variety are presented to a range of different audiences. • A range of vocabulary, grammatical constructions and rhetorical techniques are used skilfully to vary language appropriately for the task, purpose and audience.	• Sustained contributions to discussions show recognition of key ideas, an ability to summarise and sometimes shape or direct discussion in a helpful way. • There is understanding of the importance of Standard English; it is used consistently, when relevant, and conventions or features of oral communication are explained using appropriate terminology with some precision.	• Reading aloud is fluent, confident and expressive, across a range of texts, with some adaptation to suit purpose and audience. • Relationships and themes are explored with some confidence in play reading and other drama activities, through the use of a range of appropriately chosen and adapted voices and actions.
8.2	• A range of ideas and information is explored, mostly coherently, on topics that are sometimes complex, for a range of audiences. • A range of vocabulary, grammatical constructions and rhetorical techniques are used, selectively, to vary language appropriately for the task, purpose and audience.	• Contributions to discussions are developed and often sustained, showing evidence of perception and an ability to bring ideas together to move the discussion forward. • Standard English is used appropriately and consistently, when relevant, and conventions or features of oral communication are clearly explained, using some appropriate terminology.	• Clear, fluent and confident reading aloud of texts, including those with some complex ideas or unfamiliar form or vocabulary. • Some examination of characters, relationships and themes demonstrated in play reading and other drama activities, through the use of a range of appropriately chosen voices and actions.

Band	Presentation and communication	Discussion and knowledge about spoken language	Reading aloud and drama
7.3/8.1	• Information and ideas are clearly expressed, in a structured way, on a variety of topics to a less well-known audience. • A range of vocabulary, grammatical constructions and rhetorical techniques are used, with some skill, appropriate to topic, purpose and audience.	• Some developed contributions are made to discussions, building on others' points and sometimes drawing ideas together, or posing questions. • Standard English is used appropriately, when relevant, and there is some explanation of conventions or features of oral communication, using some appropriate terminology.	• Clear and fluent reading aloud of almost all texts, including those with some unfamiliar ideas or vocabulary. • Insight into characters, relationships and situations, sustained in play reading and other drama activities, through use of a range of different voices and actions.
7.2	• Information and ideas are clearly and logically expressed on familiar topics to an audience, which may include a less well-known audience. • Some range of vocabulary, grammatical constructions and other techniques are used, appropriate to the task and purpose.	• Clear and relevant points are made in discussions, showing understanding and some ability to build on others' comments. • Standard English is used, almost always appropriately, when relevant, and there is some comment on conventions of the features of oral communication.	• Clear and fluent reading aloud of most straightforward texts, including those that are unfamiliar. • Some understanding of characters, relationships and situations shown in play reading and other drama activities, through use of different voices and actions.
7.1/6.3	• Straightforward ideas on familiar topics are communicated, with some clarity, to a known audience. • Some vocabulary, grammatical constructions and other techniques are used, appropriate to the task and purpose.	• Straightforward contributions made to discussions, understanding and responding to main points. • Standard English is used, mostly appropriately, when relevant, and some conventions or features of oral communication are recognised.	• Mostly clear and fluent reading aloud of straightforward and familiar texts • Straightforward ideas about character and situations are conveyed in play reading and other drama activities, with some use of different voices and actions.

Key Stage 3 National Curriculum mapping

Reading

	National Curriculum: subject content	Unit 1: In the News	Unit 2: Language out loud	Unit 3: The power of persuasion	Unit 4: Real-world stories	Unit 5: Horror
Develop an appreciation and love of reading and read increasingly challenging material independently	Reading a wide range of fiction and non-fiction, including in particular whole books, short stories, poems and plays with a wide coverage of genres, historical periods, forms and authors. The range will include high-quality works from:	Texts 1–11	Texts 1, 2, 4, 5, 6, 10	Texts 1, 2, 3, 5, 6, 7, 8, 9	Texts 3, 5	Texts 7, 8, 11
	• English literature, both pre-1914 and contemporary, including prose, poetry and drama		Texts 3, 7, 8, 9, 11		Texts 1, 2, 4	Texts 2, 3, 4, 5, 6, 10, 12
	• Shakespeare (two plays)			Text 4		Text 9
	• seminal world literature					Text 1
	Choosing and reading books independently for challenge, interest and enjoyment					
	Re-reading books encountered earlier to increase familiarity with them and provide a basis for making comparisons				Text 8 A3	
Understand increasingly challenging texts	Learning new vocabulary, relating it explicitly to known vocabulary and understanding it with the help of context and dictionaries				Text 4 A3 Text 9 A1	
	Making inferences and referring to evidence in the text	Text 2 A1, A3 Text 3 A3 Text 4 A2 Text 5 A2 Text 6 A1 Text 7 A1 Texts 9 and 10 A1 Text 11 A2	Text 11 A3	Text 4 A1 Text 8 A1 Text 10 A1	Text 1 A1 Text 4 A1 Text 6 A1 Text 7 A1 Text 9 A2	Text 1 A1 Text 2 A1 Text 3 A1, A2 Text 10 A1 Text 11 A1 Text 12 A1

	National Curriculum: subject content	Unit 1: In the News	Unit 2: Language out loud	Unit 3: The power of persuasion	Unit 4: Real-world stories	Unit 5: Horror
	Knowing the purpose, audience for and context of the writing and drawing on this knowledge to support comprehension	Text 4 A2 Text 7 A1 Texts 9 and 10 A3, A4		Text 1 A1 Text 2 A1 Text 8 A1 Text 10 A1	Text 4 A2 Text 6 A3 Text 7 A1, A2	Text 7 A1 Text 8 A1 Text 10 A1, A3
	Checking their understanding to make sure that what they have read makes sense		Text 8 A1	Text 4 A1	Text 5 A2	Text 1 A1 Text 6 A1 Text 11 A1
Read critically	Knowing how language, including figurative language, vocabulary choice, grammar, text structure and organisational features, presents meaning	Text 1 A1 Text 2 A2 Text 3 A1, A3 Text 5 A3 Texts 9 and 10 A1, A2, A4		Text 3 A1 Text 5 A1 Text 6 A1 Text 7 A1 Text 9 A1 Text 12 A1	Text 1 A2, A3 Text 2 A2 Text 3 A1 Text 8 A1 Text 10 A1, A2	Text 1 A1, A4 Text 2 A1 Text 4 A2 Text 9 A1 Text 11 A2
	Recognising a range of poetic conventions and understanding how these have been used					Text 6 A2 Text 9 A2
	Studying setting, plot and characterisation, and the effects of these			Text 4 A2		Text 2 A1 Text 12 A1
	Understanding how the work of dramatists is communicated effectively through performance and how alternative staging allows for different interpretations of a play					Text 9 A1
	Making critical comparisons across texts	Texts 9 and 10 A2, A3, A4			Text 2 A3 Text 4 A4 Text 6 A3 Text 8 A3	
	Studying a range of authors, including at least two authors in depth each year					

Writing

	National Curriculum: subject content	Unit 1: In the News	Unit 2: Language out loud	Unit 3: The power of persuasion	Unit 4: Real-world stories	Unit 5: Horror
Write accurately, fluently, effectively and at length for pleasure and information	Writing for a wide range of purposes and audiences, including: • well-structured formal expository and narrative essays		Text 10 A2 UAT		Text 2 A3 Text 6 A3 Text 8 A3	Text 1 A4
	• stories, scripts, poetry and other imaginative writing		Text 10 A2		Text 4 A2 Text 8 A4	Text 1 A3 Text 3 A3 Text 6 A3 Text 9 A3 UAT
	• notes and polished scripts for talks and presentations		Text 5 A1 Text 9 A2	Text 9 A2		Text 10 A3
	• a range of other narrative and non-narrative texts, including arguments, and personal and formal letters	Text 1 A4 Text 3 A4 Text 8 A1, A3	Text 4 A2	UAT	Text 5 A4 Text 7 A3 Text 9 A3, A4	Text 8 A1 Text 12 A3 UAT
	Summarising and organising material, and supporting ideas and arguments with any necessary factual detail	Text 3 A2 Text 4 A3 Text 5 A3 Text 6 A3 Text 7 A2 Text 8 A4	Text 5 A2, A3	UAT	Text 10 A3	Text 1 A4 Text 2 A3 Text 11 A2
	Applying their growing knowledge of vocabulary, grammar and text structure to their writing and selecting the appropriate form	Text 1 A4 Text 3 A1, A2 Text 4 A3 Text 5 A3 Text 6 A3, A4 Text 7 A2	UAT	UAT	Text 9 A4	Text 2 A3 Text 5 A2 Text 10 A2 UAT
	Drawing on knowledge of literary and rhetorical devices from their reading and listening to enhance the impact of their writing	Text 8 A3		Text 2 A2 Text 3 A2 Text 6 A2 Text 7 A2 Text 9 A2	Text 3 A2, A3 Text 5 A4	Text 1 A3 Text 4 A2 Text 5 A1 Text 6 A3 Text 8 A2 Text 12 A2 UAT

	National Curriculum: subject content	Unit 1: In the News	Unit 2: Language out loud	Unit 3: The power of persuasion	Unit 4: Real-world stories	Unit 5: Horror
Plan, draft, edit and proof read	Considering how their writing reflects the audiences and purposes for which it was intended	Text 1 A3 Text 8 A1	Text 3 A4		Text 3 A1 Text 7 A3 Text 10 A3	
Plan, draft, edit and proof read	Amending the vocabulary, grammar and structure of their writing to improve its coherence and overall effectiveness	Text 3 A2 Text 5 A3			Text 4 A1, A2	
Plan, draft, edit and proof read	Paying attention to accurate grammar, punctuation and spelling; applying the spelling patterns and rules set out in English Appendix 1 to the key stage 1 and 2 programmes of study for English	Text 6 SPAG Text 8 A4	Texts 1 and 2 SPAG Text 4 SPAG Text 5 SPAG Text 11 SPAG			Text 1 SPAG

Grammar and vocabulary

National Curriculum: subject content	Unit 1: In the News	Unit 2: Language out loud	Unit 3: The power of persuasion	Unit 4: Real-world stories	Unit 5: Horror
Extending and applying the grammatical knowledge set out in English Appendix 2 to the Key Stage 1 and 2 programmes of study to analyse more challenging texts	Text 1 A4 Text 2 SPAG Text 3 SPAG Text 5 A1	Texts 1 and 2 A1, A2, SPAG Text 5 SPAG	Text 3 SPAG Text 7 SPAG Text 8 SPAG	Text 6 SPAG Text 10 SPAG	Text 1 A2 Text 2 SPAG Text 3 SPAG Text 4 A3
Studying the effectiveness and impact of the grammatical features of the texts they read	Text 7 SPAG	Text 1 A1 Text 10 A1 Texts 6–7, SPAG	Text 1 SPAG Text 6 SPAG	Text 4 A2, SPAG Text 7 SPAG	Text 1 A4 Text 2 A2 Text 4 SPAG
Drawing on new vocabulary and grammatical constructions from their reading and listening, and using these consciously in their writing and speech to achieve particular effects	Text 1 A3, A4 Text 1 SPAG Text 8 A4	Text 1 A3 Text 1 SPAG Text 3 A4	Text 3 SPAG Text 9 SPAG	Text 1 SPAG Text 8 SPAG	Text 5 SPAG Text 10 A2 Text 12 SPAG
Knowing and understanding the differences between spoken and written language, including differences associated with formal and informal registers, and between Standard English and other varieties of English		Text 3 A4 Text 4 A2 Text 5 A1, A2, A3 Text 8 A2 Text 11 A1 UAT	Text 8 A2 Text 11 A1		Text 12 A3

National Curriculum: subject content	Unit 1: In the News	Unit 2: Language out loud	Unit 3: The power of persuasion	Unit 4: Real-world stories	Unit 5: Horror
Using Standard English confidently in their own writing and speech	Text 8 A2, A3			Text 6 A2	
Discussing reading, writing and spoken language with precise and confident use of linguistic and literary terminology	Text 1 A1, A3 Text 5 A3, SPAG Text 9–10 A1	Text 2 A2, A3 Text 3 A1, A2, A3 Text 8 A2 UAT	Text 3 A1 Text 7 A1		Text 1 A4 Text 4 A3

Spoken English

National Curriculum: subject content	Unit 1: In the News	Unit 2: Language out loud	Unit 3: The power of persuasion	Unit 4: Real-world stories	Unit 5: Horror
Using Standard English confidently in a range of formal and informal contexts, including classroom discussion	Text 8 A2 Text 11 A1		Text 1 A2	Text 4 A3 Text 6 A2	Text 3 A2 Text 10 A3
Giving short speeches and presentations, expressing their own ideas and keeping to the point	Text 1 A3 Text 3 A3	Text 5 A1	Text 9 A3 Text 10 A2	Text 4 A3 Text 5 A1, A3 Text 9 A1	Text 6 A1 Text 10 A3
Participating in formal debates and structured discussions, summarising and/or building on what has been said	Text 2 A1, A3 Text 3 A5 Text 5 A2 Text 6 A1 Text 8 A2 Texts 9 and 10 A4 Text 11 A1, A3	Text 2 A4 Text 4 A1 Text 11 A1	Text 5 A2 Text 6 A3 Text 11 A2 Text 12 A2	Text 3 A4	Text 3 A2 Text 4 A1 Text 7 A2
Improvising, rehearsing and performing play scripts and poetry in order to generate language and discuss language use and meaning, using role and intonation, tone, volume, mood, silence, stillness and action to add impact	Text 1 A2 Text 4 A1 Text 6 A2	Text 1 A2 Texts 6 and 7 A1, A2 Text 9 A1 Text 11 A2	Text 1 A2 Text 4 A3 Text 6 A3	Text 1 A3 Text 4 A3 Text 5 A1 Text 8 A2	Text 3 A1 Text 9 A1